This book must be returned immed-
iately it is asked for by the Librarian,
and in any case by the last date
stamped below.

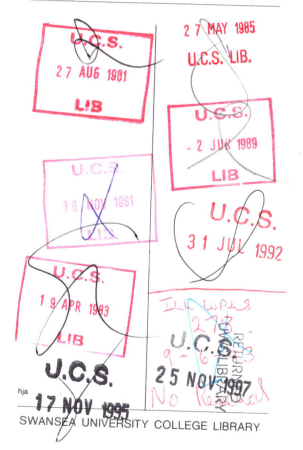

FARMING FOR PROFIT IN A HUNGRY WORLD

Capital and the Crisis in Agriculture

Farming
for Profit
in a
Hungry
World

CAPITAL AND THE CRISIS IN AGRICULTURE

by
MICHAEL PERELMAN

Preface by
Barry Commoner

LANDMARK STUDIES
Allanheld, Osmun MONTCLAIR *Universe Books* NEW YORK

ALLANHELD, OSMUN & CO. PUBLISHERS, INC.
Montclair, New Jersey

Published in the United States of America in 1977
by Allanheld, Osmun & Co., 19 Brunswick Road, Montclair, N.J. 07042
and by Universe Books, 381 Park Avenue South, New York 10016
Distribution: Universe Books

Library of Congress Cataloging in Publication Data

Perelman, Michael.
  Farming for profit in a hungry world.

  "LandMark studies."
  Includes index.
  1. Agriculture--Economic aspects--United States.
2. Food supply. I. Title.
HD1761.P38 1977   338.1'0973   76-43229
  ISBN 0-87663-807-8

Printed in the United States of America

PREFACE

Agriculture in the United States has been profoundly transformed in the last 30 years. The most obvious—and most frequently reported—change is the striking improvement in agricultural production: between 1950 and 1971 farm output increased by 52 percent, while output per unit labor increased by 257 percent. The output of crop per acre has increased about 61 percent, while cropland harvested has decreased about 10 percent. Many more people can now be fed by the food produced by a single farm worker; in 1950 about 15 people were fed per farm worker and today the figure is well over 48 people per farm worker.

But something is wrong. Since the productivity of farm labor has increased nearly three-fold and most of it is still supplied by farm families, we might expect this gain to be reflected in a comparable improvement in the economic status of the farmer. But in fact the total real income of U.S. farms decreased from $17 billion in 1950 to $12 billion in 1971 (in 1958 dollars). Because the number of farms decreased by 50 percent, the income per farm increased 43 percent, from an average of about $3,000 in 1950 to slightly under $4,300 in 1971. However, in the same period the median income of *all* U.S. families increased 80 percent, from about $4,000 in 1950 to over $7,200 in 1971. Since well over three-fourths of U.S. families live in cities, it is clear that the real income of an urban family increased considerably more than the real income of a rural family in that time. Meanwhile the total mortgage debt of U.S. farms increased from $7 billion in 1950 to $21 billion in 1971.

And, just as the increased output of U.S. agriculture has been gained at the expense of average agricultural income relative to the economy as a whole, so the gains in productivity have been achieved at the expense of a decrease in the natural fertility of the soil. In a typical modern agricultural system, in the Corn Belt for example, the nitrogen and other soil cycles have been disrupted by separating crop production from livestock production. One result is that the humus content of Midwestern soil has decreased about 50 percent on the average since farming began, reducing the available nutrients. Loss of humus also reduces the soil's efficiency in taking up the available nutrients, because humus maintains the porosity of the soil, and therefore its oxygen content—which is needed to release the metabolic energy in the roots that pulls nutrients out of the soil into the crop.

In this situation, large amounts of inorganic nitrogen fertilizer must be added to the soil each year in order to grow a successful crop—but at a price. That price is the pollution of surface waters that drain heavily fertilized land. Because nitrogen added to the soil in the inorganic form does not build up soil humus, the efficiency of nutrient uptake remains low, so that a good deal of the fertilizer leaches out of the soil into the rivers. As a result, in Central Illinois, for example, every spring the rivers carry more nitrate than the Public Health Service limits allow (excessive nitrate in the diet may increase the incidence of cancer). Moreover, as the rate of fertilizer application is increased, the efficiency with which the nitrogen it contains is converted into crop declines. In U.S. agriculture as a whole we now use about five times as much fertilizer as we did in 1947 to produce the same amount of crop.

Modern agricultural practice, such as the intensive use of inorganic nitrogen fertilizer, involves not only environmental problems, but energy problems as well. Such fertilizer contains nitrogen fixed from the air—a process that requires energy. The energy needed to produce anhydrous ammonia in the fertilizer factory comes from a nonrenewable fossil fuel—natural gas. It replaces the older practice of incorporating nitrogen from the air into the soil through legumes, which also fix nitrogen, but which use as the necessary energy a freely available, renewable, non-polluting source—the sun.

Because most modern agricultural chemicals, like nitrogen fertilizer, are energy-intensive products, the dependence of U.S. agriculture on them has had drastic economic consequences for farmers. Since the 1973 oil crisis the price of fuel has increased drastically, and with it the prices of fertilizers and other agricultural chemicals. This has left U.S. agriculture in a very vulnerable economic position. As the intensive inputs on which the farmer now depends keep rising, farmers are less able to weather the natural fluctuations in the price of their products—a situation which is serious in the Midwest at this time.

Not only is the farmer forced to pay rising prices for the industrial goods on which agricultural production has become dependent, but industry has produced synthetics—fibers, plastics and detergents—that are driving competing agricultural products off the market. The energetic relationships are, again, particularly instructive. For example, cotton can be regarded as a form of congealed solar energy. The cellulose of which cotton is composed is a large complex molecule made of numerous carbon, hydrogen and oxygen atoms. In the cotton plant, cellulose is synthesized from carbon dioxide and water, a process that requires energy, which the cotton plant obtains from the sun. The synthetic replacements are made from materials extracted from petroleum, and the energy needed to produce their complex molecules is obtained by burning fuel. Once again, solar energy loses out.

One can only admire the enterprise and clever salesmanship of the petrochemical industry, which produces both agricultural chemicals and the synthetics that compete with farm products: synthetic fiber, which competes with cotton and wool; detergents, which compete with soap, made of natural oils and fat; plastics, which compete with wood; and pesticides, that compete with birds and ladybugs, which used to be free. The giant corporations have made a colony out of rural America. Like Standard Oil forcing its products on old China, U.S. industry has molded the nation's farms into a convenient market and a weakened competitor.

These changes in the design of agricultural production are an integral part of a broad-scale post-war transformation in the technology of agricultural and industrial production and transportation: Not only do we now wash our clothes in detergents instead of soap, use man-made nitrogen fertilizer to grow food, instead of manure or crop rotation, and wear clothes made of synthetic fibers instead of cotton or wool. We also drink beer and soda out of throwaway containers instead of returnable ones; we drive heavy cars with high-powered, high-compression engines instead of the lighter, low-powered, low-compression pre-war types; we travel in airplanes and private cars and ship our freight by truck instead of using the railroads for both.

All of these changes have worsened environmental degradation: When a washer-full of detergent goes down the drain it causes much more pollution than the same amount of soap; a throwaway beer bottle delivers the same amount of beer as a returnable one, but at a much higher cost in pollution and trash, since the returnable bottle is used dozens of times before it is discarded; the heavy use of chemical nitrogen fertilizer pollutes rivers and lakes, while the older agricultural methods did not; synthetic fibers, unlike natural ones, are not biodegradable, so that when discarded they are either burned—causing air pollution—or clutter up the environment forever; the modern car pollutes the air with smog and lead, while the pre-war car was smog-free and could run on unleaded gasoline; airlines and private cars produce much more air pollution per passenger-mile, and trucks produce more pollution per ton-mile than the railroads.

Against this background it becomes clear that the sweeping post-war transformation of the U.S. farm is a crucial part of a more general transformation of the entire U.S. economy. The transformation has, indeed, greatly improved industrial and agricultural production. But it has done so at a price which for a long time remained hidden. Part of that price is the degradation of the environment, a price which remained hidden until revealed by the environmental crisis. Another part of that price is the waste and escalating cost of energy, a price which remained hidden until revealed by the energy crisis.

These costs are borne by society in the form not only of pollution and wasted energy, but also in the form of unemployment—all of which are consequences of new industrial and agricultural technologies that have been developed without adequate concern for the environment, for the conservation of resources and for the need to provide people with meaningful employment. Clearly we need to understand these costs and their relation to the benefits of modern production technology. In the present volume, Michael Perelman has made a valuable contribution to this vital task.

Barry Commoner
October, 1977

CONTENTS

ix

INTRODUCTION

Our system of agriculture is in the midst of a crisis. Its diagnosis will proceed on two different levels. It will require that we scrutinize the agricultural consequences of capitalist society as well as the social consequences of capitalist agriculture.

Part I, "The Myth of Agricultural Efficiency," describes some of the symptoms of the crisis in agriculture. The haphazard application of lethal chemicals, the abuse of the soil and the squandering of energy which are treated here are merely symptoms of a more fundamental disorder which affects society. The genesis of this disease is the system of economical organization in which farming is designed to produce profit instead of food.

Part II of the book traces out the interactions between agricultural and economic policies. It shows how both environmental and human considerations are shunted aside in favor of profit.

Part III chronicles the gradual demise of small farmers. From the point of view of capital, the ability of the small farmers to produce a bountiful supply of food with a minimum of resources limited the powers of capital. Small farmers were deemed uneconomical while policies were designed to weed them out in the name of progress. This part of the book also documents some of the costs to society of these policies.

Part IV concentrates on the fate of agriculture in the lands which have been dominated by the powerful Atlantic economies. Even the United States Department of Agriculture now admits that hunger is not to be explained by the inadequacy of production but by the irrationality of markets:

If the estimated 460 million malnourished people of the world were provided daily with additional grain equal to 500 calories, much of the world malnutrition would be alleviated.

On an annual basis, about 25 million tons of cereals would be needed, about 2 percent of the average annual world cereal production during the last decade. The world could rather easily produce 2 percent more grain. The difficult problems are not those of increasing production of food, but of distributing it.*

The first section in this part documents the role of the capitalist economies in organizing the agricultural systems in these parts of the world. The result was an economic structure in which poverty is a logical consequence. Next we move to a more detailed consideration of the beginnings of colonialism in Ireland and India. This material highlights the subsequent discussion of the recent "Green Revolution," a plan to intensify the influence of capitalism in the Third World countryside. The concluding section explores the capacity of the less developed nations to improve their agricultural situation. Drawing upon the Chinese experience, it concludes on a hopeful note.

Part V is concerned with the question of scarcity. How did premarket societies husband their resources without a pricing system? To what extent can poverty be attributed to shortages or overpopulation?

Throughout the book, I stress the importance of social relations in agricultural and economic development. By learning about what has been, hopefully we can understand what must be.

---

*United States Department of Agriculture, Economic Research Service, *The World Food Situation and Prospects to 1985*, Foreign Agricultural Economic Report No. 98 (July 1977): pp. 29-30.

PART ONE

The Myth of Agricultural Efficiency

Let us not, however, flatter ourselves overmuch on account of our human victories over nature . . . at every step we are reminded that we by no means rule over nature like a conqueror over a foreign people, like someone standing outside nature—but that we, with flesh, blood and brain, belong to nature, and exist in its midst, and that all our mastery of it consists in the fact that we have the advantage over all other creatures of being able to learn its laws and apply them correctly. . . . It required the labour of thousands of years for us to learn a little of how to calculate the more remote natural effects of our actions in the field of production, but it has been still more difficult in regard to the more remote social effects of these actions. . . . Classical political economy . . . examines mainly only social effects of human actions in the fields of production and exchange that are actually intended. This fully corresponds to the social organisation of which it is the theoretical expression. As individual capitalists are engaged in production and exchange for the sake of the immediate profit, only the nearest and most immediate results must first be taken into account. . . . In relation to nature, as to society, the present mode of production is predominately concerned only about the immediate, most tangible result; and then surprise is expressed that the removed effects of actions directed to this end turn out to be quite different, are mostly quite the opposite in character; that the harmony of supply and demand is transformed into the very . . . opposite.

—Frederick Engels, "The Role of Labour in the
Transition from Ape to Man"

1

PROLOGUE

"Would you tell me please, which way ought I to go from here?"
"That depends a great deal on where you want to get to," said the Cat.
"I don't much care where—" said Alice.
"Then it doesn't matter which way you go," said the Cat.
"—so long as I get somewhere," Alice added. . . .
                                        —Lewis Carroll, *Alice in Wonderland*

Farms today are designed to grow but one product: profit. "Efficiency" in agriculture rests on one idea: "Does it pay?" Anything else you hear is a myth.

Take a look at any of the thousands of reports produced by the United States Department of Agriculture; you will find constant references to the efficiency of U.S. agriculture. What does this really mean?

This same "efficient" system of agriculture is profligate in its consumption of energy; it must share in the blame for the twin diseases of urban life—blight and sprawl; it is contaminating the environment and providing society with a deteriorating quality of food. And we should not forget the economic plight of farm workers in any evaluation.

A realistic measure of the "efficiency" of a system must be based on consideration of its over-all impact on the present quality of life as well as its potential for the future. To speak of efficiency in agriculture without taking into account the broad range of its effects is dangerously misleading.

Developing a holistic perspective on agriculture will be a new experience for most Americans. Many of us get no closer to agriculture than the nearest supermarket. Nonetheless, each of us depends on agriculture for more than one-half ton of food every year.

We are reminded of this dependency only when higher food costs or shortages become front page news. Otherwise agriculture is taken for granted; yet whether or not we take it for granted, the ramifications of

3

agriculture go far beyond the production of food. In fact, as we shall see, current agricultural practices are consuming the very basis of our wealth, even threatening an eventual disaster in food production. To speak of agricultural efficiency without considering the risks is sheer lunacy.

To make a realistic evaluation, we must break through the restrictive circle of thought which proposes to measure agricultural performance on a superficial technical level. Clifford Hardin, the first Secretary of Agriculture in the Nixon administration, produced a typical example of this line of thought in the *1970 Yearbook of Agriculture*, perhaps the most widely distributed publication of the USDA. In the foreword to the volume, Hardin wrote:

Using a modern feeding system for broilers, one man can take care of 60,000 to 75,000 chickens. One man in a modern feedlot can take care of 5,000 head of cattle. One man, with a mechanized system, can operate a dairy enterprise of 50 to 60 milk cows.[1]

Agriculture, in short, does an amazingly efficient job of producing food.

If we grant Hardin's narrow definition of efficiency, the maximization of output per manhour, then his view appears convincing. Before hastily conceding the field to Hardin, however, we might give his words a bit more consideration. After all, no man alive can really feed 75,000 chickens by himself. In reality he is aided by many other workers who have made the cages and grown the feed. All the people employed by the food system from the worker in the fertilizer plant to the person checking out your food in the supermarket are farmers even though they may never set food on a farm; without them food would never reach the kitchen table, as society is presently organized. Including these workers, about one-quarter of the U.S. labor force may be counted as farmers.

Hardin's picture of the single farmer feeding 75,000 chickens is simply a reflection of the fact that farming has been industrialized: more and more work has been transferred from the farm to the factory. As a result of

This industrialization of farming brought about one of the largest migrations in human history. Between 1920 and 1960, 25 million people moved from farms to towns and cities.[2] By the end of the following decade, the net exodus of another 6 million people depressed the total farm population to less than 10 million people.[3] Many of the people uprooted from the farms languished in the cities without much prospect of employment. As a result, some critics charge that the forces which controlled agriculture had as much effect in growing slums and ghettos as corn and cotton.*

Of course many of the migrants from the farm prospered in the city;

---

*We might note here that political leaders as diverse as Franklin Roosevelt and Mao Tse-tung agreed that future progress required redressing the social imbalances created by excessive migrations to big cities.[4]

many others did not. In any consideration of agricultural efficiency the fate of these people must be taken into account. Agribusiness interests prefer to overlook the human costs. Every progressive step in history, they allege, produces some inevitable casualties; only the end results count. They point to the affluence of the U.S. as living proof of the benefits of the agricultural system.

Callous disregard for the health of the people who grow our food is also overlooked by the promoters of the myth of agricultural efficiency. An interesting example is the persistence of the short-handled hoe in the vegetable fields of California. For years, farm workers ruined their backs by hunching over in an unnatural position. Growers insisted that this implement was more efficient than a long-handled hoe, but the real advantage was the simplification of the job of managing the labor force. Whenever a worker tried to relax for a few minutes, his or her back would naturally become more erect. A foreman could immediately tell who was hard at work and who was not.*

Statistical measures of average wealth and income give little satisfaction to the human casualties of agriculture. In terms of fatalities alone, the costs of modern agriculture are significant. During the first two years of World War II, more Americans were killed on farms than on battlefields.[6] In the present decade, agriculture is ranked the third most dangerous occupation in the U.S.,[7] more dangerous in fact than police work (as measured by workmen's compensation figures).[8] Current measures of casualties from modern agriculture are far too conservative, however. Many—if not the majority—of pesticide exposure cases, for example, go unreported.[9]

The industrialization of U.S. agriculture has made it a major consumer of natural resources. Hardin's successor at the helm of the Department of Agriculture, Earl Butz, noted that "U.S. agriculture is the number one customer of the petroleum industry."[10] Sooner or later society must pay the price for these resources.

In addition, industrialized agriculture enjoys the benefits of massive research subsidies compared to the rest of the world. The handful of wealthy nations spend almost ten times as much on agricultural research as the rest of the world put together.[11] Public agencies in the U.S. alone employed the equivalent of 10,900 full-time scientists in 1965[12] working on 20,000 projects.[13] Moreover, this ratio seriously overstates the capacity of the Third World to direct the course of agricultural research, since many of the projects undertaken there are

---

*Earl Butz gave the following interpretation of the eventual change to the long-handled hoe: "In California, Mexican farm workers are no longer allowed to use the short-handled hoes they have used for generations; now they are required to use long-handled American-type hoes." The Secretary went on to say that ". . . this is not because the workers or the farmers want the change; but apparently because the city people, driving by, feel more comfortable watching the workers using the kind of hoes that look good through car windows."[5]

carried out for the benefit of the multinational firms which control the production of bananas, coffee and other export crops.[14] For example, the Imperial College of Tropical Agriculture in Trinidad, one of the most renowned tropical research institutes, has focused almost all of its research on traditional export crops. Clive Y. Thomas, an economist with experience in that area of the world, points out that this region has never developed even one strain of livestock bred and reared to the ecological requirements of that environment.[15]

The lack of consideration of human needs has dissipated some of the potential benefits of research. In the U.S., for example, the disproportionate power of Southern politicians has given them the power to distort the pattern of research to increase the profits of farmers in their constituancies. In a very low-keyed article by the head agronomist for the Department of Agriculture's Cooperative State Research Service, one can hear a faint plea for rationality.[16] The author hesitantly suggests as a rough rule of thumb allocating agricultural research according to the value of each crop. Based on 1970 values, for every $191 worth of tobacco grown, the Department of Agriculture spends $1 on tobacco research. For corn, $1 worth of research funds is allocated for every $452 worth of corn crop. Putting corn on an equal footing with tobacco would require expanding corn research 250 percent.

What sort of society could assign as high a priority to growing an addictive drug as it does to its most important crop, let alone give it 2 ½ times as much weight? If the more than $1 million spent on tobacco research were geared toward eliminating smoking, the priorities might be understandable; but, in fact, it went toward making tobacco production more profitable. Cotton, incidentally, fared twice as well as tobacco.

Research priorities are doubly important. Not only do they determine how much emphasis is given to growing food instead of tobacco, they also shift the relative profitability of different techniques of farming. When little thought is given to biological control of insects while millions of dollars are used to develop pesticides, we might expect chemical means of pest control to become more profitable.

Even with the irrational allocation of research funds in the U.S., the sheer bulk of available funds should create an impressive agricultural performance. In fact, the record of U.S. agriculture is far from exceptional. In spite of the unparalleled fertility of U.S. soils, nations such as Switzerland and Austria grow twice as much wheat per acre as the U.S.[17] Greece produces more rice per acre,[18] and Austria manages to harvest more than 20 percent more corn per acre than the U.S.[19] Figure 1, reprinted from a publication of the U.S. Department of State, illustrates how poorly U.S. agriculture compares in terms of yields per acre.

At the apex of the U.S. food system stands the beef industry, which consumes as much grain as all the people in India and China eat in a year.[20] In more traditional systems, animals convert inedible wastes or grasses into high quality food: we might at least raise the question of the relative efficiency of these methods of producing meat.

The myth of the efficiency of this technology ignores the pollution created by modern farming methods. American farms produce almost 2 billion tons of animal waste products.[21] They pile up in mountains which contaminate the waters and breed disease vectors. In early 1966, the Interstate Commission on the Potomac River complained that "Every time it rains . . . enormous amounts of animal wastes are washed from farmyards into the river, rendering it unsafe for swimming."[22] The commission went on to compare the sewage facilities for the 250,000 residents of the basin with the nonexistent facilities for the animals in the area which produced an amount of waste equivalent to a human population of 3.5 million.[23] The conditions in the Potomac basin are not unique.

In traditional farming systems, manure is not animal waste but a valuable asset. *The 1938 Yearbook of Agriculture*, written in an age when the Department of Agriculture had a more comprehensive vision of efficiency, estimated that the national supply of manure was capable of producing $3 billion worth of increase in crops (when prices were about 20 percent of what they are today).[24]

"The potential value of this agricultural resource is three times that of the nation's wheat crop. . . . The crop nutrients it contains would cost more than six times as much as was expended for commercial fertilizers in 1936. Its organic matter content is double the amount of soil humus annually destroyed in growing the Nation's grain and cotton crops.[25]

Meanwhile, the whole world seems hell-bent on imitating U.S. feedlot technology—results are optimistically reported from such nations as Japan.[26] Even the Soviet Union is taken in by the myth, so much so that they sound more like Earl Butz than Karl Marx, attributing the efficiency of their agriculture to the "association between agribusiness and the farm."[27] Undaunted by the problems created by feedlot technology, they press ahead in their attempt to duplicate our methods.[28]

The folly of blindly following the lead of U.S. agriculture is based on a grain of sound reasoning. Everybody realizes that improving agriculture is imperative, and the job will require all the knowledge at the disposal of the human race.

When faced with a false choice between continued stagnation and the mythical promises of U.S. agricultural technology, most nations opt for the latter. The major exception to this pattern is China, the only nation which has consciously attempted to develop a technology appropriate to its own conditions. China's success and the conditions that govern it have scarcely begun to impinge on the American consciousness. The experience of Norman Borlaug, winner of the Nobel Peace Prize for his part in the development of the "Green Revolution," is illustrative. Upon reading that China raised 200 million pigs, he was incredulous. "What would they eat?" he asked, thinking in terms of the standard U.S. practice of raising hogs on high quality grain. After seeing China with his own eyes, he estimated that number of swine at 260 million.[29]

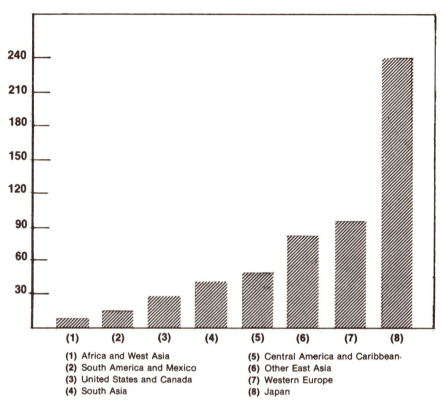

(1) Africa and West Asia
(2) South America and Mexico
(3) United States and Canada
(4) South Asia
(5) Central America and Caribbean·
(6) Other East Asia
(7) Western Europe
(8) Japan

Source: Diane Tendall, "Five Years Later," United States Department of State, *War on Hunger*, vol. 6, No. 10.(1972).

FIGURE 1
Value of food production per acre of agricultural land
in U.S. dollars (1970 estimate)

In China every possible scrap of organic material is run through the pig. What is not converted to pork becomes valuable fertilizer. Even the hair from the pig is tranformed into the bristles of high quality brushes, an important source of foreign exchange. On the other hand, our society, built on waste, even throws away much of the pork, based on one survey which found the average family discarding about 15 percent of the dollar value of its food.[30]

The success of the Chinese hog industry was described in *Foreign Agriculture*, a publication of the United States Department of Agriculture.[31] A few months after this report, one of the co-authors published a study of the Taiwanese hog industry.[32] Originally, Taiwan followed the "pre-modern feeding practices" based on the utilization of table wastes and the by-products of the sugar industry. Under the influence of the most up-to-date techniques in animal husbandry. Taiwan turned to "scientifically formulated" feeds containing large amounts of high protein soybean mean. Today, Taiwan imports 90 to 95 percent of its hog feed, creating a sizable drain on the economy.

The economic and environmental costs of uncritically adopting U.S. agricultural technology in the Third World are incalculable. Perhaps not just millions, but billions of people would be driven from the countryside to already overcrowded cities. The amount of agricultural chemicals poured upon the land would multiply beyond belief. Finally, the resources required for implementing this policy could put an unbearable strain on the world economic system.

I write this book as a plea for rationality.

REFERENCES

1. Clifford M. Hardin, "Foreword," in United States Department of Agriculture, *Contours of Change, The Yearbook of Agriculture, 1970* (Washington, D.C.: United States Government Printing Office, 1970), pp. xxxiii-xxxiv.

2. Dale Hathaway, "Migration from Agriculture: The Historical Record and its Meaning," *American Economic Review*, Vol. 50, No. 2 (May 1960), pp. 379-91; Reprinted in *Agriculture in Economic Development*, Carl Eicher and Lawrence Witt, eds. (New York: McGraw-Hill, 1964), p. 214.

3. United States Department of Agriculture, *Agricultural Statistics, 1975* (Washington, D.C.: United States Government Printing Office, 1975), p. 430.

4. Franklin D. Roosevelt, "Actualities of Agricultural Planning," in Charles A. Beard, ed., *America Faces the Future* (Cambridge, Mass: Harvard University Press, 1932), pp. 326-47; and Mao Tse-tung in *Miscellany of Mao Tse-tung's Thought* (Arlington, Va.: Joint Publication Research Service, Nos. 61269, 1 & 2, 1974).

5. Earl Butz, "Speech to the Indiana Farm Bureau Cooperative Association," (March 17, 1976), cited in *Nutrition Action* (November 1976), p. 12.

6. Anon., "Be Careful," *Horticulture* (July 1976), 3. This feature is a reprint of an item which appeared during World War II.

7. Neal Smith, "The Third Most Dangerous Occupation," *Congressional Record* (September 17, 1959), 35944-49.

8. This point is brought out by Michael Eden Gertler, "Notes on Agricultural Planning and Farm Depopulation in Canada," Senior Honors Thesis, School of Urban and Regional Planning (University of Waterloo, July 1975), pp. 34-35.

9. See Joel Swartz, "Poisoning Farm Workers," *Environment* (July 1975), 26-33; and Richard E. Howitt and Charles V. Moore, "Internalizing Health Effects of Pesticides," University of California, Davis, paper presented at the American Agricultural Economics Association Meetings, Columbus, Ohio (August 10-13, 1975).

10. Cited in Anon., "Farm Fuel: Rationing is not expected this summer," *Sacramento Bee* (June 9, 1973), p. 30.

11. Joseph Willett, Director, "Foreign Demand and Competition Division, Economic Research Service," speech before the Canadian Agricultural Economics Society, Agricultural Institute of Canada, Quebec City (August 6, 1974).

12. T. W. Schultz, "The Allocation of Resources in Agricultural Research," in Wesley Fishel, ed., *Research Allocation in Agricultural Research* (Minneapolis: University of Minnesota Press, 1971), pp. 27, 90-120.

13. Ned Bayley, "Research Resource Allocation in the Department of Agriculture," in Fishel, *op. cit.*, p. 218; and Harlow J. Hodgson, "Scope and Character Public Plant

Breeding Research in the U.S.," *Agricultural Science Review*, Vol. 9, No. 4 (Fourth Quarter 1971), pp. 36–43.

14. W. A. Lewis, *Aspects of Tropical Trade*, 1883–1975 (Stockholm: Almquist and Wicksell, 1969), p. 25.

15. Clive T. Thomas, *Dependence and Transformation: The Economics of the Transition to Socialism* (New York: Monthly Review Press, 1974), p. 106.

16. Hodgson, *op. cit.*

17. *Agricultural Statistics, op. cit.*, p. 10.

18. *Ibid.*, p. 24.

19. *Ibid.*, p. 34.

20. Francis Moore Lappe, "Fantasies of Famine," *Harpers* (February 1975).

21. Cecil H. Wadleigh, *Wastes in Our Relation to Agriculture and Forestry*, Miscellaneous Publication No. 1065 (Washington, D.C.: United States Department of Agriculture, March 1968).

22. *Ibid.*, p. 42

23. *Ibid.*

24. Cited in *ibid.*, pp. 40–41.

25. *Ibid.*, p. 41.

26. Harold D. Smedley, "U.S.-Style Feedlots Are Success Story in Japan," *Foreign Agriculture* (October 6, 1975); and Anon., "U.S. Ranchers Supply Feedlots Expertise," *ibid.* (February 9, 1976), p. 4.

27. Anon., "Meeting in Moscow; Interview with Quentin W. West, Administrator of the U.S. Department of Agriculture, Economic Research Service," *The Farm Index* (February 1974), pp. 12–16.

28. Anon., "Soviet Livestock Complexes Help to Boost Meat Output," *Foreign Agriculture*, Vol. 13, No. 27 (July 7, 1975).

29. Anon., "U.S. Team's Long Look at Agriculture," *RFI Illustrated*, Vol. 2, No. 2 (March 1975).

30. William L. Rathje, "The Garbage Project," *Archaeology*, No. 7 (October 1974), pp. 236–41.

31. Frederick W. Crook and Sheldon Tsu, "People's Republic of China Reports Hog Numbers up Sharply," *Foreign Agriculture* (April 29, 1974).

32. Sheldon Tsu, "Taiwan Hog Raising—Boom Industry with a Few Problems," *Foreign Agriculture*, Vol. 21, No. 48 (December 2, 1974). See also Anon., "U.S. Still Major Supplier of Taiwan's Grain Imports," *Foreign Agriculture*, Volume 14, No. 50 (December 13, 1976), p. 5.

2

ENERGY EFFICIENCY

We look at the progressive farmer of today as an associated businessman in the chemical industry. . . . After all, these men are producing proteins, fats, celluloses, carbohydrates—all of which are processed chemicals. The goal of this chemical plant operator is not to grow a crop of lettuce, a herd of steers, etc., but to maximize his return on his investment.[1]

—T. J. Army and M. E. Smith,
representing the chemical industry

As Clifford Hardin pointed out, U.S. agriculture has been extremely successful in eliminating jobs on the farm; he neglected to add the costs of this transformation. Today agriculture is the largest user of petroleum of any single industry.[2]

In fact, in terms of energy, U.S. agriculture is scandalously inefficient. Farmers burn as many calories of fossil fuel in their machines as the entire population consumes in the form of food; in other words, modern farming U.S.-style consists in transforming fossil fuel into food.[3] Adding the energy cost of producing these machines as well as the fertilizers, pesticides and other purchased farm inputs casts agriculture in an even more damaging light; for each calorie of food the system harvests, it burns about 2½ calories of fossil fuel.

In our society very little food is eaten on the farm. Without a further energy subsidy, it would rot in the countryside. About one-half of all trucks transport food and agricultural items.[4] About 17 percent of all railroad tonnage consists of food and agricultural items.[5] The monetary cost of intercity truck and train transport alone amounted to more than $7 billion in 1974.[6]

Since food takes a relatively long time to go through the complex marketing system, ·much of it is packaged and processed. The food processing industry is the fourth largest consumer of energy of all the Standard Industrial Classification groupings of the Department of Commerce. MacDonald's Hamburgers operations alone consumed the equivalent of 12.7 million tons of coal, enough to supply the combined power

11

needs of Pittsburgh, San Francisco, Washington, and Boston for an entire year.[7]

Our society uses more energy in processing, packaging and transporting food than in growing it. Combining all these energy costs leads to an astounding result: for each calorie of food produced in the U.S., more than six calories of fossil fuel are consumed. While the agribusiness establishment crows about its efficiency in moving workers off the farm, it is very defensive about discussing energy efficiency. Here the U.S. wins a booby prize.

In the Orient, care of the land is a fine art. A substantial portion of its land has been in continuous cultivation for 40 centuries; although much of their land is marginal, yields in China and Japan are comparable to or higher than our own.

In the area where I live, rice is planted, fertilized and sprayed from the air, according to standard American practice. Visitors are often surprised at the thick haze which hangs over our region after the standing rice straw is burnt. Since a local rice paper mill closed down many years ago, the farmers have made no serious effort to turn the stubble into useful products instead of pollution. In China, rice stubble was used for mats or baskets and sometimes it was burned as a cooking fuel. Heat from the stove was drawn off through pipes and led to large black blocks of subsoil which held the heat through the night while the family slept upon them.[8] Sooner or later, the beds began to crumble; the heat and the nutrients from the smoke had opened the blocks up to microbial life. What the blocks lost in usefulness as beds they gained in value as fertilizer. Back they went to the fields to nourish the next crop of rice, beginning the cycle once again.

Romanticizing the life of Chinese peasants would be as misleading as the starry-eyed vision of efficiency publicized by the Department of Agriculture. Those people worked long hard hours, and their poverty was appalling. On the other hand, their poverty was not entirely due to their methods of cultivation. Since the Chinese have eliminated the wastefulness of the landlords and nobility and have mobilized the energies of the people, hunger has been eliminated from China.[9] Today, the Chinese are turning to more mechanized forms of agriculture in hopes of releasing more of the population to build the industry, science and culture of the future, but they still cherish the values which turned rice straw into cooking fuel, bed warmers and fertilizer. According to the modern Chinese ethic, "There is nothing in the world which is absolute waste."[10]

In terms of energy efficiency, traditional Chinese agriculture is the world's champion. According to one estimate, traditional Chinese wet rice agriculture at its best could produce 53.5 calories in the form of food for each calorie of human energy expended in farming.[11] (Notice that we have not even included the calories of human energy in our calculations of the energy input of U.S. agriculture.) For each unit of energy the wet rice farmer puts out, more than 50 are harvested; for each unit of energy consumed in the U.S., only about 1/6 calorie of food results. On the basis of these numbers, traditional Chinese agriculture is about 300 times as efficient as our own in terms of energy.

In fact, this ratio is (based on 1970 energy data) if anything too conservative. True, U.S. agricultural exports were left out of the picture, but exports have tended to be nonprocessed crops such as wheat, corn or soybeans, while U.S. imports have consisted of a high percentage of processed foods.* One study suggests that correcting for exports would not affect the figure by much more than 5 percent.[12] On the other hand, since 1970, energy use has been climbing. In 1970, for example, the average tractor sold was rated at 72 horsepower compared to 97 horsepower in 1975, an increase of about 25 percent.[13]† Although the data on energy cost neglected the role of non-food crops such as cotton or tobacco, including them would not come to much more than 10 percent even though tobacco is one of the most energy-intensive crops, according to Department of Agriculture figures.

Another consideration will offset the cost of non-food crops many times over. After food is shipped to the store, shoppers carry their meals home in 200-horsepower automobiles. Although the amount of energy consumption of this sort which can be attributed to agriculture is not easily quantifiable, it is considerable.

Even the modern farm family specializing in a single crop travels to the supermarket for an increasing portion of its food. In 1941, the value of home-grown food for an average farm family was equivalent to 20 percent of its income, declining to 10 percent in the early post-war period. By 1955, 60 percent of its food was purchased commercially.[16] As of 1973, the average farm family spent more than $2,000 for food.[17]‡ Add to the farmers' shopping trips those of the ex-farmer and the children and grandchildren of ex-farmers and you will have a substantial use of gasoline. Be sure to include the workers who have to commute to the fertilizer factory in the calculation, since the transfer of work from the farm to the factory has also meant the physical separation of residence and workplace.**

---

*Although in 1970 exports were much less than today, a substantial portion of our crops were exported, nonetheless.

†The Department of Agriculture estimates that most farms with over 1500 acres would increase their profits by purchasing a four-wheel with horsepower ratings exceeding 200.[14] The *Wall Street Journal* goes one step further in describing 450-horsepower tractors which can plow almost 60 acres per hour.[15]

‡Think back to the Department of Agriculture's description of the efficient farmer. Imagine that the family of the owner of the broiler factory described by Clifford Hardin once grew its own tomatoes while the tomato farmer raised chickens in the backyard. Today, each purchases the other's product. Even if the total number of chickens and tomatoes raised between them were unchanged, their efficiency, measured in terms of products sold per worker, would improve. In fact, even the more realistic measures of efficiency used by the Department of Agriculture will register an improvement in efficiency in this example.

**If we consider that agriculture is even partially responsible for the sorry state of the cities, than our calculations must include a portion of the enormous number of automobile trips caused by the need to escape the unpleasant surroundings of urban life.[18]

Modern urban life imposes many other demands besides commuting. The Nobel prize-winning economist Simon Kuznets estimated that even in 1929, 20 to 30 percent of all consumer outlays represented costs not required in a rural civilization.[19] These activities required energy as well as money.

The Department of Agriculture's response to the charge of energy inefficiency is that *farmers* burn only 3 percent of the fuel in our society.[20] Even though, as we have seen, the fuel used on the farm represents only a portion of the total energy consumed by the food system, the percentage directly charged to the food production system falls somewhere around 20 percent. This number is kept relatively small, not so much because agriculture conserves energy, but because the rest of our society consumes such incredible quantities of fuel.

We have no reason to believe that the energy efficiency of U.S. agriculture will not continue to get worse. Corn production per unit of energy declined 24 percent between 1954 and 1970.[21] Between 1940 and 1972, tractor horsepower increased sixfold and the quantity of fuel fivefold.[22] Since yields rose far less dramatically, energy efficiency fell. Even the Department of Agriculture seems to expect energy efficiency to continue to deteriorate. A 1973 estimate by the Administrator of its Economic Research Service predicts that the demand for agricultural fuel will increase 45 percent by 1980.[23]

Our measures of energy inefficiency prove that as a model for world development, the U.S. system is suicidal. Just imagine all the nations of the world trying to imitate the U.S. food system with its elaborate marketing and distribution network; to do so would require 80 percent of the world's annual energy expenditures *just* to produce and market food.[24] Optimistic agriculturists, taken in by the myth of agricultural efficiency, are not dismayed by the global energy costs of a U.S.-style food system. Carried away by their fancy, they paint a future of agro-nuclear complexes[25] without mentioning that the cost of the nuclear capacity to produce enough power to grow and distribute in this fashion would come to more than $600 billion (assuming $1000/kw capacity).[26] No nation, not even the U.S., can come up with that sort of money.

While energy inefficiency points to a fundamental fallacy of U.S. agriculture, energy cannot be the sole criteria of agricultural efficiency. Fruits and vegetables are bound to be more inefficient in terms of energy than corn. Are we to conclude that we should eliminate these energy-consumptive foods from our diet? Absolutely not. Measuring efficiency solely in terms of energy is no more accurate than applying the "man-hour" criterion popularized by the Department of Agriculture.

Nevertheless, consideration of energy efficiency is vital. Reservoirs of fossil fuels and minerals run dry; while farming, properly conducted, has the potential to repeat itself indefinitely. Unlike other industries, agricultural production can be expanded without depleting its future productive capacity. In fact, numerous studies indicate that farming might have the potential for economically producing a significant amount of fuel, over and above its harvest of food.[27]

Before farming became just another industry, the great founders of economic theory singled out agriculture as an occupation of special importance.[28] They saw that in agriculture, workers intensified their powers of production by learning how to draw more efficiently upon natural forces; while in industry, workers required sophisticated machinery to accomplish the same end. In evaluating the energy efficiency of agriculture, we should take note of how effectively it succeeds in harnessing these natural forces instead of relying on manufactured inputs.

The value of these natural forces is not insignificant. In a rare attempt to assess the value of nature, three southern scholars estimated the value of tidal marshland.[29] Based on market values, tidal marshland is next to worthless unless it is filled and covered tith subdivisions. These market values ignore many important functions of the tidal marshes which act as nurseries for fish and purify waste water from cities. The monetary value of these services which the tidal marshes produce free of charge was estimated at $2,500-4,000 per acre per year.

Today, agriculture uses more mechanical work per employee than does industry.[30] More importantly, the capital requirements of agriculture are rising faster than those of industry.[31]

TABLE 2-1

Indices of Labor and Purchased Inputs in Agriculture (1967 = 100) in 1967 Dollars

	Labor	Mechanical Power and Machinery	Agricultural Chemicals
1935	299	33	8
1940	292	42	13
1945	271	59	20
1950	217	85	30
1960	145	98	50
1970	90	100	110
1975	81	104	126

Source: United States Department of Agriculture, Economic Research Service, "Changes in Farm Production and Efficiency, A Special Issue Featuring Historical Series," Statistical Bulletin No. 561 (September 1976).

While the operator of a broiler factory can produce 75,000 chickens, he does so not by the efficiently harnessing natural forces but by siphoning off more steel, more fuel and more electricity from the city than his predecessors did. By 1975, the energy bill for the poultry and egg industry was estimated to run almost $650 million, increasing at a rate of 15 percent per year.[32] Marketing the products required even larger amounts of fuel.[33]

While the Department of Agriculture and the agribusiness establishment publicly ignore the problems of energy inefficiency, privately they recognize the problem. At a working conference on research to meet U.S. and world food needs, sponsored by the Department of Agriculture's Agricultural Research Policy Advisory Committee held in 1975, the participants concluded that the nation's "most urgent agricultural research need . . . is to find ways to grow more food using less energy."[34]

The costs of energy-intensive farming are beginning to become apparent on the farm itself. Some farmers in Pecos, Texas, have to discontinue production because they cannot afford the natural gas costs of pumping irrigation water from 500 feet below the ground.[35] In the poultry industry which was singled out for its efficiency by Secretary Hardin, a recent study found that individual operations could save from 20 to 50 percent of its energy bill through more efficient use of ventilation, shading and other simple modifications.[36]

More obvious signals of the need for change came from the supermarket. Because of the energy inefficiency of the food system, food prices are more sensitive to energy costs than most other consumer goods.[37] As energy prices vault higher, so will food costs. Not only will energy prices increase the cost of food for U.S. families, they will make food scarcer.

Currently, agricultural exports amounting to more than $20 billion per year are the major means of paying for imported energy. Food exports can be expanded either by inducing farmers to grow more or by coercing U.S. citizens to eat less. Both methods spell still higher prices.

Besides higher prices, modern agriculture threatens to worsen existing economic problems. Current business publications complain of shortages of capital while workers protest the lack of jobs.[38] How can we describe as efficient a system of agriculture which requires more and more capital while providing fewer jobs? Yet from the very beginning, American agriculture has been designed to minimize employment.

This objective grew out of the historical conditions in which American agriculture was rooted. Now we will turn our attention to these roots.

REFERENCES

1. T. J. Army and M. E. Smith, "Research and Development in Farm Related Firms—Its Impact on Agriculture," Center for Agricultural and Economic Development, Report No. 24 (Ames: Iowa State University, April 1965, p. 133.

2. Committee on Agriculture, House of Representatives, *Food Costs*—Farm Prices, A Compilation of Information Relating to Agriculture, 92nd. Cong., 1st Session (July 1971).

3. John S. and Carol P. Steinhart, "Energy Use in the U. S. Food System," *Science*, Vol. 184 (April 19, 1974), pp. 307-16.

4. *Ibid.*, p. 309.

5. Richard E. Briggs, statement, in "Energy Requirements for Food and Fiber," Hearings before the *Subcommittee on Department Operations, Investigations and Oversight of the House Committee on Agriculture*, House of /representatives, 94th Cong., 1st Session (March 17-18, 1975), p. 85.

6. United States Department of Agriculture, *1974 Handbook of Agricultural Charts*, Agriculture Handbook No. 477 (Washington, D.C.: U.S. Government Printing Office, October 1974), p. 30.

7. Bruce Ingersol, "Fast Foods Draining U.S. Resources," *San Francisco Examiner and Chronicle* (November 12, 1972), p. A24.

8. See F. H. King, in J. B. Bruce, ed., *Farmers of Forty Centuries: or Permanent Agriculture in China, Korea, and Japan* (London: J. Cape Ltd., 1949).

9. Victor D. Lippit, *Land Reform and Economic Development in China: A Study in Institutional Change and Development Finance* (White Plains, N.Y.: International Arts and Sciences Press, 1975).

10. Writing Group of the Tientsin Municipal Revolutionary Committee, "Multiple Use: Important Policy for Industrial Production," *Peking Review*, No. 6 (February 1971), p. 7.

11. Cited in Roy Rappaport, *Pigs for the Ancestors* (New Haven: Yale University Press, 1967, p. 262, referring to Marvin Harris, "Cultural Energy," unpublished ms.

12. Steinhart and Steinhart, *op. cit.*

13. Duane Paul, "Farm Machinery Sales and Prices Likely to Slow in 1976," Agricultura Outlook, (April 1976), pp. 6-7.

14. Anon., "4-Wheel Drive adds New Dimension," *The Farm Index*, Vol. 15, No. 8 (August 1976), p. 11.

15. Karen Arrington, "What's Big, Yellow, Plush, Very Powerful and Travels Fast?" *Wall Street Journal* (August 17, 1976), p. 1.

16. Gabriel Kolko, *Wealth and Power in America, An Analysis of Social Class and Income Distribution*, (New York: Praeger, 1962), p. 17.

17. Fred C. Throp, "Family Expenditures: The Farm Family Living Survey," in 1976 U.S. Agricultural Outlook Papers Presented at the National Agricultural Outlook Conference Sponsored by the U.S. Department of Agriculture, Prepared for the Committee on Agriculture and Forestry, United States Senate, 94th Cong., 1st Session (18 December 1975): pp. 312-18.

18. See Wilfred Owen, *The Accessible City*, Washington, D.C.: The Bookings Institution (1972), pp. 6-7.

19. Simon Kuznets, *Economic Change* (New York: W. W. Norton, 1953), pp. 195-96.

20. See, for example, United States Department of Agriculture, Economic research Service, *The U.S. Food and Fiber Sector: Energy Use and Outlook: A Study to the Energy Needs of the Food Industry*, prepared for the Subcommittee on Agriculture and Forestry, United States Senate, 93rd Cong., 2nd Session (September 20, 1974).

21. David Pimentel, L. E. Hurd, A. C. Belotti, M. J. Forster, I. N. Oka, O. D. Sholes, and R.J. Whitman, "Food Production and the Energy Crisis," *Science*, Vol. 182, No. 4111 (November 2, 1973), pp. 443-49.

22. *The U.S. Food and Fiber Sector, op. cit.*, p. 8.

23. Quentin West, "Food Shortages: A Poor Man's Energy Crisis," a paper presented at the Oklahoma State Fair Energy Forum (September 29, 1973).

24. Steinhart and Steinhart, *op. cit.*

25. Perry R. Stout, "Editorial," *California Agriculture*. Vol. 26, No. 12 (December 1972).

26. Based on figures from Steinhart and Steinhart, *op.cit.*, and the assumption of $1,000/kw capacity and 3412 BTU's kw hrth.

27. For example, see Malvin Calvin, "Solar Energy by Photosynthesis," *Science*, Vol. 184 (1974): pp. 375-81.

28. Adam Smith, *An Inquiry Into The Nature of Causes of the Wealth of Nations* (New York: Random House, 1937.

29. James G. Gosselink, Eugene P. Odum and R. M. Pope, "The Value of the Tidal Marsh" (Baton Rouge, La.: Lousisana State University, Center for Wetlands Resources), Publication No. LSU-SG-74-03 (May 1974).

30. See Allen G. Smith, "Comparative Investment per Worker in Agriculture and Manufacturing Sectors of the Economy," *American Journal of Agricultural Economics*,

Vol. 53, No. 1 (February 1971): pp. 101-2; and Paul Zarembka, "Manufacturing and Agricultural Production Functions and International Trade," *Journal of Farm Economics*, Vol. 38 (November 1966): pp. 952-66.

31. Michael Perelman, "American Agriculture and the Prophecy of Increasing Misery: Comment," *American Journal Agricultural Economics*, Vol. 56, No. 1 (February 1974); p. 165-67.

32. Anon., "Fuel for Fowl," *Agricultural Situation* (March 1976), p. 6.

33. *Ibid.*

34. Reported in *Agricultural Situation* (October 1975) and the Report of a Working Conference sponsored by the Agricultural Research Policy Advisory Committee of the U.S. Department of Agriculture, "Research to Meet U.S. and World Food Needs," Held at Kansas City, Missouri (9-11 July 1975), p. 281.

35. Anon., "Crisis on the Pecos," *Newsweek* (19 April 1976): p. 75. Also Dudley Lunch, "Losing Land to Energy Costs," *Business Week* (4 October 1976): pp. 20E-20F.

36. United States Department of Agriculture, Economic Research Service, *Energy Use and Conservation in the Poultry and Egg Industry*, Agricultural Economic Report No. 354 (October 1976).

37. Thomas Van Arsdall, "Energy Requirements in the U.S. Food System," *Agricultural Outlook* (March 1976), pp. 18-20.

37. Anon., "The Capital Crisis, The $4.5 Trillion America Needs to Grow," *Business Week* (September 25, 1975).

PART TWO

Developing Agriculture for Profit

The moral of history . . . is that the capitalist system works against a rational agriculture, or that a rational agriculture is incompatable with the capitalist system (although the latter promotes technical improvements in agriculture), and needs either the hand of the small farmer living by his own labour or the control of associated producers.

—Karl Marx, *Capital*

3

THE ROOTS OF AGRICULTURE IN THE UNITED STATES

Where land is in such plenty men very soon become farmers, however low they set out in life. Where this is the case, it must at once be evident that the price of labour must be very dear; nothing but a high price will induce men to labour at all, and at the same time it (enables) . . . . them to take a piece of waste land. By day-labourers, which are not common in the colonies, one shilling will do as much in England as half-a-crown in New England.

—Anonymous author of *An American Husbandry* published in London, 1773.[1]

The impulse to mechanize, as well as the neglect of the land, developed as a response to an economic environment in which land was cheap and wages high. The connection between land prices and wages was clear to any employer. So long as workers had the option of farming instead of working for wages, employers had no choice but to offer a standard of living above what workers in Europe could command.

Anything which could limit the wage rate would improve profits. As early as 1636, a committee of Puritans attempted to remedy the high rate of wages with a proposed code "agreeable to the word of God."[2] By 1776, the New England states initiated another drive against "the most extravagant Price of Labour," but they too failed in their efforts.[3]

In Europe the economic environment was very different. A British farm worker in 1830, for example, could purchase about 1/10 acre of land with his annual salary; an Illinois farm worker could afford 80 acres for a year's wages.[4] An English farm worker had to put in three times as many hours to earn enough to buy a bushel of wheat as an American farm worker.[5]

In response to the relatively high labor cost, U.S. farmers sought every conceivable technique for minimizing the amount of labor used on the farm, while in England every nook and cranny was farmed with care.*

---

*We must be careful in using the term "high" to describe U.S. wages. In the last part of the Eighteenth Century, a common laborer with a wife and child sometimes earned less per head than the cost of keeping the three of them in the poor house.[6]

Because of the uniqueness of economic conditions in the U.S., the British reading public devoured a flood of books produced by English travelers describing farming methods in the U.S.[7]

Travelers were unamimoùs on one point. Yields in U.S. farming were far below the British norm. Pennsylvania wheat farms harvested about half as much per acre as a well-run English farm.[8] Although only a few of the travelers recognized that low yields were accompanied by a high output per worker,[9] they sensed the novelty of U.S. agriculture. The reaction of John Robert Godley, writing in 1844, was generally representative of the English descriptions of farming on this side of the Atlantic:[10] "It is long before the English eye becomes reconciled to the lightness of the crops and the careless farming (as we should call it) which is apparent." Most visitors were quick to grasp the cause. Godley was no exception; he wrote, "Where land is so plentiful and labour so dear as it is here, a totally different principle must be pursued to that which prevails in the populous countries, and that the consequence will of course be want of tidiness, as it were, and finish, about everything which requires labour."[11]

Although much has changed in the last 100 years, the relationship between English and American agriculture has not.

As the Department of Agriculture is fond of pointing out, at today's prices a worker in London spends 50 percent more time on the job than a U.S. worker does to earn enough money to buy a loaf of bread.[12] Land in England is still used more extensively for growing food. In the United Kingdom, 80 percent of all land is used for crops and grazing; in this country, less than half is put to these uses.[13] As a result of the more intensive farming practices in England, wheat yields continue approximately to double the U.S. average.[14]

Keen observers such as Godley knew that farms did not just grow food; they also grew workers who hired themselves out for employment in the factories.[15] English workers were so plentiful that the wage rate frequently dipped below the minimum required for human survival.* How could workers in the U.S. be forced to do factory work so long as they had the option to set off on their own as farmers?

In Britain as well as the U.S., factory workers were at the forefront of the struggle for land reform.[19] If some of their fellow workers had the opportunity to start small farms, they hoped to see a reduction in the competition for jobs.†

The land reform movement, especially in England, never succeeded. Workers had no option but to enter those "dark satanic mills." Everything about the factory was foreign to the farm worker. These laborers, accustomed to pacing themselves, balked at the discipline of the facto-

---

*The term "plentiful" is relative. During harvest time farmers considered labor to be scarce.[16] They relied on temporary Irish immigrants.[17] Farm workers in the South complained that the farmers "keep us here like potatoes in a pit, and only take us out for use when they can no longer do without us."[18]

†Settlers in the U.S. were sometimes willing to use force to gain access to land.[20]

ry.* To maintain a steady flow of labor from the farms, laws had to be framed to prevent workers from drifting into vagrancy or falling back on the degrading welfare system of that age. Those who refused to accept employment were subjected to whipping or branding with a red-hot iron.[23]

On the job, the whip was used to stimulate industry as well as to prevent drowsiness; the latter was required for the children, who tired after ten or more hours of constant labor. Admirers of the captains of industry praised them as if they were captains of infantry. Boswell, the famous biographer of Samuel Johnson, described the industrialist, Mathew Boulton, as "an iron captain in the midst of his troops"; while a Scottish writer promoted the industrialists, arguing that their role "required a man of Napoleonic Nerve and Ambition, to subdue the refractory tempers of workpeople accustomed to irregular paroxysms of diligence."[24]

The recruiting sergeant for these industrial armies was poverty. First-rank economists such as Thomas Malthus, most famous for his doctrine of population, were quite frank on the subject. "It is want of necessaries," Malthus explained to his readers, "which mainly stimulates the labouring classes to produce luxuries."[25] William Temple, in his *Essay on Trade and Commerce,* published in 1770, envisioned a noble life of labor for the children of the poor:

When these children are four years old, they shall be sent to the country workhouse [usually recommended by authors of the time to resemble prisons as much as possible], and there taught to read two hours a day and be kept fully employed the rest of their time in any manufactures of the house which best suits their age, strength and capacity. If it be objected that at these early years, they cannot be made useful, I reply that at four years of age there are sturdy employments in which children can earn their living; but besides, there is considerable use in their being, somehow or other, *constantly employed at least twelve hours a day,* whether they earn their living or not; for by these means, we hope that the rising generation will be so habituated to constant employment that it would at length prove agreeable and entertaining to them [emphasis added].[26]

An earlier writer elaborated on the relationship of rich and poor. John Bellers, known for his proposal for a College of Industry, explained the importance of Temple's plan for childcare. Bellers pointed out that "if the poor labourers did not raise much more food and manufacture than

---

*Arthur Koestler describes the incompatibility between industrial rhythms and peasant consciousness in his *Darkness at Noon:*[22]

"I," said Gletkin in his usual correct voice, "was sixteen years old when I learnt that the hour was divided into minutes. In my village, when the peasants had to travel to town, they would go to the railroad station at sunrise and lie down to sleep in the waiting room until the train came, which was usually at about midday; sometimes it only came in the evening or next morning. These are the peasants who now work in our factories.... (Without strong discipline) the whole country would come to a standstill, and the peasants would lie down to sleep in the factory yards until grass grew out of the chimneys and everything became as it was before."

what did subsist them, every Gentleman must be a Labourer, and every Idle Man must starve."[27] As Marx pointed out, workers were treated as "part of the movable fittings of the factory."[28]

In light of English conditions, farming in the U.S. must have appeared to Godley as pursuing a "totally different principle." The politicians and economists of Godley's day sided with his interpretation of the situation. About the same time as Godley was touring this nation, they were actively trying to modify the pattern of colonization in Australia and New Zealand. These devout followers of the free market were taking active measures to artificially create a scarcity of land in these colonies lest the pattern of U.S. development be repeated.*

In the words of one of the major figures in the English Colonial Office, Herman Merivale, ". . . in densely peopled colonies the labourer, although free, is naturally dependent on the capitalist; in thinly peopled ones, the want of natural dependence must be supplied by artificial restrictions."[31] The best-known spokesman for artificial dependence was Edward Gibbon Wakefield,† who hailed the policy of creating an artificial scarcity of land as "systematic colonization"; according to Wakefield, this policy should be valued for its encouragement of "natural slavery, . . . that natural subordination in which the greater part of mankind always have been and probably always will be."[32] In fact, it was little more than a plan to limit the areas of settlement; by making land less available, its price would rise.

The economists and parliamentarians who followed Wakefield were practical men, many of whom joined with him in his investment schemes for colonial development. They knew the importance of a cheap wage and acted accordingly. As many as 50,000 convicts were sent to the American colonies prior to 1776.[33]

Today the historical fears of labor shortages have turned to hysterical scenarios of overpopulation. The name of Thomas Robert Malthus has become a rallying cry for those haunted by the specter of overpopulation. Few of his contemporary followers realized Malthus was an ambiguous prophet of Malthusianism. In fact, he was a far stronger advocate of poverty. His original tract, *An Essay on the Principle of Population as It Affects the Future Improvement of Society*, published in 1798, was not primarily concerned with population control; actually, he denounced the use of contraceptives, even by married couples, as a vice,[34] although he was silent on the vices of industrialists who purchased the children of paupers in "lots of fifty, eighty or a hundred" to be "sent like cattle to the

---

*Landholdings of the poor in the Massachusetts Bay Colony were limited, partly for the purpose of preventing what Governor Winthrop termed "the neglect of the trades."[29] Later, in 1763, the English did try to limit westward settlement in the American colonies to win over the Indians who feared losing their lands. Because of the fierce opposition of speculators and settlers, the Proclamation of 1763 was unenforceable.[30]

†Wakefield was a distant relative of the famous historian who wrote *The Decline and Fall of the Roman Empire,* and associate of John Robert Godley. He educated himself on the subject of colonies while serving a prison sentence for attempting to trick a wealthy young schoolgirl into marriage.

factory where they remained imprisoned for many years."[35]

The key to Malthus' *Essay* is the second part of the title, "as It Affects the Future Improvement of Society." Malthus' father, a close friend of Rousseau, defended the ideas of William Godwin, one of the handful of writers courageous enough to defend egalitarian society in an age when England was abandoning any pretense of civil liberties. Godwin's *Political Justice,* appearing only four years after the French Revolution of 1789, outraged the younger Malthus. His father's acceptance of Godwin's doctrine of human perfectability set Malthus on the attack.[36] Not only is poverty needed as a spur to industry, but, Malthus added, poverty is also the major check on the rise of population, since as wages increase families can afford more children. Remove this check and the teeming masses will breed faster than food supplies increase. Poverty, he concludes, is the inevitable state of mankind.

Malthus, like Godley, was writing in a particular historical context. From feudal times until the industrial revolution, shortages of labor were an overriding concern. During the industrial revolution, new technology was being developed at breakneck speeds. In some industries, shortages of labor continued to be troublesome; while in other places, caring for indigents was more of a problem. Malthus, sensing that labor, unlike other raw materials, cannot be reproduced for immediate use in the factories, saw that the balancing of the reproduction of labor with employers' demand required delicate institutional adjustments; hence, the repudiation of contraception coupled with warnings about overpopulation.

Malthus' pen magically transformed poverty from an irrational defect of society into a natural consequence of the debased mentality of the poor. For Malthus, poverty is not rooted in the relationship between employer and worker, but in the carnal desires of man and woman. The English ruling class rewarded Malthus by appointing him the world's first professor of political economy. This appreciation grew out of their belief, clearly expressed for the well-to-do readers of *The Examiner,* who opened up their paper on the day after Christmas, 1830, to read that it was commendable to teach that "want and labour spring from the niggardliness of nature and not from the inequality which is consequent of the institution of property."[37]

This idea could make little headway in the U.S., where abundant resources were everywhere to be found. Employers were far more concerned with the problem of labor shortages. Although indentured servants and convicts were invaluable in supplying needed labor,[38] the most effective remedy for labor shortages came from Africa. Ships hauled cargoes of blacks to work the fields of the South.

The prevailing view of the time was expressed by a lobbyist for the planters of Georgia who wanted to introduce slaves into the last free state in the South. He argued that ". . . it is clear as light itself, that negroes are as essentially necessary to the cultivation of Georgia, as axes, hoes or any other utensil of agriculture."[39]

The importance of these slaves cannot be overestimated; the tobacco and cotton they grew amounted to over half of U.S. farm exports in 1800.[40] These crops not only supported wealthy planters, but the Northern financial interests which controlled the marketing system. By transferring the profits skimmed off the cotton and tobacco trade into manufacturing investments, the Northern bankers were able to transform the sweat of the slaves into the vital fluids of industry.

Even slaves were not sufficient to eliminate the high cost of labor, however. The constant stream of immigrants helped but did not suffice. Although the workers' standard of living was low, it never sank to the level of the European worker. Employers were obsessed with eliminating this differential, which ate into their profits. They searched the four corners of the earth for immigrants.

Labor-saving inventions were an important source of relief for employers. The demand for inventions of all kinds, was so brisk that tinkerers and inventors of all sorts threw themselves into the effort to develop newer and better machines.[41] No sooner would one invention appear than another would improve on it. The Secretary of the Treasury reported in 1832 that the garrets and outhouses of textile mills were stuffed with discarded machinery.[42]*

Labor-saving technology proved to be an effective weapon in the struggle to hold down wages. In agriculture, labor-saving technology increased the area a single worker could farm, as well as the output of grain per worker. Both results helped solve the problem of high wages. By increasing the area farmed by the average worker, labor-saving agricultural technology helped to absorb the reservoir of cheap, unused land. By increasing the amount of grain a single farmer could work, labor-saving technology helped to glut the market with grain. As the price of grain fell, farmers' income suffered, making agriculture a less attractive venture. In short, labor-saving technology on the farm accomplished, to some extent, what employers had sought in vain to do by law and decree—namely, shut off the escape route from the factory.† The difference between the U.S. and England narrowed, as a result, but did not entirely disappear.

If the American farmer had been self-sufficient, the deteriorating market conditions would have been without effect; but in the U.S., farmers were never self-sufficient. True, land was cheap; but land is only one of the requisites of production. The families who emigrated to the west traveled in oxcarts loaded down with tools, seeds, poultry, utensils and simple furniture.[46] A typical farm in the middle of the nineteenth century cost about $1,000 to establish.[47]‡

---

*Since equipment became obsolete in such a short period of time, business had no interest in paying for durability.[43] Unlike England, where machinery was built from steel whenever possible, wood was the common building material in the U.S.[44]

†The escape route was not available to any and all workers,[45] but although only a small number of workers were actually able to set out as farmers, they still could relieve the downward pressure on wages.

‡To some extent technical change lowered the cost of provisions;[48] but more importantly, it developed more expensive technology.

Few of the workers who set out to become farmers could lay their hands on $1,000 without going into debt. With interest rates running as high as 120 percent, farmers were continually short of the cash to pay off their debts.[49] *The New England Farmer* wrote about the credit needs of its readers:

A farmer sells his pork, butter, cheese, grain, etc. from January to April. The cost of producing these was paid (or ought to have been) the summer or autumn before. His sheep are sheared in May, and should be able to convert their fleeces immediately into money (which he cannot always do). Still the whole expense of producing this wool, excepting about two months spring pasturing, was paid the year before, a considerable portion of it the August before.[50]

The paper concedes that a farmer can get by for a considerable period without much money, but only by slighting the farm, hiring less labor and harvesting fewer crops. Strapped for money, the farmer is forced to sell his produce at reduced prices while buying from the store "wholly on long credit . . . . paying a price, say, twenty to thirty percent more than the cash price. His dealings with the blacksmith, the shoemaker, and mechanics in general are after the same fashion. And thus, he passes his life continually pinched for want of a little money, incessantly harassed by duns, and once in a while appalled by the tap on the shoulder, though gentle it may be, of the practiced hand of the constable."[51]

The harder farmers struggled to pay off their debts, the worse conditions became, since the markets for agricultural produce were so limited. About 1820, for example, about 80 percent of all food products from northern farms was consumed by the rural population.[52] Although urban populations grew, they could not keep up with the expansion in farm production. As Charles Boone outlined the predicament about one hundred years ago in a meeting of fellow Illinois agriculturalists, the farmer:

. . . was an overproducer because he wanted to get out of debt. But when he produced the extra quantities, they depressed the prices and kept him in debt still.[53]

Economists have long supported Boone's contention. The prices of food are sensitive than those of most commodities. The more food the farmers brought to the market, the more prices fell; and with the fall in prices, the farmers had to produce still more food just to stay in the same place.

Farmers looked to the federal government for relief. They agitated for expansion of the money supply. More money meant higher prices, and higher prices deflated the value of their debt. They demanded that the tariffs be lowered; by allowing European manufacturers to freely enter this nation, Europe could be encouraged to lower its restrictions on agricultural imports from the U.S. Northern industrial and financial interests resisted these demands. The plight of the farmer was profitable for them. Lack of competition from European manufacturers allowed them to charge higher prices for their products. Abundant money supplies would weaken their financial strength.

Not only was federal assistance practically nonexistent in questions of monetary policy and tariffs, it was not forthcoming in response to the pleas for lower railroad rates. Only one demand of the farmers rallied the government to their cause. The economic interests of the nation were almost unanimous in their demands that the government adopt an active role in promoting the exports of U.S. agriculture. Senator Sidney Breeze of Illinois voiced their sentiments when he proclaimed:

Illinois wants a market for her agricultural productions; she wants the markets of the world. Ten counties of that state could supply all the home market. We want a foreign market for our produce which is now rotting in our granaries.[54]

By the time the U.S. emerged as a major exporter of crops grown by farm families instead of slaves, problems of labor scarcity had subsided except during the brief periods when the economy was running close to its maximum capacity. The cost of outfitting a farm prohibited many workers from moving into farming. In addition, streams of immigrants flowed into the American cities. Most important, business knew that it could profit from its involvement in foreign agricultural trade. The stakes of these markets were high. In 1869, for example, the value of tallow and butter exports exceeded the value of iron and steel sent abroad.[55]

These markets, seen as the natural outlet for U.S. production, were vitally important for their existing suppliers. Farmers in England or Germany bristled at the thought of cheap U.S. grain flooding their markets. The economic problems of the farmers led to international conflict among nations. The story of the influence of agriculture in shaping U.S. foreign policy is told in great detail by William Appleman Williams,[56] who reminds us that not all politicians were blind to the pitfalls. Many years ago, Thomas Jefferson warned the nation about the dangers of solving domestic problems by foreign trade with the prophetic words:[57] "Our commerce on the ocean and in other countries must be paid for by frequent war."

No matter how aggressively the government pursued foreign markets, the problem of farm surplus persisted because of the continuing rapid increase in farm production. The dim prospects of farming limited the alternatives to factory work. The decline in the possibilities for farming was symbolized by what the superintendent of the census announced as the cessation of the "continuity in the line of settlement," or what the historian Frederick Jackson Turner popularized as the end of the frontier.[58] As the age of cheap land drew to a close, labor had to confront capital in a direct struggle over wages to improve its lot. Workers had to strike against their employers instead of striking out on new careers as farmers.

The "totally different principle" of U.S. agriculture observed by Godley shattered on the increasing scarcity of cheap land. One perceptive U.S. farmer, speaking only one year after the publication of Godley's book, saw what was hidden to Godley: "In very truth," he said, "when enough (farmers) have been driven into manufacturing ... they would be numerous enough to manufacture two or three times as much as this country could consume and the surplus would have to find a foreign market."[59] Once the farm surplus turned into a surplus of goods in general, the momentum generated in the drive for agricultural exports continued as a policy to expand manufacturing exports as well. The U.S. was eventually drawn into conflict with the other great industrial nations in a world struggle over markets which culminated in World War I.

REFERENCES

1. Anon., *An American Husbandry*, London (1773); reprinted as Henry J. Carmen, ed., *An American Husbandry* (New York: Columbia University Press, 1939), pp. 53-54.

2. Jonathan Grossman, "Wage and Price Control During the American Revolution," *Monthly Labor Review*, Vol. 96, No. 9 (September 1973), pp. 3-9.

3. *Ibid.*

4. Paul W. Gates, *The Farmer's Age: Agriculture 1815-1860* (New York: Harper Torch Books, 1960), p. 276.

5. *Ibid.*, p. 276.

6. Philip S. Foner, *History of the U.S. Labor Movement*, Vol. 1 (New York: International Publishers, 1947).

7. On this literature, see Gates, *op. cit.*, pp. 428-39.

8. *Ibid.*, p. 43.

9. *Ibid.*

10. John Robert Godley, Letters From America, 2 vols. (London: Murray, 1844) cited by J. S. Mill, in *Works*, Vol. II (Toronto: University of Toronto Press, 1965), pp. 174-75.

11. *Ibid.*

12. Anon., "The Time It Takes," *Agricultural Situation* (January/February 1976), p. 13.

13. Cynthia A. Breienlohner, United States Department of Agriculture, Economic Research Service, "Structural Changes in Western European Agriculture," Foreign Agriculture Economic Report No. 114 (November 1975), p. 19; and Orville Krause and Dwight Hair, "Trends in Land Use and Competition for Land to Produce Food and Fiber, Perspectives on Prime Land," United States Department of Agriculture, *Background Papers for Seminar on Retention of Prime Lands* (1975), pp. 1-26, p. 3.

14. U.S. Department of Agriculture, *Agricultural Statistics* (Washington, D.C.: U.S. Government Printing Office, 1975), p. 20.

15. William Lazonick, "Karl Marx and the Enclosures in England," *Review of Radical Political Economy*, Vol. 6, No. 2 (Summer 1974), pp. 1-59.

16. E. L. Jones, "The Agricultural Labour Market in England, 1793-1862," in his *Agriculture and the Industrial Revolution* (New York: Halstead Press, 1974), pp. 210-33.

17. Nassau Senior, *A Letter to Lord Howick on a Provision for the Irish Poor*, 2nd ed., London (1831) cited in R. D. Collison Black, *Economic Thought and the Irish Question, 1817-1870* (Cambridge: Cambridge University Press, 1960), p. 102.

18. E. P. Thompson, *The Making of the English Working Class* (New York: Vintage, 1963), p. 223.

19. *Ibid.*, pp. 231, 295; and Foner, *op. cit.*, pp. 444-45.

20. Edward Countryman, "Out of Bounds of the Law, Northern Land Rioters in the Eighteenth Century," in Alfred F. Young, ed., *The American Revolution, Explorations in the History of American Radicalism* (DeKalb: Northern Illinois University Press, 1976), pp. 37-70.

21. E. P. Thompson, *op. cit.*, p. 305; and his "Time Work-Discipline, and Industrial Capitalism," in M. W. Flinn and T. C. Smout, *Essays in Social History* (Oxford: Clarendon Press, 1974), pp. 39-77; and Paul Mantoux, *The Industrial Revolution in the 18th Century, An Outline of the Beginnings of the Modern Factory System in England* (New York: Harper & Row, 1961), pp. 233, 375-76, 409, and 432.

22. Arthur Koestler, *Darkness at Noon* (New York: Macmillan, 1941), p. 160.

23. Paul Mantoux, *The Industrial Revolution in the Eighteenth Century, An Outline of the Beginnings of the Modern Factory System in England* (New York: Harper and Row, 1961), p. 432.

24. *Ibid.*, p. 376; and Stephen A. Marglin, "What Do Bosses Do? The Origins and Functions of Hierarchy in Capitalist Production," *The Review of Radical Political Economics*, Vol. 6, No. 2 (Summer, 1974), p. 85.

25. Thomas R. Malthus, *Principles of Political Economy*, 2d ed. (London: John Murray, 1836), p. 215.

26. See Thompson, *op. cit.*, p. 267. Cited in Edgar S. Furniss, *The Position of the Laborer in a System of Nationalism* (New York: Kelley, 1957), pp. 114-15.

27. Wesley C. Mitchell, *Types of Economic Theory*, Vol. I, Joseph Dorfman, ed. (New York: Augustus M. Kelley, 1967), p. 115.

28. Karl Marx, *Capital, A Critique of Political Economy*, Vol. I (Chicago: Charles Kerr, 1906), p. 632.

29. Carter Goodrich and Sol Davison, "The Wage Earner in the Westward Movement, Part 1," *Political Science Quarterly*, Vol. 50, No. 2 (June 1935), p. 168.

30. Francis Jennings, "The Indian's Revolution," in Alfred F. Youngs, ed., *The American Revolution: Explorations in the History of American Radicalism* (DeKalb: Northern Illinois Press, 1976), pp. 319-48.

31. Herman Merivale, *Lectures on Colonization and Colonies* (London, 1841), Vol. 2, p. 314, cited in Karl Marx, *Grundrisse* (New York: Vintage, 1974), p. 834. See also Karl Marx, *Capital*, Vol. 1 (Chicago: Kerr, 1906), p. 792.

32. Bernard Semmel, *The Rise of Free Trade Imperialism* (Cambridge: Cambridge University Press, 1970), p. 111 citing 2d Report of the Committee on South Australia, v. LV (1841), p. 238. This connection between slavery and availability of labor is historically correct. Perry Anderson points out that the Periclean reforms which saved the Athenian peasantry from debt bondage were promptly followed by a sharp increase in the use of slave labor. See Perry Anderson, *Passages from Antiquity to Feudalism*, London: NLB (1974): p. 36. Dobb says that when labor became scarce in England after the Black Plague, the ruling class tried to reimpose old feudal obligations rather than pay the higher wage rates which could be earned in a condition of labor scarcity. See Maurice Dobb, *Studies in the Development of Capitalism*, New York: International Publishers (1963): p. 57. Evsey Domar suggests the general hypothesis that slavery or serfdom is prevalent in history when labor is scarce; when the bargaining power of labor is low, markets are preferred. See Evsey Domar, "The Causes of Slavery or Serfdom: A Hypothesis," *The Journal of Economic History*, Vol. 30, No. 1 (March 1970), pp. 18-32.

33. See Tom Fulton, "Agricultural Labor in the United States: A Brief History," (United States Department of Agriculture, Economic Research Service, Agricultural History Group, October 1975), p. 9. See also J. J. Tobias, *Crime and Industrial Society in the 19th Century* (New York: Schocken Books, 1967), p. 61.

34. See Leo Rogin, *The Meaning and Validity of Economic Theory, A Historical Approach* (New York: Harper & Brothers, 1956), p. 196; and Marx, *Capital, op. cit.*, p. 695. The French economist, J. B. Say, was taken aback when Malthus wrote to him about his fears of labor shortages. See Maurice Dobb, *Theories of Value and Distribution Since Adam Smith, Ideology and Economic Theory*, Cambridge at the University Press (1973): p. 93.

35. Mantoux, *op. cit.*, p. 413.

36. John Maynard Keynes, *Essays in Biography* (New York: W. W. Norton, 1963), p. 98.

37. Mark Blaug, *Ricardian Economics* (New Haven: Yale University Press, 1958), pp. 144-45.

38. Anon., "Farm Labor's Niche in History," *The Farm Index*, Vol. 15, No. 2 (February 1976), pp. 14-15.

39. Cited by Paul S. Taylor, *Georgia Plan: 1732-1752* (Berkeley: University of California, Institute for Business and Economic Research, 1972).

40. Anon., "Farming for World Markets," *The Farm Index*, Vol. 14, No. 11 (November 1975), pp. 12-16.

41. Charles Kennedy, "Induced Bias in Innovation and the Theory of Distribution," *Economic Journal*, Vol. 74 (September 1964), pp. 541-47.

42. H. J. Habakkuk, *American and British Technology in the Nineteenth Century, The Search for Labour-Saving Inventions* (Cambridge: Cambridge University Press, 1967), p. 56.

43. *Ibid.*, pp. 47 and 57-59.

44. *Ibid.*, pp. 57-59.

45. Goodrich and Davison, *op. cit.*

46. S. Gideon, *Mechanization Takes Command* (New York: Oxford University Press, 1948), p. 144.

47. Clarence Danhof, "Farm Making Costs and the 'Safety Valve': 1850-1860," *Journal of Political Economy*, Vol. 49 (June 1941), pp. 217-59.

48. Carroll W. Pursell, "Comments on Science and Technology in Agriculture," *Agricultural History*, Vol. 46, No. 1 (January 1972), pp. 91-94.

49. Gates, *op. cit.*, p. 73.

50. *Ibid.*, p. 405.

51. *Ibid.*, p. 406.

52. Clarence Danhof, *Change in Agriculture, The Northern United States, 1820-1870* Cambridge: Harvard University Press, 1969), p. 9.

53. William Appleman Williams, *The Roots of the Modern American Empire* (New York: Vintage Books, 1969), p. 162.

54. *Ibid.*, p. 91.

55. *Ibid.*, p. 118.

56. *Ibid.*, p. 118.

57. *Ibid.*, p. 2.

58. Stanley Lebergott, "Labor Force and Employment, 1880-1960," *Output, Employment, and Productivity in the United States After 1880,* (New York: National Bureau of Economic Research, 1966), p. 119.

59. Williams, *op. cit.*, p. 90.

4

CORN AND THE SELLING OF THE SOIL

Imagine a train more than 20,000 miles long, with over 2 million boxcars full of corn. . . . That's the size of the 1969 corn crop.

—Glen D. Simpson in *The Yearbook of Agriculture*, 1970.

The railroads and ships which carried the produce of American lands to far-off peoples were not carrying a surplus; in reality, they were hauling away the fertility of the land. Bountiful harvests of cotton and tobacco ravaged the lands of the South. Its agricultural potential was undermined. True, the Southeastern and Delta states continue to produce crops, but this production is made possible by very costly infusions of manufactured inputs required to take the place of the natural fertility of the land. These states contain only about 8 percent of the farmland in the nation, but they consume 17 percent of the nitrogen fertilizers used in the U.S.[1] and 20 percent of the pesticides.[2]

In the North, worn-out soils were commented on as early as 1700.[3] Soil depletion frequently lowered wheat yields, sometimes by more than 50 percent,[4] but once the rich land of the Corn Belt was opened up to farming, the problem of soil depletion seemed obsolete. These lands seemed to be truly inexhaustible. Of course, they were not. The reservoirs of fertility only served to obscure the effects of soil mismanagement.

Both the mismanagement of the soil and the economic forces which made it rational are bound up in the history of corn. By the time the European settlers reached this continent, the breeding of corn had been in progress for several millennia. Descended from rather commonplace grasses, corn plants were continually selected for the size of their cob. By 5000 B.C., the cob had reached about one inch. Archaeological evidence shows a gradual increase in size until the plant comes to resemble what we now know as corn. The selection of corn as a staple was exceedingly fortunate; not only does corn fall in a special class of plants which utilizes a more efficient photosynthetic process than most other crops, but corn is well adapted to an economy where labor is in short supply. In the words of Governor Bradford at Plymouth, "And sure it was God's good providence that we have found this Corne, for else we know not how we should have done."[5]

Unlike wheat, which must be harvested at the precise moment of maturation, corn harvesting can be spread out over time without serious crop losses.[6] Corn is also less susceptible to plant disease and destruction by parasites.[7] Most importantly, the prairie soils of the U.S. are perhaps the best soils in the world for growing corn.[8]

For the U.S. farmer, selling corn was a great deal more difficult than growing it. Unlike the situation in Europe, where farmers and consumers lived close to each other, in the U.S. great distances separated the farmer from his markets, domestic as well as foreign. In the 1850's, for example, grain grown in Lawrence, Kansas, only 30 to 40 miles from the Missouri river, was worth nothing without the railroads because the cost of transporting the grain to the river was more than dealers paid for it there.[9] Representative John Adam Kasson of Iowa protested, "The great burden of the West is that it costs so much to get articles to market that it leaves almost nothing as a profit."[10] Even the *American Railroad Journal* admitted that the Illinois surplus of wheat and corn, worth $40,000,000 in New York,

> . . . did not net the producers more than $12,000,000. This vast difference is due to the charges for transportation alone. Illinois turns her vast resources to small account, for the want of more and better avenues to market.[11]

Here, too, corn had the edge over other grains. Sometimes, the farmer's only recourse was to bring his grain to market in the form of livestock; and, as a feed, corn is more suitable than wheat or most other grains.[12] As one observer exclaimed, "For what is a hog but fifteen bushels of corn on four legs?"[13] Around Cincinnati, where the meat packing industry first developed, corn prices sank to six cents per bushel in some districts; in others, they fell so low that corn was burned as a fuel instead of wood.[14] With prices so depressed, farmers often hogged down their fields rather than expend the time and energy to harvest their corn.[15]* The resulting production of hogs was so great that the packing industry could not cope with the bulk. Only the most valuable parts of the carcass were used; the rest were thrown into the river.[17] To process the enormous supply of meat, the packing industry developed the assembly line long before its debut in Detroit.

We have already seen how U.S. farmers chose methods of farming corresponding to the structure of prices. Early American farmers such as George Washington concurred with Godley that U.S. farming was characterized by "cultivating much rather than cultivating well."[18] The

---

*The traditional American razorback hog was noted for its ability to fend for itself foraging in the woods. With the advent of the packing industry, the costless razorbacks lost their commercial value.[16]

fate of the corn, haphazardly grown, hogged down and ultimately transformed into pork dumped into the river, dramatizes the performance of U.S. agriculture. While the outlet per acre of U.S. farming was scandalously low, the product per worker was impressive by European standards.

This result is consistent with economic theory. With prices reduced well below European norms, farmers had to sell more crops to earn a standard of living comparable to a European farmer. Given the level of wages, farmers predictably attempted to spread their labor as well as that of their hired workers over as large an area as possible. Although this strategy of farming conforms to economic theory, in practice its consequences were seriously detrimental to this society, since one of the most effective labor-saving techniques was what some called "land butchery."[19]

Just as the factories profited from the continual scrappage of machines, so, too, the farmers benefited from the scrapping of the land. From the beginning of colonization of this part of the world, little thought was given to the care of the soil. Visitors commented on the settlers' "aversion to trees";[20] farmers were forever clearing the land, farming it, only to abandon it a few years later. After all, it took less time to clear new land than to care for the soil. Jefferson, for example, figured that it made no sense to fertilize his land "because we can buy an acre of new land cheaper than we can manure an old acre."[21] Others considered the idea of manuring the land "simply ridiculous"—"with the present scarcity and high price of labor, how is the farmer to find time and money or labor to manure his farm . . . .?"[22]

The consequences of this sort of thinking were visible to the naked eye. When the unspoiled lands of Oklahoma were opened to settlement, observers could recognize the more luxuriant crops as soon as they crossed over the Kansas border. As might be expected, the difference did not last for long.[23]

Even those who saw the dangers inherent in the continued disregard for the land could do nothing about it. The low price of food was predicated on the minimization of labor. Any time or labor expended on the care of the soil would just push up the immediate costs of production, putting the farmer at an economic disadvantage which he could probably ill afford. One of the most perceptive British travelers writing on U.S. agriculture, Patrick Shirreff, observed:

The farming of a country is affected by local circumstances and farming in Britain and in the remote parts of America may be considered the extreme of the art. In the one country the farmer aims to assist and in the other to rob nature. When the results of capital and labor are low, compared with the hire of them, they are sparingly applied to the soil, in which case nature is oppressed and neglected if I may be allowed to use such terms; and when they are high compared with their hire, she is aided and carressed. Both systems are proper in their respective countries.[24]

Shirreff was correct that both systems were proper, if that term simply means conducive to the short-run profitability of farming; but how can agriculture be described as proper when it destroys its own basis—the soil? Or perhaps we could say that the illusion of propriety is possible only so long as farmers could draw upon a pool of unexhausted soil fertility.

The thought of running out of fertile soil was foreign to most farmers. By the time the western frontier had reached the prairie soils of the midwest, farmers were more convinced than ever that they had found a soil which could not be exhausted. When they carved blocks of topsoil from the ground to build their sod houses, they saw how deep and rich the soil was. Of course, they were wrong. Today, the depth of the topsoil, once measured in feet, is calculated in inches.[25]

The consequences of soil depletion moved westward with the frontier. By 1800, yields were suffering even in the more fertile areas of the east.[26] By the 1860's, soil depletion was making itself felt as far west as Iowa.[27] Not only were yields falling off as a result of inadequate care of the soil, but plant diseases and insects were taking a greater toll of the crops.[28]

Yields of corn, like most other crops, suffered. True, overall production per acre remained constant between 1870 and 1902, but only because worn-out soil continued to be taken out of production while virgin land was put to the plow.[29] Then between 1902 and 1925, yields increased slightly because less fertile land like that found in Texas and Oklahoma was taken out of production. After that time, yields gradually fell off until the 1930's.

In the subsequent years, yields of corn as well as other crops zoomed upwards even though the organic content of midwest soils had declined about 50 percent in the last hundred years.[30] True, some of the increases in corn yields after 1937 resulted from nothing more than the discontinuation of production in some of the lower-yielding Southern states;[31] climatic improvement also contributed to the increases in corn yields.[32]

While other cultures rose and fell according to how well they managed their topsoil,[33] U.S. agriculture continues to prosper even though about one-third of our topsoil is lost to erosion.[34] More importantly, the Department of Agriculture persists in its claim of agricultural efficiency even though the quality of soil management is deteriorating. The Department of Agriculture's own statistics, assembled before the problem of erosion worsened in the last few years, show that more than two-thirds of our agricultural land is not adequately managed with respect to soil conservation;[35] but then conservation has never figured heavily in the American image of efficiency, not nearly so much as profitability. Even the Department of Agriculture at one time recognized that "the success and prosperity of the American farmer are due to the unbounded fertility of the soils, the cheapness of farm lands and the privilege of utilizing modern inventions in machinery rather than to systematic organization and efficient management."[36]

Two Stanford researchers who studied technical change in corn production amplified on this relationship between soils, machines, and efficient management in agriculture; they concluded that crop production is

... essentially an extractive operation, transforming natural wealth into another form of capital, as does any form of mining. The trend of decreasing yields despite movement towards better land suggests that increases in the total production of corn between 1870 and 1937 were, to a large degree, brought about by fertility-depleting operations. Capital in soil fertility was transformed into animals and machines which, in turn, enabled the process to be accelerated."[37]

The continued marketing of the fertility of the soil was incompatible with good farming; but in U.S. agriculture, farming was all too often a lesser concern than profits from speculation.

REFERENCES

1. United States Department of Agriculture, Economic Research Service, "1975 Changes in Farm Production and Efficiency, A Summary Report," Statistical Bulletin 548 (1975).

2. Helen T. Blake and Paul A. Andrilenas, "Farmers' Use of Pesticides in 1971," United States Department of Agriculture, Economic Research Service, Agricultural Economics Report No. 296 (November 1975), p. 4. For a more detailed discussion of soil exhaustion in the South, see Eugene D. Genovese, *The Political Economy of Slavery* (New York: Vintage, 1967), pp. 85-99.

3. See Richard Wilkenson, *Poverty and Progress: An Ecological Perspective on Economic Development* (New York: Praeger, 1973), pp. 152-53.

4. *Ibid.*, pp. 152-53.

5. Cited in Walton C. Galinat, "The Evolution of Corn Culture in North America," *Economic Botany*, Vol. 19 (1965), pp. 350-57, reprinted in Stuart Streuver, *Prehistoric Agriculture* (Garden City, N.Y.: Natural History Press, 1971), p. 535.

6. See D. B. Grigg, *The Agricultural System of the World, An Evolutionary Approach* (Cambridge: Cambridge University Press, 1974), p. 179; and Paul W. Gates, *The Farmer's Age: Agriculture 1815-1860* (New York: Harper Torch Books, 1960), p. 170.

7. Gates, *op. cit.*, p. 169.

8. *Ibid.*, p. 172.

9. James C. Malin, "The Grassland of North America: Its Occupance and the Challenge of Continuous Reappraisals," in William L. Thomas, Jr., ed., *Man's Role in Changing the Face of the Earth*, Vol. I (Chicago: University of Chicago Press, 1956), p. 357.

10. Cited in William Appleman Williams, *The Roots of Modern American Empire* (New York: Vintage Books, 1969), p. 119.

11. Cited in Williams, *op. cit.*, p. 97.

12. Cited in Gates, *op. cit.*, p. 169.

13. J. S. Wright, *Chicago: Past, Present, and Future* (Chicago: University of Chicago Press, 1970), p. 213, cited in Williams, *op. cit.*, p. 145.

14. Siegfried Gideon, *Mechanization Takes Command, A Contribution to Anonymous History* (New York: Oxford University Press, 1955), p. 215.

15. Gates, *op. cit.*, p. 218 and Gideon, *op. cit.*, p. 215.

16. Clarence Danhof, *Change in Agriculture, The Northern U.S., 1820-1870* (Cambridge, Mass.: Harvard University Press, 1969), p. 178.

17. Gideon, *op. cit.*, p. 215.

18. H. J. Habakuk, *American and British Technology in the Nineteenth Century: The Search for Labour-Saving Inventions* (Cambridge: Cambridge University Press, 1967), p. 101.

19. Fred A. Shannon, *The Farmer's Last Frontier, Agriculture, 1860–1897* (New York: Farrar & Rinehardt, 1945), p. 169.

20. Gates, *op. cit.,* p. 3.

21. *Ibid.,* p. 101.

22. Shannon, *op. cit.,* p. 170.

23. *Ibid.,* p. 169.

24. Patrick Shireff, *Tour Through North America* (Edinburgh, 1835), p. 341, cited by Clarence H. Danhof, in *Change in Agriculture, The Northern U.S., 1820–1870,* (Cambridge: Harvard University Press, 1969), p. 50.

25. Gates, *op. cit.,* p. 172.

26. Y. Hayami and V. Ruttan, *Agricultural Development: An International Perspective* (Baltimore: Johns Hopkins Press, 1971), p. 140.

27. *Ibid.;* see also Gates, *op. cit.,* p. 168.

28. Danhof, *op. cit.,* p. 50.

29. James O. Bray and Patricia Watkins, "Technical Change in Corn Production in the U.S.," *Journal of Farm Economics,* Vol. 46, No. 4 (November 1964), pp. 751–65.

30. Barry Commoner, "Nature Under Attack," *Columbia Forum,* Vol. 11, No. 1 (Spring, 1968).

31. Bray and Watkins, *op. cit.*

32. Louis M. Thompson, "The Impact of Agricultural Drought in the Corn Belt and High Plains of the United States, A Report to the National Oceanic and Atmospheric Administration," Columbia, Mo. (November 9, 1973).

33. See Edward Hyams, *Soil and Civilizations* (New York: Thames and Hudson, 1952); Tom Dale and Vernon Gill Carter, *Topsoil and Civilization* (Norman: University of Oklahoma Press, 1955); Genovese, *op. cit.,* Chap. 4; and Marx, *Capital,* Vol. 1, Chap. 15, Sec. 10.

34. National Academy of Sciences, *The Life Sciences* (Washington, D.C.: National Academy of Sciences, 1970), p. 1961.

35. United States Department of Agriculture, Conservation Needs Inventory Committee, "Basic Statistics of the National Inventory of Soil and Water Conservation Needs," United States Department of Agriculture, Statistical Bulletin No. 317 (1972).

36. Willet M. Hays and Edward G. Parker, *The Cost of Producing Farm Products,* United States Department of Agriculture, Bureau of Statistics, Bulletin No. 48 (1906), p. 9.

37. Bray and Watkins, *op. cit.,* pp. 760–61.

5

SPECULATION

The farmer has been something of a pioneer.... And it has been an essential trait of this American pioneering spirit to seize upon so much of the country's natural resources as the enterprising pioneer could lay hands upon. . . .

Subtraction has been the aim of this pioneer spirit, not production; and salesmanship is its line of approach, not workmanship.

—Thorstein Veblen, "The Independent Farmer"[1]

The most perceptive observer of speculation in the U.S. was Thorstein Veblen. In fact, Veblen is probably the most important economist the U.S. has ever produced.

Born in a family of Norwegian immigrants, Veblen was contemptuous of the careless farming techniques of the U.S.[2] He looked at the heart of U.S. agriculture and realized that the economic pressures of agriculture explained only a part of the behavior of farmers in this society. Veblen, more than any other important economist, realized that farming in this society had never been separate from land speculation. True, the farmer suffered under economic pressures more severe than the typical industrialist. Low prices, excessive costs of transportation and credit, as well as the uncertainty of harvests, combined to make farming a risky and not very lucrative business. But land speculation . . . that was something else.

Veblen's 1923 essay, "The Independent Farmer," continually returns to the theme of the farmers' "timeworn make-believe that they are still individually self-sufficient masterless men."[3] As Veblen saw the farmer, he was so caught up in his hunger for speculative profits that he blinded himself to "the system of business interests in whose web the farmers are caught."[4] He offered his "unwavering loyalty" to the system in which he saw himself acting like any other independent businessman. Unfortunately for him, most of the other businessmen were not independent at all. Their units of operation were "drawn on a large scale . . . massive, impersonal, imperturbable and in effect, irresponsible, under the established law and custom, and they are interlocked in an unbreakable framework of common interest."[5]

Veblen's ironic essay pictures the farmer deluded by his fantastic vision of the world around him. All around him, bankers, railroad magnates and food processors profit from their "effectual collusive control of the market,"[6] while the foolish farmer does little more than identify with the very people who are most adept at exploiting him. Some day he, too, will share in the prosperity of the system, at least so he believes. The poor farmer turned a deaf ear to the warning that it is certain that all cannot become rich in this way. All cannot be shavers—some must be fleeced."[7]

Veblen seems to have exaggerated the uniformity among farmers. Wheat farmers, for instance, are more vulnerable to fluctuations in the marketplace. Not surprisingly, they are more prone to organize for reform. Corn growers are more insulated from the market; they can distribute their labor relatively evenly over the year; they are less vulnerable to the weather than wheat growers; and they can always feed their corn to hogs if they find the price of corn unacceptable. Where wheat is grown, populism tends to take root more easily; in the Corn Belt, McCarthyism flourished.[8]

In spite of Veblen's oversimplification of the differences between farm groups, his insights into the overall nature of farm management were devastatingly accurate. True, some farmers may have felt close to the soil, but the English traveler, James F. W. Johnson, never saw them. He found in his wanderings "scarcely any such thing as local attachment—the love of a place, because it is a man's own."[9] "Speaking generally," he continued, "every farm is for sale."[10]

Fred Shannon points out that the 1910 census found 54 percent of the farm population living on tracts they occupied for five years or less.[11] He continues:

There was not the remotest chance of getting acquainted with the soil in that interval. A lifetime was hardly enough. . . . In the best farming regions of Europe the tendency is to value old soils because the family, through generations, has learned to understand them.[12]

This emphasis on speculation made for an irrational farm economy. Naturally, the larger the farm the greater the speculative profits. In the farmer's eye, the potentional of these profits often outweighed the consequences of expanding the farm beyond what could be justified in terms of growing crops efficiently. Many a would-be land baron, dreaming of a sunny future of speculative profits, eked out a living as a land-poor farmer. Even this fate was not possible for the misguided speculator who went too deeply in debt to keep the creditors at bay.

Generally, for society as a whole, speculative development is disorderly development. Some farmers went so far as to withhold land from farming —adding on more land to their farms than they could hope to cultivate.[13] Large tracts of land, known as "speculative deserts," lay unused.[14]

In making land artificially scarce, speculators limited the opportunities for prospective farmers. To the extent that speculation barred workers from becoming farmers, the pressure to force workers into unattractive occupations became more severe. The workers who were able to become farmers as well as the farmers who sold out to move farther west had to cultivate land in more remote districts. As a result, the transportation burden became more extreme. The long distances also made education more difficult for farm children.[15] Veblen attributes the high rate of insanity among women on the farm to the "dreary isolation" of agricultural life.[16] Paul Gates, a historian reknowned for his work on agriculture and land politics, suggests that a more orderly development of the land might have forestalled the pressure for the creation of the Kansas-Nebraska territories which played such an important role in the sequence of events leading up to the Civil War.[17] Finally, we should add that since speculation encouraged the expansion of farm size, it must bear some of the blame for the neglect of the soil.

Veblen added another negative consequence to the list of problems generated by a speculative psychology in agriculture. Unlike most other economists, Veblen understood that "farming is team-work."[18] Cooperation, not competition, is the key to efficiency in agriculture. Even Earl Butz has recognized that "farm cooperatives and farm organizations [provide] the best alternative for maintaining control of farming in the hands of farmers."[19] Unfortunately, the farm cooperative movement has never developed to its full potential or has been corrupted by bureaucratic control. Farmers themselves have never learned to control the institutions which control their lives. Some of the blame must be traced to the individualistic mentality fostered by decades of the false lure of speculative profits.

Veblen's insight did not stop there. He called for teamwork in farm production itself. Since Veblen, economists have been mute on the subject of cooperative and collective farming and even Veblen did not go into much detail on this subject. Hopefully, the ongoing success of Chinese agriculture will turn our attention to the potential of cooperation in farm production.

In spite of every effort to cut corners and reap the benefits of speculation, the farmer, in general, was not particularly successful at the business of farming. Veblen ironically credits the farmers with being "good losers . . . gracefully accept[ing] the turn of things . . . and . . . count[ing] on meeting with better luck or making a shrewder play next time."[20]

Veblen was not alone in recognizing that the cards were stacked against the farmer in the marketplace. John Scott, president of the Iowa Board of Trade, spoke of the farmer as the object of "the sport of the bulls that toss and the bears that squeeze."[21] Even Lincoln noted that agriculture "clad in homespun" is generally "elbowed aside by capital, attired in ten-dollar Yorkshire."[22] The farmers, unfortunately, never saw the market in these terms. Instead, they got caught up in speculative designs. In Veblen's words, "Their passion for acquisition has driven them to work, hard and painfully, but they have never been slavishly attached to their work; their slavery has been not to an imperative bent of workmanship and human service, but to an indefinitely extensible cupidity which strives to work when other expedients fail."[23]

The farmers' mishandling of the soil, together with their unwillingness to combine their market power, have put them more and more at the mercy of the market. Their struggle for survival will be told now by returning to the history of corn production.

REFERENCES

1. Thorstein Veblen, "The Independent Farmer," in Max Lerner, ed., *The Portable Veblen* (New York: The Viking Press, 1948), pp. 395–406.

2. See Joseph Dorfman, *Thorstein Veblen and His America* (New York: The Viking Press, 1940), Chap. 1.

3. Veblen, *op. cit.*, p. 398.

4. *Ibid.*, p. 399.

5. *Ibid.*

6. *Ibid.*, p. 396.

7. Paul W. Gates, *The Farmer's Age: Agriculture 1815–1860* (New York: Harper Torch Books, 1960), p. 276.

8. Jeffrey M. Paige, *Agrarian Revolution, Social Movements and Export Agriculture in the Underdeveloped World* (New York: The Free Press, 1975), p. 36.

9. Gates, *op. cit.*, p. 400.

10. *Ibid.*, p. 400.

11. Fred A. Shannon, *The Farmer's Last Frontier: Agriculture 1860–1897* (New York: Farrar & Rinehardt, 1945), p. 9.

12. *Ibid.*

13. Gates, *op. cit.*, p. 199.

14. *Ibid.*

15. *Ibid.*, p. 113 and Veblen, *op. cit.*, p. 403.

16. Veblen, *op. cit.*, p. 403. See also Anon., "Women in Agriculture," *The Farm Index*, Vol. 15, No. 1 (January 1976).

17. Gates, *op. cit.*, p. 199.

18. Veblen, *op. cit.*, p. 396.

19. Earl Butz, Address at FS Services, Inc., Annual Meeting, Chicago (22 September 1972).

20. Veblen, *op. cit.*, p. 405.

21. Cited in William Appleman Williams, *op. cit.*, p. 152.

22. *Ibid.*, p.115.

23. Veblen, *op. cit.*, p. 404.

6

THE INDUSTRIALIZATION
OF CORN

The barbarous Indians, which know no better, are constrained to make a virtue of necessitie, and thinke it a good food: whereas we may easily judge, that it nourisheth but little, and is of hard and evill digestion, a more convenient food for swine than for men.

—John Gerard, English Herbalist
of the late sixteenth and early seventeenth century[1]

The extensive use of tractors in farming is a recent phenomen. It first took on economic importance during World War I, when labor on the farm became scarce once again.* In spite of the dramatic changes brought about by the tractor, its economic advantage was slight enough that animals continued to contribute a significant portion of agricultural power until comparatively recently. As late as 1952, the number of horses and mules on U.S. farms exceeded the number of tractors.[3] A 1956 English study concluded that the horse was more economical than the tractor in nations as advanced as Great Britain.[4]†

Mechanical power has several advantages over animals. In the first place, it allows one worker to farm a larger area than is possible with horse-drawn equipment. The tractor has an undeniable appeal, given the pressure to increase output per worker. Farm animals consume food every day whether they work or not.[6] As a result, tractors tend to be more economical where farming is less intensive. Also, remember that some

*Raymond Wik points out that E. D. Swinton, the British inventor of the tank, was inspired by watching a Caterpillar in Antwerp.[2]

†This study should be somewhat qualified. The tractor was feasible on some farms as early as the 1890's. Its practicality at the time was generally limited to specialized grain farms. Since the early tractors were not capable of dealing with row crops, they were dropped from the rotation. The hauling of dung from the stalls was eliminated because the tractor could not enter through the narrow gates. The net effect of early mechanization in England was a movement toward a stockless grain farm.[5]

farm animals were used to pull wagons. As the truck and the car replaced the wagon, the amount of work remaining for the plow horse diminished and the average cost per hour of work increased substantially. Finally, timeliness is crucial in agriculture. With corn, for instance, delaying the planting by a single day between May 15 and June 1 can drop yields by about one bushel per acre.[7] Since the tractor allows the farmer to complete his operations in less time, we must credit the tractor with another decided advantage.

While these advantages cannot be denied, something else is at stake. Farming is not just technical or biological; farm work is part of a more general economic process in which human labor power is combined with land and other resources. Purely technical aspects of agriculture cannot be analyzed independently of the way labor, land and other resources are treated. Some of this treatment reflects natural conditions; some does not. Take the case of labor.

The use of the tractor shifts labor from the fields to the factory. Instead of breeding, raising and caring for animals on the farm, workers under the strict supervision of the factory assemble tractors. Since the factory worker is more easily disciplined than the farm worker, transferring work to the factory increases the amount of work that employers can extract from workers.

Most of the important economists of the nineteenth and early twentieth century would have agreed on the benefits of transferring agricultural work to the factory. In their eyes, farm labor could never develop the productivity of industrial labor, because of the nature of farm work. This difference had nothing to do with the social relations between employer and worker; so far as they were concerned, improvement in the productivity of agricultural labor was limited by its irregularity.*[10] More recent analysis of the factory process lends credibility to our earlier thesis, that ease of supervision was fundamental to the success of the factory.[11] More importantly, almost all of these economists were wrong in their prediction that the nature of farm work would inevitably lead to stagnation in agricultural production.[12] Only Marx had the foresight to anticipate that agricultural technology would outstrip industrial technology as a consequence of the application of manufactured products to agricultural production.[13]

The importance of the relationship between workers and employers in agriculture cannot be overstated. We will come back to this point several times in the course of this book: so long as workers do not have a vested interest in making agriculture productive, discipline will be required. Since discipline is harder to maintain in the field than in the factory, agricultural technology will tend to rely more and more on work which can be done in the factory. The net result of this process is an industri-

---

*Throughout the rest of the book we will return to the subject of social relations,[8] which will be used in the same sense as in a study of Bertell Ollman, in which he points out that Marx defined society as "the human being himself in its social relations."[9]

alized farming which consumes more resources and is less in touch with ecological relationships.

The treatment of resources in this economy reinforces this tendency. We have already discussed the mining of the soil; most of these industrially based agricultural technologies involve the mining of our fossil fuel reserves as well. So long as these resources are priced cheaply, the market will tend to confirm the correctness of current agricultural practices just as it had confirmed the mining of soil.

The Department of Agriculture argues that the tractor releases land which otherwise would have to be used for producing feed for farm animals. The horses and mules used on U.S. farms in 1939 required 81 million acres of land to produce their feed.[14] At the present level of mechanization, using horses for all our farm horsepower would require 20 to 50 times more cropland for grazing than we cultivate at this time.[15] As a matter of fact, the potential for increasing the quantity of food for human consumption has never been realized; about 91 percent of all U.S. production of cereal, legume and vegetable protein suitable for human use is fed to animals,[16] with substantial losses in quantity in the final product.*

The soil, compacted from the weight of the tractor and deprived of the droppings from the horse, fared worse than ever, even though another war-related situation obscured the problem.

As in the case of the tractor, in the early development of the nitrogen industry, military considerations played an important role. Prior to World War I, the Chilean nitrate deposits were the major source of nitrogen explosives as well as commercial fertilizers. When the Germans found themselves cut off from the Chilean nitrate, they developed a process which utilized free nitrogen in the air. In the U.S. Section 124 of the 1916 National Defense Act, mandated that the government involve itself in nitrogen technology.[17]†

The government also authorized the Tennessee Valley Authority to produce and distribute fertilizers in 1935. Although the purpose was ostensibly to aid farmers, its military significance was no secret. Besides supplying military plants with nitrogen, during the second world war the TVA became the largest military supplier of another important fertilizer, phosphorous, which is also used for explosives.[19]

Fertilizer, like tractors, became a standard component of farm operations after World War I, although part of its application must be attributed to government subsidies.[20] These subsidies of chemical fertilizers are, in effect, government-sponsored disincentives to use manures. While this policy might be justified on military grounds, manufactured fertilizer is very costly in terms of energy. For example, in growing an acre of corn, the major item in the energy budget is the manufacturing of nitrogen fertilizer, which accounts for about one-third of the energy cost

*Animal products, in addition, are luxury items which for the most part benefit the affluent minority.

†About 10 percent of all nitrogen is used for explosives.[18]

of corn production.[21] Just as in the case of the tractor, the industrialization of fertilizer represents the replacement of a biological process by a highly supervised industrial process. The fertilizer industry, like the farm implement industry, is highly capital-intensive and makes possible a significant increase in farm production with a minimum employment of labor. Our dependence on manufactured fertilizers is so great that they are responsible for between one-third and one-half of the crop production in the U.S.[22]

Reliance on tractors and manufactured fertilizer consumes far more resources than farming with animals and manure, which utilize biological processes. Government programs designed to raise the price of agricultural products encouraged farmers to overlook these costs. In fact, until the 1970's everybody seemed too taken up with the sudden rise in the yields of corn and other crops to pay attention to the underlying production process.

The single development most commonly credited with the vigorous climb in corn yields was the introduction of hybrid corn. From the time of the early experiments of Cotton Mather, a clergyman better known for his unstinting efforts to eradicate witches from the Massachusetts colony, European settlers have searched for improved breeds of corn. By 1877, researchers reported 50 percent increases in yield from hybrids.[23]

To some extent, the higher yields from hybrid corn can be traced to a more aggressive root system which is able to extract fertility previously inaccessible to other strains of corn. Had it not been for the application of fertilizers, hybrid corn would have accelerated the rate of soil depletion.

On the other hand, the ability of hybrid corn to produce a greater quantity of grain was not matched by an ability to produce the same quality; the increased yields were achieved at the expense of protein content. Agronomists refer to this phenomenon as the inverse nitrogen law, which states that the more nitrogen we find in a crop, the less we can expect its yield to be.[24] Similarly, the higher the yield, the less the percentage of nitrogen we can expect to find. Nitrogen is found in all proteins; it may be taken as a rough proxy for the protein level of corn.

Low-yielding Indian corn has shown a protein content from 12 to 15 percent. Indian corn is uniformly richer in every essential mineral than commercially grown corn of today.[25]* Teosinte, widely believed to be an ancestor of corn, has an even higher protein content ranging from 19 to 23 percent.[27] In addition, so-called primitive strains of corn had a much higher quality of protein than modern corn, which is especially low in lysine.[28] With the introduction of hybrid corn, yields increased but protein content fell from about 10 percent to about 8.7 percent in 1946.[29]

According to William Albert Albrecht, once the head of the Department of Soil Science at the University of Missouri,[30]

. . . in 1911, before the hybridization practice was common, the mean concentra-

---

*Native Americans were able to further enhance the nutritional quality of corn by cooking it with ashes.[26]

tion in this feed grain was reported at 10.30% for a single grain. By 1950, the top grade among five then listed contained 8.8%, while the lowest had 7.9%. By 1956, among 50 tested corn grains from the outlying experiment fields of the Missouri Experiment Station, one sample of these hybrids reached a low of 5.15% of "crude" protein, or a value of just half what it had been 45 years ago.*

Since that time, the protein content of corn has increased as a result of more intensive fertilizer use, but recent work on the effects of fertilizer suggests that this recovery in overall protein content was accompanied by a fall in the levels of lysine and tryptophan.[36]

Although 10 percent is normal in hybrid corn, some samples have been found to contain as little as 7 percent protein.[37] In some cases, hybrid corn fails to pick up essential trace elements such as boron and cobalt, when these elements are present in the soil.[38] Sulphur, which is required for the proper functioning of ruminants, is also deficient in hybrid corn.[39] These deficiencies severely limit the nutritional quality of corn.

When hybrid corn was first introduced, livestockmen complained about the poor performance of hybrid corn as a feed.[40] Since 1950, the efficiency of hogs as a converter of calories of food has considerably declined.†[41] The decline in cattle efficiency since 1950 has been about 50 percent.[43] This falling off of feed efficiencies for hogs and cattle is especially interesting because the corn is supplemented with very high protein food. Until recently, the chief supplement was fish caught off the coast of Peru. By 1967, fishmeal accounted for about one-third of all U.S. broiler feed.‡[44] A few years ago, the U.S. imported enough protein in the form of fishmeal to bring the Latin American protein consumption up to the level enjoyed by Southern Europeans. U.S. livestock are exceedingly well fed; while in Peru, a substantial number of babies begin life with serious, and possibly irreparable, brain damage as a result of malnutrition.[46]

Today, after years of overfishing, the catches have drastically fallen off. No one knows whether they will recover.[47]

Today, soybeans are supplanting fishmeal to some extent; enough soybean protein alone was fed to U.S. livestock in 1972 to satisfy the requirements of 200 million people for a year.[48] But for about three

---

*The same situation has developed with other grains. Volunteer oats contain as much as 37 percent protein;[31] higher yielding cultivated varieties contain an average of only 17 percent. The average protein level of the common Peruvian-Bolivian potato is 3.24 percent. Some varieties run as high as 5.83 percent. In the U.S., the average is only 1.89 percent.[32] In 1969, Georg Borgstrom wrote that the common wheat varieties of that day contained 20-25 percent less protein than varieties grown before the end of World War II.[33] This downward trend seems to be continuing. Between 1962 and 1973, the protein content of Montana wheat dropped by an additional 6 percent.[34] Some wheat is currently being harvested in the U.S. which is so low in protein that it is unfit for milling, according to the U.S. Department of Agriculture.[35]

†This trend has continued even though lard yield per hundred pounds of live weight has declined during the last 20 years.[42]

‡In an earlier age, many of these fish would have been eaten by the large bird population in the area. Their droppings would have accumulated as part of the Chilean guano deposits.[45]

decades the major success of the most powerful agricultural nation of the world has depended on subsidies of protein from lands where malnutrition is common. Such is the nature of progress.

Hybridization changed the nature of corn production. Farmers no longer planted seeds from their own harvest. Specialized firms produced seeds for sale. Corn was not just bred to suit the needs of society or even farmers; it was designed for the convenience of the seed growers as well. Hybridizing corn requires removing the tassels from much of the corn so that it gets fertilized by another breed. Manually cutting the tassels of corn used to cost seed growers between $100 and $200 per acre.[49]

To avoid this cost, seed growers turned to genetic engineering. In 1925 in Davis, California, an onion plant was observed with no male organs.[50] By 1931, corn breeders discovered the same trait in a corn plant.[51] In 1945, another line of male sterile corn was discovered in Texas. This gene, dubbed Texas Male Sterile or Tms, was incorporated in all hybrid corn together with another gene discovered by D. F. Jones, which restored the tassels in subsequent generations. This development in genetic engineering replaced the 125,000 high school students who earned some extra money cutting tassels from the corn.[52]

In 1958, one of the giants in corn breeding, D. F. Jones, discoverer of the restorer gene, warned his fellow workers that they were courting disaster in their reliance on genetic engineering:

> Genetically uniform pure line varieties are very productive and highly desirable when experimental conditions are favorable and the varieties are well protected from pests of all kinds. When these external factors are not favorable, the results can be disastrous due to some new virulent parasite.[53]

Three years later two researchers in the Philippines confirmed Jones' warning.[54] Corn containing the Tms gene was virulently attacked by *Helminthosporium maydis*. Other corn was relatively immune. American workers ignored this omen. By 1970, no more warnings were needed. *Helminthosporium maydis* struck the U.S. corn crop. About 15 percent of the corn crop was lost. South Carolina lost about 43 percent of its crop, and Illinois, where about one-quarter of the nation's corn crop is grown, lost about 24 percent.[55] These losses were far less than what might have occurred had the weather not taken a favorable turn during the growing season. Even so, the 1970 losses from this fungus cost the nation about $1 billion.

Seed growers should have worried that male sterility is known to alter the transport and synthesis of DNA and RNA in the male organs of plants.[56] When *Helminthosporium maydis* struck, it upset the workings of the mitochondria, small oddly shaped bodies whose action allows chemical reactions to take place inside the cells which house them.[57] Somehow, the incorporation of the male sterile gene weakens the resistance of the mitochondria to the fungus. Other corn plants were relatively immune.*

---

*The problem of genetic uniformity is not limited to corn. Marquis wheat, for example:[58]

. . . was not very resistant to rust, and the bad rust year of 1916 doomed Marquis as a reliable variety. However, plant breeders were able to cross Marquis and Kota (a resistant Russian wheat) to produce the first artificially rust-resistant wheat. It was called Ceres. Meanwhile, the black stem rust fungus had developed, and in 1935 the millions of fields of Ceres wheat were severely damaged.

Thatcher, another wheat with Marquis parentage produced by American wheat breeders, became the most important wheat on the Great Plains of North America. Unfortunately, Thatcher was not resistant to leaf rust and had to be discarded as a profitable variety. New rust-resistant varieties replaced Thatcher, but the fungus again produced a new race, called 15B by the plant pathologists. This strain of black stem rust, first observed in Iowa in 1939, had become very troublesome by 1950. In 1953, race 15B devastated the spring wheat crops of North America with losses of up to 75 percent in durum wheats and 35 percent of the bread wheats.

The devastation of the 1970 corn crop reminds us of the dangers in the industrialization of agriculture. A field may be plowed with a tractor instead of a horse without altering the fundamental biological processes of farming. The same holds true, to a lesser extent, for the replacement of manures by chemical fertilizers. Once agriculture turns to genetic engineering for improvements, it runs grave risks. Nature cannot be manipulated just to suit the convenience of employers. With so many people depending on hybrid corn, proper plant breeding requires a careful consideration of the plant as a whole, not just one or two desirable traits.*

What does economic theory have to say about the development of hybrid corn? In the same year that D. F. Jones issued his warnings on the genetic dangers of hybrid corn, Zvi Griliches, a statistical economist from Harvard University, attempted to estimate the social benefits from research on hybrid corn.[60] Griliches claims that he took special pains to make his calculations as conservative as possible. In spite of this caution, he estimated that for every dollar invested in research on hybrid corn, society earned a dividend of 700 percent per year.

Griliches' paper has served as the model for innumerable imitations, but it fails to prove anything. As we have seen, hybrid corn was a different product produced by different inputs than open-pollinated varieties. Any valid analysis of hybrid corn would have to take into account its suscepti- bility to disease, its lower nutritional value and, most of all, its depen- dence on the continued mining of resources necessary to produce the fertilizer, tractors, and other industrial inputs which are integral parts of the economy of hybrid corn.† Only if we assume that the market is

---

*In addition, genetic uniformity makes crops more vulnerable to man-made disasters. The U.S. military routinely studies the resistance of Russian and Chinese plants to disease.[59] Apparently, their interest stems from the ease with which a nation's food supply could be demolished through the intentional introduction of a pathogen. Besides the simplicity of this technique, it offers the further advantage of the near impossibility of detection.

†This point was made by G. K. Boon:

One needs a clear definition of the product whose production costs are to be prepared. Ideally, the definition of the product includes an exact description of the type of raw materials, the quality desired, the precise measurements where possible, an exact indication of all those conditions which may influence the comparison. The products, although made by alternative methods, must be of equal quality.[61]

capable of accurately reflecting all these factors can we regard Griliches' work seriously.

As one of the very few critics of Griliches argues:[62]

To conclude, as Griliches has done, that the rate of return on the development of hybrid corn in the U.S. was of the order of 700 percent may well be correct within the calculus of that approach. Add warts and "social" evaluations, and (no doubt) the figure will change a little. What remains unaltered, however, is that to accept that sort of framework for analysis is also to suppose that one is asking the right questions in the right way.

With upward revaluation of resources consumed in hybrid corn production, some of the apparent efficiency of this technology would be expected to vanish. Indeed, something of the sort appears to be occurring. Although corn is the most efficient food plant (in terms of food to calories of fossil fuel input), this characteristic owes more to its photosynthetic abilities than to any aspect of corn production. David Pimentel and his associates at Cornell calculated that each calorie of fossil fuel committed to corn production resulted in 2.7 calories of corn.[63] Most of this efficiency is dissipated by feeding corn to animals. Also, modern technology works against the natural efficiency of corn. Between 1945 and 1970, the calorie output per unit of energy input has declined by 24 percent.[64]

This deterioration of agricultural efficiency makes less and less sense with rising energy prices. A recent survey of Corn Belt farmers indicates that those who use manure instead of chemical fertilizer, and crop rotation instead of pesticides, do at least as well as those who purchase these expensive materials.[65]* Are the chickens coming home to roost?

*This study is not offered as conclusive proof of our proposition that the seeming efficiency of hybrid corn would evaporate with rising energy prices. The study does not indicate that either set of farmers used open-pollinated varieties.

REFERENCES

1. Cited in Charles B. Heiser, Jr., *Seed to Civilization, The Story of Man's Food* (San Francisco: W. H. Freeman, 1973), p. 99.

2. Raymond Wik, "Some Interpretations of Agriculture in the Far West," *Agricultural History*, Vol. 49, No. 1 (January 1975), pp. 84–86.

3. Wayne D. Rasmussen, "A Postscript: Twenty-five Years of Change in Farm Productivity," *Agricultural History*, Vol. 49, No. 1 (January 1975), pp. 84–86.

4. Keith Dexter, "A Study of the Economic Costs of Production: An Analysis of Horse and Tractor Costs," *Journal of Agricultural Economics*, (June 1956), pp. 75–81.

5. See Paul A. David, "The Landscape and the Machine: technical interrelatedness, land tenure and the mechanization of the corn harvest in Victorian Britain," pp. 145–205 in Donald N. McCloskey, ed., *Essays on a Mature Economy, Britain After 1840*, (Princeton: Princeton University Press), p. 185; and E. Whetham, "Mechanization of British Farming, 1910–1945," *Journal of Agricultural Economics*, Vol. 21, No. 2 (May 1970), pp. 6–7.

6. See Naum Jasney, "Tractor Versus Horse as a Source of Farm Power: Their Competition in Various Countries of the World," *American Economic Review*, Vol. 25, No. 4 (December 1935), pp. 708-23.

7. Earle E. Gavett, "Agriculture and the Energy Crisis," presented at the National Conference on Agriculture and the Energy Crisis, University of Nebraska (April 10-11, 1973). Earle E. Gavett is the leader of the Farm Labor and Mechanization Group, Production Resources Branch of the Economic Research Service of the U.S. Department of Agriculture.

8. Bertell Ollman, *Alienation: Marx's Conception of Man in Capitalist Society* (Cambridge: Cambridge University Press, 1971), Chap. 2.

9. Karl Marx, *Grundrisse* (New York: Vintage, 1974), p. 712.

10. John Stuart Mill, *Principles of Political Economy*, Vol. II of his *Collected Works*, J. M. Robson, ed. (Toronto: University of Toronto, 1965), p. 142; Alfred Marshall, *Principles of Political Economy* (London, 1936), p. 209; and John M. Brewster, "The Machine Process in Agriculture and Industry," *Journal of Farm Economics*, Vol. 32, No. 1 (February 1950), pp. 69-81.

11. Stephen A. Marglin, "What Do Bosses Do? The Origins and Functions of Hierarchy in Capitalist Production," *The Review of Radical Political Economics*, Vol. 6, No. 2 (Summer, 1974).

12. Michael Perelman, "American Agriculture and the Prophecy of Increasing Misery: A Comment," *American Journal of Agricultural Economics*, Vol. 56, No. 1 (February 1974), pp. 165-67.

13. *Ibid.*

14. Gavett, *op. cit.*

15. Harold J. Barnett, "The Myth of Our Vanishing Resources, *Trans-Action* (June 1967), pp. 7-10; reprinted in Roger Revelle, Ashok Kholsa and Morris Vinoskis, eds., *The Survival Questions: Man: Resources and His Environment* (Boston: Houghton, Mifflin, 1971), pp. 180-86.

16. David Pimentel, William Dritschilo, John Krummel, and John Kutzman, "Energy and Land Constraints in Food Production," *Science*, Vol. 190 (November 21, 1975), pp. 754-61.

17. Jesse W. Markham, *The Fertilizer Industry: Study of an Imperfect Market* (Nashville: Vanderbilt University Press, 1958), p. 211.

18. Subcommittee on Department Operations of the Committee on Agriculture, House of Representatives, *Fertilizer Shortage Situation, Hearings*, 93d Cong., 1st Session, September 26, and October 3, 4, and 9, 1973 (Washington, D.C.: U.S. Government Printing Office, 1974), p. 12.

19. Markham, *op. cit.*, p. 219.

20. *Ibid.*, p. 211.

21. David Pimentel, L. E. Hurd, A. C. Bellotti, M. J. Forester, I. N. Oka, O. D. Sholes, and R. J. Whitman, "Food Production and the Energy Crisis," *Science*, Vol. 182, No. 4111 (November 1973), pp. 443-49.

22. University of California Task Force, "A Hungry World: The Challenge to Agriculture," (Berkeley and Davis: University of California, Division of Agriculture, July 1974), p. 97.

23. D. D. Harpstead, "Man-Moulded Cereal—Hybrid Corn's Story," in *That We May Eat: Yearbook of Agriculture, 1975* (Washington, D.C.: United States Department of Agriculture, 1975), pp. 213-24.

24. See Hugh Nicol, *The Limits of Man, An Inquiry Into the Scientific Bases of Human Population* (London: Constable, 1967), p. 33: "In 1900 Lawes and Gilbert published a voluminous paper in which they pointed out *inter alia* that in non-leguminous crops such as cereals and turnips, in the state in which they are usually harvested, a characteristic effect of nitrogenous fertilizer is to increase yields per acre of starch, sugar, and fat—the non-nitrogenous constituents. . . . [t]his magisterial statement has not been mentioned in any textbook as far as I know," (J. B. Lawes and J. H. Gilbert, *Phil. Trans. Roy. Soc.*, B, Vol. 192

abundant resource endowment in U.S. agriculture, Americans tend to give the credit to land grant colleges and government research as well as price supports.[35]

In conclusion, we can say that American agriculture is truly efficient in adapting itself to the price system. It minimizes the use of labor by reliance on huge fossil fuel subsidies and neglect of resources, exactly the type of behavior sanctioned by the price system.* In this sense, economists are correct in speaking of agricultural efficiency, but only in a limited sense. In the words of one of the highly respected Brookings Institution reports, "An economic system should be judged by how it affects the lives of its citizens, and not by how well it maximizes money profits or measured output."[37]

What can be said for the rationality of a society which plans to minimize the use of labor when faced with massive unemployment? What sensible person could advise society to squander the resources upon which it depends? Obviously, such advice would be dismissed out of hand. Yet the price system forces each firm to behave in a way which is irrational for society as a whole.

Economists know that families are motivated not just by desire to gain immediate consumption, but to leave an estate for their descendants.[38] The market hinders society from caring for its future;† instead, it encourages the accelerated mining of its natural wealth.

About 100 years ago, Karl Marx prophesied:[40]

From the standpoint of a higher economic form of society, private ownership of the globe by single individuals will appear quite as absurd as private ownership of one man by another. Even a whole society, a nation, or even all simultaneously existing societies taken together, are not the owners of the globe. They are only its possessors, its usufructuaries, and, like *boni patres familias* (good fathers of the family), they must hand it down to succeeding generations in an improved condition.

---

*In the words of the editors of *Business Week*, "Ever since James Watt's steam engine in 1769 launched the Industrial Revolution, Western capitalism has managed to surmount its economic and social problems with a simple reduction in energy costs to make economic growth possible at extremely rapid rates."[36]

†Arrow and Fisher have shown that the market cannot adequately allow for the irreversible consequences of environmental damage.[39]

REFERENCES

1. Warren C. Scoville, "Did Colonial Farmers 'Waste' Our Land?" *Southern Economic Journal*, Vol. 20 (October 1953), pp. 178-81.

2. Karl Marx, *Capital*, Vol. 1 (Chicago: Kerr, 1906), Chap. XV, Sec. 10; and Vol. 3 (New York: International Publishers, 1967), p. 813; and his *Theories of Surplus Value*, Part 3 (Moscow: Progress Publishers, 1971), p. 309.

3. Marx, *Capital*, Vol. 1, *op. cit.*, pp. 260 and 292-93.

4. Kenneth E. Grant, "Erosion in 1973-1974: The Record and the Challenge," *Journal of Soil and Water Conservation*, Vol. 30, No. 1 (January-February 1975).

5. James Ridgeway, "Stripmine," *The Elements* (May 1976). David Pimentel *et al.* estimate that about 2.1 billion gallons of gasoline per year are required to offset the effects of erosion on the land. See David Pimentel, Elinor C. Terhune, Rada Dyson-Hudson, Stephen Rochereau, Robert Samis; Eric A. Smith, Daniel Denman, David Reifschneider and Michael Shepard, "Land Degradation: Effects on Food and Energy Resources," *Science*, Vol. 194 (October 8, 1976), pp. 149-55. In addition, these authors point out that the sediment from land in the U.S. costs society about one-half billion dollars annually.

6. Lowell D. Hill and Steve Erickson, "Economics of Agricultural Energy Use," *Ag World*, Vol. 2, No. 3 (April 1976), pp. 1-6.

7. Earl Cook, "Saving the Environmental Goat with the Energy Cabbage," *Exxon Magazine* (Spring, 1974).

8. See United States Department of Agriculture, Economic Research Service, "The U.S. Food and Fiber Sector: Energy Use and Outlook; A study of the Energy Needs of the Food Industry," prepared for the Subcommittee on Agricultural Credit and Rural Electrification of the Committee on Agriculture and Forestry, U.S. Senate, 93d Cong., 2d Session (September 20, 1974), p. 21.

9. *Isaiah* 55:1.

10. E. J. Mishan, "The Evaluation of Life and Limb, A Theoretical Approach," *Journal of Political Economy*, Vol. 79, No. 4 (July/August 1971).

11. J. A. Kay and J. A. Mirlees, "The Desirability of Natural Resource Depletion," in D. W. Pearce, ed., *The Economics of Natural Resource Depletion* (London: Macmillan, 1975), pp. 140-76.

12. Carlo M. Cippola, *Before the Industrial Revolution, European Society and Economy, 1000-1700* (New York: Norton, 1976), pp. 109-111.

13. Karl Marx,"Preface to the Critique of Political Economy," in Karl Marx and Frederick Engels, *Selected Works in Three Volumes* (Moscow: Progress Publishers, 1969), Vol. 1, p. 361.

14. H. C. Darby, "The Clearing of the Woodland in Europe," in William L. Thomas Jr., *Man's Role in Changing the Face of the Earth* (Chicago: University of Chicago Press, 1970), pp. 200-201.

15. George Perkins Marsh, *Man and Nature: or Physical Geography as Modified by Human Action* (Cambridge, Mass: Harvard University Press, 1965), pp. 192-94.

16. William Petty, (Charles Hull, ed.), *Economic Writings* (New York: Kelly, 1963), Vol. 1, pp. 285-90. See also Richard Cantillon, "Essay on the Nature of Trade in General," in Ronald Meek, ed., *Precursors of Adam Smith* (Totowa, N.J.: Rowman and Littlefield, 1974), pp. 8-13.

17. Kenneth E. F. Watt, *The Titanic Effect: Planning for the Unthinkable* (Stamford, Conn.: Sinauer, 1974), p. 153.

18. Eugene Ayres, "The Age of Fossil Fuels," in William L. Thomas, Jr., *Man's Role in Changing the Face of the Earth* (Chicago: University of Chicago Press, 1970), pp. 367-68.

19. Cited in Cippola, *op. cit.,* pp. 267-68.

20. See Bernard Semmell, *The Rise of Free Trade Imperialism* (Cambridge: Cambridge University Press, 1970), pp. 181-83.

21. Nassau Senior (S. Leon Levy, ed.), *Notes on Senior's Industrial Efficiency and Social Economy* (New York: Henry Holt, 1928), p. 244.

22. Paul Bairoch "Agriculture and the Industrial Revolution," in C. Cippola, ed., *The Fontana Economics History of Europe*, Vol. 3. *The Industrial Revolution* (London: Fontana, 1973), p. 490.

23. Stanley Lebergott, "Labor Force and Employment, 1800-1960," in National Bureau of Economic Research, *Output, Employment and Productivity in the U.S. After 1800*, Vol. 30, "Studies in Income and Wealth" (New York: NBER, 1966), p. 128.

24. M. H. Toulmin, "Letter to editor," *Monthly Magazine*, Vol. 12 (1802) cited by Thomas Spence, "Britain Independent of Commerce," reprinted in his *Tracts on Political Economy* (New York: Viking, 1933), p. 33.

25. Robert Solow, "The Economics of Resources or Resources of Economics," *American Economic Review*, Vol. 44, No. 2 (May 1974), pp. 1-14.

26. Nicholas Georgescu-Roegen, *The Entropy Law and Economic Process* (Cambridge, Mass.: Harvard University Press, 1971).

27. J. S. Mill said that Parliament would be guilty of a "criminal dereliction of duty" if it did not arrange to pay off the national debt before coal deposits were exhausted. Cited by William D. Gramp, "Economists and Politicians: Some Cautionary History," Paper presented at the American Economic Association Meetings, Dallas (December 29, 1975), p. 15, citing *Hansard*, Vol. 181 (April 17, 1866), p. 1525. Alfred Marshall concurred with the idea. See Alfred Marshall (A. C. Pigou, ed.), *Memorials of Alfred Marshall* (New York: Kelly and Millman, 1956), p. 322, reprinting a letter to the *Times* (April 22, 1901). See also Senior, *op. cit.*, p. 221, where he referred to the British potential for steam power as the greatest element in the nation's wealth. For a general survey of the importance of coal, see E. A. Wrigley, "The Supply of Raw Materials in the Industrial Revolution," *Economic History Review*, 2d Series, Vol. 15, No. 1 (August 1962), pp. 1-16.

28. William Stanley Jevons, *The Coal Question*, 2d ed. (London: Macmillan, 1866), p. 173.

29. Adam Smith (E. Cannon, ed.), *An Inquiry into the Nature and Cases of the Wealth of Nations* (New York: Random House Modern Library, 1937), p. 423.

30. John Rae, *Statement of New Principles on the Subject of Political Economy* (Boston, 1834), reissued, R. Warren James, ed., 2 vols. (Toronto: University of Toronto Press, 1965).

31. *Ibid.*, p. 12.

32. *Ibid.*, p. 206.

33. William Scoville, *op. cit.*, pp. 180-81.

34. Anon., "Tax Briefs," *Wall Street Journal* (June 9, 1976), p. 1.

35. Charles O. Meiburg and Karl Brandt, "Agricultural Productivity in the United States," *Food Research Institute Studies in Agricultural Economics, Trade, and Development*, Vol. 3, No. 2 (May 1962): pp. 63-85.

36. Anon., "How OPEC's High Prices Strangle World Growth," *Business Week* (December 20, 1976), pp. 44-50.

37. Richard R. Nelson, Merton J. Peck and Edward D. Kalchick, *Technology; Economic Growth and Public Policy*, (Washington, D.C.: Brookings Institution, 1967), p. 147.

38. Franco Modigliani and Richard Brumberg, "Utility Analysis and the Consumption Function: An Interpretation of Cross Sectional Data," in *Post-Keynsian Economics*, Kenneth K. Kurihara, ed. (New Brunswick, N.J.: 1954), pp. 388-436.

39. See Kenneth J. Arrow and Anthony L. Fisher, "Preservation, Uncertainty and Irreversibility," *Quarterly Journal of Economics*, Vol. 78, No. 2 (May 1974).

40. Karl Marx, *Capital*, Vol. III (New York: International Publishers, 1967), p. 776.

APPENDIX ON PRICES

Value is determined . . . in an apparently rational way, by costs of production and its social utility. Subsequently, it turns out that value is entirely fortuitous and need have no connection either with cost of production or with social utility.

—Karl Marx and Frederich Engels,
"The Holy Family," 1844.[1]

In the last section, we discussed the ability of markets to take account of the future. The challenge of this sort of reasoning is serious but not insurmountable. Depletion taxes and other patchwork measures could conceivably correct for the insufficient weight put on future needs. On the other hand, the fact that any correction is needed at all raises more serious questions which threaten the entire framework of conventional economics.

As a result, the justification of markets totally falls apart. Even some of the most vigorous defenders of the market have been driven to admit that the theoretical demonstrations of the benefits of the market memorized by generations of obedient students do not prove anything at all. The only defense left to advocates of the market, even according to its proponents, is a "faith" that it will work well.[2]

This debate has been carried out on a very theoretical level so far because the participants have not yet sorted out its practical ramifications. This much is clear: Prices are not a measure of scarcity.

If prices are not a measure of scarcity, what do they measure? The answer is that they reflect the relative powers of economic forces, or what Marx termed "the respective powers of the combatants."[3]

Scarcity, of course, affects these powers, but it is by no means the sole determinant. This debunking of prices may very well turn out to be the most important development in economics in the twentieth century. The rest of this appendix is devoted to an elaboration of the debate itself. It may be skipped without any loss in continuity.

Although the debate itself is very modern, it actually begins about 150 years ago.

The story begins with David Ricardo, the most brilliant economist England ever produced. Ricardo was a successful financier whose letters to the editor of the *Morning Chronicle* sparked the interest of the most important economic thinkers of the day. Ricardo became the most influential spokesman for indirect farming, basing his argument in terms of how much a worker could produce. This method of quantifying economic activity in terms of labor raised thorny technical problems which have troubled generations of economists.

Just about 100 years after the death of Ricardo, Piero Sraffa, a meticulous Italian scholar transplanted to Cambridge University in England, produced a draft of a manuscript intended to clarify Ricardo's meaning.[4] For almost 40 years, he polished and refined, until his slim volume was ready for publication in 1960. Sraffa's compact book created a furor. Not only did he piece Ricardo's work together, he showed that standard economic theory could produce inconsistent and contradictory results. Much of the argument is very technical, but its meaning can be made fairly clear with a simple example.

Imagine a nation in which the farmers spend two hours a day selling their crops at roadside stands. During this time, they hire a worker to take their place in the fields. As labor costs rise,* they find that they can save some money by selling at a discount to a middleman who will market their crops for them. As labor prices go up still further, the middleman comes back to them demanding a greater discount. He explains that higher wages make the cost of operating his stores unprofitable. Faced with this demand, the farmers may find it more profitable to rehire their replacements while they market their own crops once again.†

The major virtue of the market is supposed to be its capacity to allocate scarce resources through the workings of supply and demand. Sraffa brings these concepts into question. If we accept conventional economic theory, then we should expect that when the wage rate rises, less labor will be hired. When an increase in wages leads farmers to turn to a middleman to market their produce, we might infer that this new arrangement requires less social labor than the direct marketing by farmers. When a further increase makes them abandon their arrangement with the middleman, we could then infer that direct marketing requires less labor than the use of a middleman.

Of course, direct marketing cannot use more labor in the first case and less in the second, since we are assuming that the farmers are returning to the original state of affairs. Conventional theory leaves no way of getting out of this contradiction.

Direct marketing may be profitable at one level of wages, unprofitable at a higher level and then profitable once again when wages increase another notch because farmers are not concerned with the amount of

---

*Assume that wage rates are equal in both farming and food distribution.

†Although our example is not intended to describe current trends, recent events do make it seem a bit reasonable now that direct marketing is becoming more popular among farmers.[5]

labor used by the middleman; rather, they are affected by the cost of labor. To simplify his explanation, Sraffa follows a common procedure among economists, assuming that all firms earn the same rate of profit. Then he shows that for every worker employed by the middleman, the going wage is paid.

Assuming a rate of profit of 10 percent, for each worker employed by a trucking company hired to move the produce, the middleman has to pay the wage rate plus 10 percent. For each worker employed by a garage which services the trucks, the middleman will have to pay the going wage plus the 10 percent profit earned by the owner of the garage, plus the profit which the trucking firm expects to earn on its outlay. All in all, the middleman will have to pay for the wage rate of this worker plus a markup of 21 percent when all the profits are totaled together. Using this line of reasoning, Sraffa shows that the cost of labor to the middleman and the amount of labor involved in marketing may move in opposite directions.

The numbers in the last paragraph are not as important as the fact that prices cannot be counted on to reflect the amount of resources involved in production. The market, he concludes, is not an adequate mechanism to allocate labor; rather, in the tradition of Ricardo, Sraffa suggests that wages or profits are set by socio-political forces. In the U.S., for example, the scarcity of labor allowed the nineteenth century workers to extract higher wages because they could threaten to withdraw their labor and begin a farm. In England, during the industrial revolution, wages and working conditions were so low that the health of the working class degenerated to the point that Parliament seriously worried that the people would not be able to breed enough healthy children to carry on the industrial system. The government had to move in with protective legislation lest the working class be annihilated in the process of working.[6]

Sraffa's analysis of the socio-political determination of wages can be extended to the realm of natural resource prices. The rapid deterioration of the environment in the absence of government control implies that here, too, the market is incapable of functioning rationally.

This sort of Sraffian reasoning drew a vigorous response from Cambridge, Massachusetts, especially from Robert Solow. Solow retorted that the level of wages and profits is not determined by socio-political struggle but by how much society desires to save for the purpose of augmenting future production.[7] According to Solow's image of the economy, production is like putty which can be formed into consumption goods or tools and equipment. In making this assumption, he runs smack into Sraffa's objection that prices are not sufficiently accurate to lump everything together in this fashion.* Solow and his group admit that examples such

*Kelvin Lancaster concludes:

The only conclusion to a study of the problem of aggregation in economics is that there is no single conclusion. . . If any conclusion is to be drawn at all it is that the problems of aggregation in economics are usually swept under the rug.[8]

as our case of food marketing might cause a problem in treating consumption, in general, as a single quantity, but they assume that the market will do a reasonably good job of measuring consumption in terms of market value.

Solow's analysis depends on a second assumption. Society does not decide how much to save; individuals do. Although social and political struggles lead to tax laws and other benefits for those who have sufficient income to save, the basic decision of how much a person wants to save rests with the individual.

Solow rests his case on the ability of the market to allocate resources between the present and the future. This assumption depends upon the capacity of what Smith termed "the invisible hand," yet in his 1974 lecture Solow comes to the same conclusion as John Rae: The market gives insufficient consideration to the future when social decision-making is replaced by a hodgepodge of individual profit-seeking decision makers. Some sort of social corrective is needed to bring the behavior of the individuals into line with what is best for society as a whole. In admitting to this fatal flaw* in his method of social valuation, Solow abdicates the field to Sraffa.

*Remember that the major defense of Solow was that the rate of profit is not arbitrary because it reflects society's willingness to provide for the future.

REFERENCES

1. Karl Marx and Frederick Engels, "The Holy Family," in Karl Marx and Frederick Engels, *Marx and Engels: 1844–45*, "Collected Works" (New York: International Publishers, 1975), Vol. 4, p. 32.

2. C. E. Ferguson, *The Neoclassical Theory of Production and Distribution* (Cambridge: Cambridge University Press, 1969), p. 269.

3. Karl Marx, "Wages, Price and Profit," in Karl Marx and Frederick Engels, *Selected Works in Three Volumes* (Moscow: Progress Publishers, 1969), Vol. 2, p. 73.

4. Piero Sraffa, *The Production of Commodities by Means of Commodities* (Cambridge: Cambridge University Press, 1960).

5. Anon., "Direct Marketing: The Results So Far," *Economic and Social Issues*, Co-operative Extension, University of California (December 1975–January 1976).

6. Karl Polanyi, *The Great Transformation* (Boston: Beacon Press, 1957).

7. Robert Solow, *Capital and the Rate of Return* (Amsterdam: North Holland, 1963).

8. Kelvin Lancaster, "Economic Aggregation and Additivity," in S. Krupp, ed., *The Structure of Economic Science* (Engelwood Cliffs, N.J.: Prentice Hall, 1966), pp. 201–15.

PART THREE

Capital Conquers
The Countryside

[T]he capitalist mode of production . . . implies . . . the subordina-tion of the various spheres of production to the control of the capitalists. . . . But this . . . runs into greater obstacles, whenever numerous and large spheres of production not operated on a capitalist basis (such as soil cultivation by small farmers), filter in between the capitalist enterprises and become linked with them.

—Karl Marx, *Capital*

8

THE HUMAN DIMENSION OF TECHNICAL PROGRESS

THE LOSS OF SELF-SUFFICIENCY

One can only speak of the *productivity* of capital if one regards it as the embodiment of definite social relations of production.

Karl Marx, *Theories of Surplus Value*[1]

From a social point of view . . . the working-class even when not directly engaged in the labour-process, is just as much an appendage of capital as as the ordinary instruments of labour.

Karl Marx, *Capital*[2]

Small farms are bad for business, especially for big business.

Early American farm culture took pride in its ability to keep its money expenses at a minimum.[3] This attitude might have been an adjustment to the sad lot of many small farmers, but it did make some sense because the seasonal nature of farm work made for long periods of idleness for the men. On the other hand, much of the burden of self-sufficiency fell on the shoulders of the women, whose work tended to be less seasonal. According to an 1862 report by the newly formed Department of Agriculture, on more than three out of four farms, "the wife works harder, endures more, than any other on the place."[4] In a later survey, women also complained of the isolation and loneliness of farm life.[5]

The effort to be self-sufficient was also encouraged by the low price of farm produce and the high cost of transport; most farmers could make a table or a chair in fewer hours than would be required to grow an equivalent value of food. Families who relied on their own efforts instead of the market as a source of material goods must also have had an easier time getting through the depressions which periodically swept through the economy.

By the end of the nineteenth century, the farmer had lost much of his independence. In 1891 W. A. Peffer, a populist senator from Kansas, commented:

A great many men and women now living remember when farmers were largely manufacturers; that is to say, they made a great many implements for their own use. . . . Then the farmer produced flax and hemp and wool and cotton. These fibers were prepared upon the farm; they were spun into yarn, woven into cloth, made into garments, and worn at home. . . . A hundred dollars average probably was as much as the largest farmers of that day needed in the way of cash to meet the demands of their farm work, paying for the hired help, repairs of tools, and all other incidental expenses.[6]

Although American farmers were never totally self-sufficient, their efforts in this direction made them notoriously bad customers for industry. Also, as we saw earlier, small farms had a particularly detrimental effect on labor supply—and hence on wages—from the point of view of business interests.

Anything which served to encourage large farming assisted business in several ways. In the first place, the large farm depends on technology, which displaces labor. For each tractor used on a farm, for instance, farm employment is reduced by three or four persons.[7] Also the larger the farm, the more hired labor instead of independent farmers will work the land.[8] An index of the decline of the self-sufficient farm is suggested by the fact that about 70 percent of the male workers on the farm in 1851 were hired.[9]

The hired worker has minimal ties to the land. His employment will possibly be seasonal; even if he works full time, his winters will not very likely be occupied in producing consumer goods. He will more often than not obtain his material needs from the market.

Workers displaced from the land worked in factories mostly producing farm inputs or consumer goods for the farm population. At first, urban workers retained some of their farm habits. Except in the crowded tenement districts, town and city dwellers produced some of their own food. Sometimes their lots looked like barnyards with chickens, rabbits, and sometimes pigs, goats, or even cows. Even in Manhattan, pigs and goats were seen along the East River. For many urban workers, contact with their rural roots was strengthened by family ties with small farmers nearby. An 1890 study of the coal, iron and steel regions suggests that about 30 percent of the families purchased no vegetables other than potatoes. Another survey conducted between 1889 and 1892 showed that less than half of the working class families purchased any bread; instead, they bought an average of more than one-half ton of flour per year.[10]

The urban workers' tradition of self-sufficiency created problems for business. Besides minimizing their dependence on the market, it made labor discipline more difficult. Workers who grew their own food or could count on help from local farmers could hold out longer during strikes and lockouts.[11]*

---

*The decline in factory workers' self-sufficiency was a mixed blessing for employers. Adam Smith pointed out in 1776 that workers who farmed or gardened for themselves required less money to support themselves.[12] Henry Ford followed the same logic during the Great Depression. He required that every Ford employee maintain a garden or face dismissal.[13]

As the urban environment grew more congested, gardening and farming in the city became more complicated; urban workers lost contact with their heritage of rural skills. Dependence on the market was reinforced.

In fact, even farmers lost many of their rural skills. They turned to the market for an ever-increasing portion of their means of production. As early at 1860, the farm implement industry was among the ten largest industries in the U.S.[14] Farmers began to rely on the market for consumer goods as well. As reduced farm employment bloated the urban population, competition for jobs in the city grew more intense, so much so that industry no longer had to depend on immigration. This competition for jobs helped keep wage levels in check. Relatively cheaper wages and cheap sources of power combined to make the prices of manufactured goods more attractive compared to the time and effort involved in home production. Farm families began to depend on the market so much that they even began to purchase substantial portions of their food in stores.[15]

Relations of production also changed with the scale of farming. An Irish essayist of 150 years ago wrote, "The large farmer says to his laborers, *go* to your work; but when the small farmer has occasion to hire them, he says *come*; the intelligent reader will, I daresay, understand the difference."[16] The difference in the relationship between boss and worker in the factory and on the farm is also self evident. Changes in occupation and work relationships produce altered patterns of thought and behavior. The use of words like "city slicker," "hayseed," and "hick" indicates how sharply the differences are felt.

The decay of the self-sufficient family, brought about by the transfer of work from farm to factory, illustrates the close connection between social and technical change. The self-sufficient farm family evolved into the modern household—fetching its groceries in a station wagon.

The strain and tension of modern urban life became so draining that people began to feel the necessity to turn more and more to the market to purchase convenience or diversion instead of taking care of their own needs. For example, the modern family is willing to pay more money to buy so-called convenience foods to cut down on time required for food preparation.[17] These convenience foods appear to serve their purpose since the average time spent in preparing food in an urban household fell by 30 minutes between the 1920's and the late 1960's.[18] The family never really got to enjoy this time, however, since the increasing complexity of urban life required an extra 36 minutes per day for marketing and record keeping.[19]

To pay for the felt necessities of urban living, more and more families require two wage earners. Presently, 20 million families depend, at least in part, on income earned by the wife.

Naturally, housework after a day on the job represents a real burden. To cut back further on the time spent in the kitchen, modern families are even balking at preparing convenience foods. About 35 cents of each dollar spent for food goes for meals eaten away from home.[20] By 1980, business expects to see one-half of the national food budget go for institutional food.[21]

In other words, by extracting more of the family's vitality on the job, business helps to ensure that the working class will be better customers during its leisure hours. The greater the tedium and boredom on the job, the more the working class will buy an imaginary escape through the consumption of more commodities and entertainment. We are prone to see tractors and TV dinners as just material objects, but they are more. The production and utilization of these things involves subtle and perhaps even unnoticed changes in personal relationships.

With each family member free to spend a share of the income as he or she please, the family becomes a collection of individual consumers. Many people are troubled by the breakdown in traditional family life, while to others, the family seems to be outmoded. No matter how we feel about the family, we must recognize the role of factory life, modern consumer goods and the market in changing the environment of the household.

TECHNOLOGY, RESEARCH, AND SOCIAL PRIORITIES

Machinery, gifted with the wonderful power of shortening and fructifying human labor, we behold starving and overworking it. The newfangled sources of wealth, by some strange weird spell, are turned into sources of want. . . . At the same pace that mankind masters nature, man seems to become enslaved by his own infamy. Even the pure light of science seems unable to shine but on the dark background of ignorance.

Karl Marx, "Speech at the Anniversary of the People's Paper, 1856"[22]

The human ramifications of agricultural technology are especially far-reaching because the majority of people in the world depend on agriculture for their livelihood. Despite the enormous potential for causing social and economic dislocation, innovations in agriculture are rarely developed with serious thought being given to their over-all effects.

One early technical development proved so disastrous for many farmers that some even joined rioting workers in burning their own equipment. In 1830, when unemployment was already severe, a threshing machine was widely adopted in England. For most farmers the machine cost more to utilize than the hand labor it was designed to save. The rationale for the machine, as far as farmers were concerned, had nothing to do with saving labor or improving efficiency; they needed the machine to speed up the flow of wheat to the market.

At that time the first grain to reach the Canadian maritime provinces sold for a premium of 15 to 20 percent for three or four weeks after the beginning of the harvest. Unless the small and medium size farmers adopted the threshing machine, they could not hope to get their grain to market as fast as the larger growers.[23] Society gained little from speeding up the race to market, while the riot, arson and subsequent punishments involved hardships for many individuals.

Today, threshing machines are an integral part of agricultural technology. Few, if any, Americans question their use. The importance of the thresher is suggested by the threefold increase in output per worker in U.S. grain fields between 1840 and 1911.[24] Economists estimate that almost half of this increase in productivity can be traced back to the reaper and the thresher.[25]

The introduction of mechanization in the nineteenth century was bound to be more painless in the U.S. because the continual shortages of labor made employment a less pressing problem. Furthermore, mechanization did not always displace labor; it allowed the same number of workers to farm more land, so long as a surplus of cheap land was available. Nevertheless, the social repercussions of mechanization of U.S. agriculture were undeniable. We have already discussed the impact on the farm family. The consequences for the farm labor force were more immediate.

Whenever the bargaining power of farm labor improved, farmers responded to the demands for higher wages with a burst of mechanization. The adoption of the tractor during World War I, which we discussed in the last chapter, is a case in point. During the Crimean War in the 1850's, when the demand for U.S. grain—and consequently the demand for labor—soared, farmers used their profits to purchase reapers, thus reducing their dependency on labor.[26]

As with so many other inventions, the reaper had been on the market for decades before farmers began to adopt it. In normal times, it was not an economical investment; but when labor became restive, the reaper practically became a necessity.[27] The farmers knew what they were buying. In the words of one of Cyrus McCormick's salesmen, the new technology would serve to "place the farmer beyond the power of a set of drinking Harvest Hands with which we have been greatly annoyed."[28] Mechanization seems to have served the same purpose in England where its pace was relatively slow until the efforts of farm workers' organizations appeared successful in the 1870's.[29]

Until recently, farm workers' organizations in the U.S. have not been very strong. Besides the constant pressure of mechanization, the power of farm workers has been undermined by the immigration of foreign-born migrant workers. In California, for example, crops were harvested by a string of nationalities beginning with Chinese, Japanese, Filipinos, Hindus, finally ending with Braceros from Mexico. Only when this artificial flooding of the market was limited during the middle of the 1960s could the farm workers make much progress in bettering their standard of living.

The agricultural science establishment anticipated the potential strength of farm workers' organizations once immigration was restricted.[30] As Jack Hanna, the breeder who developed tomatoes hard enough to withstand the ordeal of mechanical harvesting, remarked, "I'd seen nationality after nationality out in the fields and I felt that someday we might run out of nationalities to exploit."[31]

Just when the workers began to organize successfully in the California tomato fields, scientists and engineers at the Davis campus of the University of California coordinated their energies to put the finishing touches on a mechanical tomato harvester.* The developers of the tomato harvester insist that their work was not intended to injure the farm workers. They claim that the harvester was necessary to save the domestic tomato industry from Mexican competition.†

Two economists at the Berkeley campus of the University of California attempted to assess the social consequences of the tomato harvester. Neglecting the quality differential of the tomatoes, they calculated that the return to society from the research spent on this technology varied from a high of 929 percent per year (compared with Grilliches' 700 percent for hybrid corn) to a low of minus 8 percent—depending on which set of assumptions they adopted.[34] The crucial determinant of the rate of return was the probable fate of the displaced farmworkers. If they had no difficulty in finding new employment, the upper rate is realistic; otherwise, the lower rate is closer to the truth.

Presently, most of the fresh market tomatoes are still hand-picked, although the Davis group is still hard at work in their efforts to make the fresh market tomatoes more economical to harvest by machine. Like the processing tomatoes, the fresh market crop must be bred to resist bruising during the trip to market in giant dump trucks. To further minimize bruising, fresh market tomatoes are picked before they are ripe and then artificially ripened with ethylene gas,‡ a chemical which is released by plants under stress.[35] This process reduces the vitamin A and vitamin C content of the tomato.[36]

As a result of the intensive work in breeding the tomato for mechanized harvesting and distribution, the U.S. has developed a product unfit for people. In a nationwide survey, the Department of Agriculture found consumers more dissatisfied with tomatoes than any of the other 30 products studied. They especially criticized the price, ripeness, taste, and appearance of the tomato.[37]

We should not be surprised that technology developed for the interests of a small group of businessmen often does nothing to further the best interests of society, even if we forget the hardship involved for farm labor. A recent Presidential Commission on Productivity headed by the Secretary of Commerce came to much the same conclusion:

It sometimes appears that efforts to maximize productivity by individual firms in one sector are counter-productive for the system as a whole. The effect of most of these mechanical harvesters has been a lower cost to the consumer. In some instances, however, the resultant gain to the grower may be more than offset by

---

*The timing of mechanization if the South suggests that new technology was used to defend against the prospect of blacks bettering their lot as a result of the civil rights movement.[32]

†Tomato harvesters have since become relatively common in the northwest of Mexico.[33]

‡Ethylene gas was discovered in 1864 when German scientists discovered it was responsible for the defoliation of shade trees near leaky gas mains.

processors' losses due to the increased man-hours required to find and discard damaged, immature, and otherwise unsaleable fruit that handpickers could have discarded in the fields. Machine harvesting also dictates that transportation equipment and processing plants work at peak capacity for short periods and at low capacity at other times—thereby reducing productivity for haulers and processors . . . .

A simple food item like an orange is handled 17 separate times from tree to table. More productive material handling equipment, however, requires minimizing the number of shapes and sizes to be handled, thereby making offsize products unusable.[38]

The Commission found an especially outrageous example of the irrational operation of profit-maximizing technology in the California tomato fields.[39] Scientific effort in plant breeding managed to increase the 1971 yields by an additional 450,000 tons—all in the form of extra water retained by the crop. The individual grower was paid for this extra production. About 86 percent of the harvest then went to processors who had to remove the water to convert the tomatoes to tomato sauce, catsup, and other products.[40] The consumer pays the water bill.

Agricultural science suffers from a particularly acute narrowness of vision. In general it limits its concern to assisting agricultural businesses in their immediate problems.[41] For example, we discussed the 1970 crisis involving hybrid corn, which caught science almost totally unprepared. In the two years before the epidemic, only six publications appeared on the subject of the fungus that attacked the corn. In the year of the blight, eighteen were published; in the following two years, 91 publications were cranked out on this subject.[42] Agricultural scientists too often adopt the economic problems of business as intellectual problems of science. Just as business' response to economic problems often fails to serve the general social interest, the intellectual solutions of science and technology often run counter to the needs of society. A good example is a mechanical lettuce harvester being developed by researchers at the Davis campus. The harvester uses radioactive isotopes to shoot X-rays through the lettuce heads to determine maturity automatically.[43] The production of this machine depends upon an expensive investment of scientific talent as well as costly material and technology.

A Davis engineer who has worked on the lettuce harvester for the last 13 years admits that the machine is not worth the social costs; the chief advantage of the machine, according to the engineer, Roger Garrett, is that it "won't strike, it will work when they want it to work."[44] To put this machine into perspective, we might mention that back in 1965, when development of the harvester was underway, the Secretary of Labor estimated that *doubling* the wage rate in the lettuce fields would result in a cost increase of only one cent per head.[45]

While millions of people go without jobs, the agricultural research establishment measures its success by how many jobs it can eliminate. The direction of this process is determined, according to the administrator of the Department of Agriculture's Economic Research Service:

... in light of raw power—economic power, political power, the power naturally accruing to those privileged enough to have an effective voice. The poor and disadvantaged do not have this kind of power. Yet, we are publicly supported research organizations.[46]

The impact of the present orientation of science and technology is clearly seen in the percentages of farm receipts received by labor. In 1949, this figure stood at 72 percent. Less than two decades later, in 1968, it had fallen to 33 percent.[47]

Although farm workers have made some progress in terms of wages, their economic situation is still appalling. According to the 1970 census, males with Spanish surnames earned only half as much in agriculture as in industry.[48] Farm workers employed a full year averaged little over $4,000 in 1972; the average annual wage for all farm workers was only about $1,000 that year.[49] Not only are wages of farm workers well below urban standards, opportunities for economic advancement are almost nonexistent.

In California, with the largest farm income in the nation, the aggressive development of mechanization has resulted in the lowest proportion of farm population in the nation.[50] Mechanization is not only lowering the farm labor bill, it is cutting back on the number of farms. Between 1960 and 1976, one half of the farms in the state disappeared. The corporate domination of agriculture was all but completed.

REFERENCES

1. Karl Marx, *Theories of Surplus Value*, Part 3 (Moscow: Progress Publishers, 1971), p. 265.

2. Karl Marx, *Capital*, Vol. 1 (Chicago: Kerr, 1906), p. 628.

3. Clarence Danhof, *Change in Agriculture: The Northern U.S., 1820-1870* (Cambridge, Mass.: Harvard University Press, 1969), pp. 16-17.

4. Anon., "Women in Agriculture," *The Farm Index*, January 1976, and Vivian Wiser, "Women in American Agriculture," in *1976 U.S. Agricultural Outlook*, paper presented at the National Agricultural Outlook Conference sponsored by the U.S. Department of Agriculture, held in Washington, D.C., November 17-20, 1975, prepared for the U.S. Senate, Committee on Agriculture and Forestry, 94th Congress, 1st Session (December 18, 1975), pp. 89-94.

5. *Ibid.*

6. W. A. Peffer, *The Farmer's Side: His Troubles and Their Remedy*, (New York: 1891), pp. 56-7.

7. Victor Stoltzfus, "Amish Agriculture: Adaptive Strategies for Economic Survival of Community Life," *Rural Sociology*, Vol. 38, No. 2 (Summer 1973), pp. 196-206.

8. See Anne Rochester, *Why Farmers Are Poor: The Agricultural Crisis in the United States* (New York: International Publishers, 1940), p. 85.

9. Bruce F. Johnston and Peter Kilby, *Agriculture and Structural Transformation: Economic Strategies in Late-Developing Countries* (New York: Oxford University Press, 1975), p. 188.

10. Harry Braverman, *Labor and Monopoly Capital: The Degradation of Work in the Twentieth Century* (New York: Monthly Review Press, 1974), pp. 273-74.

11. *Ibid.*, p. 273.

12. Adam Smith, *An Inquiry into the Nature and Causes of the Wealth of Nations*, Cannan Edition (New York: Random House, 1937), pp. 116-17.

13. Keith Sward, *The Legend of Henry Ford* (New York: Atheneum, 1927), p. 128.

14. Paul Gates, *The Farmer's Age: Agriculture, 1815-1860* (New York: Harper & Row, 1960), p. 292.

15. See Part 1.

16. Cited by John Stuart Mill, *Principles of Political Economy*, reprinted as Vols. II and III of his *Collected Works*, John M. Robson, ed. (London: Routledge & Kegan Paul, 1965), Vol. II, p. 144.

17. Larry Traub and Dianne Odland, "Convenience Foods—1975 Cost Update," United States Department of Agriculture, *1975 Agricultural Outlook*, papers presented at the National Agricultural Outlook Conference prepared for the Committee on Agriculture and Forestry, United States Senate, 93d Congress, 2d Session (December 23, 1974).

18. Kathryn Walker, "Homemaking Still Takes Time," *Journal Home Economics*, Vol. 61, No. 8 (October 1969), pp. 621-24.

19. *Ibid.*

20. See Anon., "America's Eating Out Splurge," *Business Week* (October 27, 1974).

21. *Ibid.*

22. Karl Marx,"Speech at the Anniversary of the People's Paper, 1856," in Karl Marx and Frederick Engels, *Selected Works in Three Volumes* (Moscow: International Publishers, 1970), Vol. 1, pp. 500-502.

23. The following discussion is based on E. J. Hobsbawn and George Rude, *Captain Swing* (New York: Pantheon Books, 1968), pp. 362-63.

24. See William N. Parker and Judith L. V. Klein, "Productivity Growth in Grain Production in the United States, 1840-60 and 1900-10," in Dorothy S. Brady, ed., *Output, Employment and Productivity in the United States After 1800*, Vol. 30 (New York: National Wealth," Vol. 30 (New York: National Bureau of Economic Research, 1966).

25. *Ibid.*

26. See Paul David, "The Mechanization of Reaping in the Antebellum Midwest," in H. Rosovsky, ed., *Industrialization in Two Systems: Essays in Honor of Alexander Gershenkron* (New York: Wiley & Sons, 1966), p. 3-28; reprinted in Nathan Rosenberg, ed., *The Economics of Technical Change* (London: Penguin, 1971).

27. *Ibid.*, p. 233.

28. *Ibid.*, p. 246. Paul S. Taylor cites other evidence of this attitude toward workers and machines. See Paul S. Taylor, "Origins and Growth of Migratory Seasonal Labor in Agriculture," pp. 3892-916 in Part 5B of Subcommittee on Migratory Labor of the Committee on Labor and Public Welfare of the U.S. Senate, *Farmworkers in Rural America, 1971-1972*, 92d Congress, 1st and 2d Sessions (1971-1972), esp. pp. 3896-97.

29. Paul A. David, "The Landscape and The Machine: Technical Interrelatedness, Land Tenure and Mechanization of the Corn Harvest in Victorian Britain," in Donald N. McCloskey, ed., *Essays on a Mature Economy: Britain After 1840* (Princeton: Princeton University Press, 1971), pp. 145-205, p. 181.

30. Anon., "The New Sophistication of Agricultural Science," *Business Week*, Industrial Edition (September 27, 1976).

31. James E. Bylin, "The Innovators: Role of the University as a 'Hidden Partner' in Invention Growing," *Wall Street Journal* (June 17, 1968); and William H. Friedlander and Amy Barton, *Destalking the Wily Tomato: A Study in the Social Consequences of California Agricultural Research* (Davis: University of California, Department of Applied Behavioral Sciences, June 1975), p. 23.

32. See Johnston and Kilby, *op. cit.*, pp. 205-6.

33. Ed McCaughen and Peter Baird, "Harvest of Anger: Agro-Imperialism in Mexico's

Northwest," *NACLA's Latin America and Empire Report,* Vol. 10, No. 6 (July/August 1976), pp. 2–30.

34. Andrew Schmitz and David Seckler, "Mechanized Agriculture and Social Welfare: The Case of the Tomato Harvester," *American Journal of Agricultural Economics,* Vol. 52 (November 1970), pp. 569–77, p. 574.

35. Anon., "Plants Under Stress," *Agricultural Research,* Vol. 24, No. 10 (April 1976), p. 15.

36. Statement of Alice Shabecoff in *Farmworkers in Rural America, 1971–1972,* Subcommittee on Migratory Labor of the Committee on Land and Public Welfare, 92d Congress, 1st and 2d Sessions (July 22, September 21 and 22, and November 5, 1971; and January 11–13 and July 19–20, 1972), Part 4A, p. 2291.

37. Charles R. Handy and Martin Pfaff, "Consumer Satisfaction with Food Products and Marketing Services," United States Department of Agriculture, Economic Research Service, Agricultural Economic Report No. 281 (March 1975).

38. National Commission on Productivity, *Preliminary Study of Problems and Opportunities, Productivity in the Food Industry* (Washington, D.C.: Government Printing Office, 1972), p. 8.

39. *Ibid.*

40. *Ibid.*

41. Nicholas Wade, "Agriculture: Socially Oppressed and Poverty Stricken," *Science,* Vol. 180 (May 18, 1973); and Jim Hightower, *Hard Tomatoes, Hard Times* (Cambridge, Mass.: Shenkman, 1973).

42. Paul E. Waggoner, "Agricultural Research," editorial in *Science,* Vol. 181, No. 4099 (August 10, 1973).

43. Anon., "Harvesting Lettuce Electronically," *California Agriculture,* Vol. 22, No. 7 (January 1974); and Anon., "New Machine to Harvest Lettuce," *San Francisco Chronicle* (July 19, 1975), p. 5.

44. Paul Barnett, "Lettuce Harvester Could Displace Salinas Farmworkers," *Cal Aggie,* University of California at Davis (May 22, 1975).

45. Donald E. Wise, "The Effect of the Bracero on Agricultural Production in California," *Economic Inquiry,* Vol. 12, No. 4 (December 1974), pp. 547–58.

46. Quentin M. West, "Economic Research Trade-Offs Between Efficiency and Equity," *Agricultural Science Review,* Vol. 11, No. 1 (1st Quarter 1973), pp. 31–34.

47. T. P. Lianos and Q. Paris, "American Agriculture and The Prophecy of Increasing Misery," *American Journal of Agricultural Economics,* Vol. 54, No. 4, Part 1 (November 1972), pp. 570–77.

48. United States Bureau of the Census, *1970 Census of Population: Special Reports,* "Industrial Characteristics," PC(2)-7B (June 1973), Table 44, p. 359.

49. United States Department of Agriculture, Economic Research Service, *The Hired Farm Working Force of 1972, A Statistical Report,* Agricultural Economic Report No. 239 (March 1973), pp. 5–6.

50. "Research Notes," *California Agriculture* (April 1976).

9

THE NEW FEUDALISM

Times are changing mister, don't you know? Can't make a living. Cropland isn't for little guys like us any more . . . Nothing to do about it. You try to get three dollars a day in some place. That's the only way.

—John Steinbeck, *Grapes of Wrath*, 1939

I was raised on a farm, Mr. President. I am one of the world's most successful farmers. (Laughter) I left the farm as early as I could possibly get away, and I have never gone back since, demonstrating in advance a keen knowledge of farming.

—Senator Huey Long, 1935[1]

Even in the early nineteenth century not all farms were the small-scale family enterprises were were describing. Among the earliest large agricultural ventures were two established by a subsidiary of the Hudson Bay Company in the 1860s. After a few successful years, their fortunes took a turn for the worse. The company finally liquidated in 1870.[2] The most famous of all nineteenth century bonanza farms was the factory-like operation of Oliver Dalrymple, who moved into the vacuum left by the failure of the infamous financier, Jay Cook, when his scheme to develop the Red River Valley in the Dakota Territory collapsed.[3] Dalrymple's six farms comprised 75,000 acres run by an army of 600 workers. His operations set a pattern for similar enterprises in the territory until the draught and low prices of the 1880's brought most of them to bankruptcy.

The lesson of the bonanza farms is easily forgotten. Today, economists presume that the trend of increasing farm size will continue unabated, yet a study of history shows that large scale farming is not an exclusively modern phenomenon. Farm sizes have fluctuated over the centuries. As early as the middle of the 4th century B.C., Rome passed a law limiting individual ownership of land to a maximum of 300 acres. By the end of the third century, it was openly violated.[4] One Roman noble, Lucius Domitius Ahenobarbus, owned over 200,000 acres. This land was not necessarily in one parcel. Typically, Roman latifundia were made up of a large number of medium-sized villa estates which may or may not have been contiguous. These estates would frequently exceed 300 acres. Pliny the Younger owned one consisting of more than 3,000 acres.[5]

The economy built upon the giant Roman latifundia collapsed when the supply of slave labor dried up. The feudal period saw the reintroduction of large scale patterns of landholding but these farms could not compete with the more efficient market-oriented peasant farms. The advantage of these small farms was not lost on the economists who observed them. One of the most perceptive economists of all time, Adam Smith, writing in 1776, pointed out that to "improve land with profit, like all other commercial projects, requires an exact attention to small savings and small gains, of which a man born to a great fortune, even though naturally frugal, is seldom capable."[6] Smith's observation seemed self evident to him. He asked his readers to "compare the present conditions of those [large] estates with possession of the small proprietors in their neighbourhood, and you will require no other argument to convince you how unfavourable such extensive property is to improvement."[7]

In California, 45 corporations now own 3.7 million acres, or nearly half the farm land in that state; 19 corporations own about 21 percent of the timberland.[8]

On a national scale, only one percent of the nation's farms account for 24 percent of all farm sales. Government figures show that:

In 1964, the 94 topscale vegetable farms accounted for 23 percent of the sales of the nation's 23,207 commercial vegetable farms. The 68 topscale field crop farms (other than cash-grain, tobacco, and cotton farms) with $1 million or more sales accounted for 16 percent of sales from the Nation's 35,130 commercial field crop farms. The 322 topscale livestock farms (other than poultry farms, dairy farms, and ranches) accounted for 11 percent of all sales by the 514,529 commercial livestock farms. The 81 topscale ranches accounted for 20 percent of all sales by the 66,282 commercial ranches. The 43 topscale miscellaneous farms accounted for 8 percent of all sales by the 78,528 commercial miscellaneous farms.[9]

Even a small family-type farm requires an enormous investment. The Department of Agriculture estimates that a technically optimum one-man farm generally costs much more than a quarter of a million dollars.[10] In the case of a California vegetable farm, the capital involved falls just short of one half million dollars, according to a report done several years ago when land and equipment costs were considerably lower.[11] In the period of 10 to 15 years before the Department of Agriculture compiled these figures, the amount of land required for a one-man farm increased by about 50 percent.[12]

With the costs of farming well beyond the means of all but the most affluent, labor has no choice but to remain in the factory. Only the large, capital-intensive farm can survive in the rough and tumble world of the American marketplace—at least, so agribusiness spokesmen would have us believe. According to the ex-president of the Bank of America, Rudolph A. Peterson,

What is needed is a program which will enable the small and uneconomic farmer—the one who is unwilling or unable to bring his farm to the commercial level by expansion or merger—to take his land out of production with dignity.[13]

A spokesman for Gates Rubber Corporation was a little more blunt: "The economists say that forty percent of the people in agriculture are going to have to leave the farms eventually—we're just helping some of them to make the change."[14] Such spokesmen neglect to add that the rules of this marketplace have been stacked against the small independent farmer.

In the first place, business charges more to small farmers when they purchase fertilizer, farm services, and biocides (see Table 9-1). Lack of money is a continual problem for small farmers.[15] This problem is compounded by banks which consistently charge higher rates to small farms (see Figure 2).

According to one study of midwestern corn farms, the large operations' ability to get favorable prices gave them an advantage of almost $14 per acre over a medium-sized farmer.[16]

Another major advantage enjoyed by the large farms lies in the tax structure. The small farmer who earns an income from working the land depends upon this money for a livelihood. Wealthy individuals or corporations, however, can wait for an eventual return on investment.

TABLE 9-1

Relationship Between Farm Size and Cost of Capital and Other Purchased Inputs

Farm Size (acres)	Interest on Operating Capital (6% norm)	Volume Discount on Fertilizers	Volume Discount on Insecticides	Volume Discount on Crop Dusting and Aerial Spraying	Total Difference from Base Cost per Acre
80	6.88%	0%	0.0%	0.0%	$0.56
160	6.52%	4%	0.0%	0.0%	-$0.25
320	6.47%	4%	5.0%	0.0%	-$0.53
640	6.47%	4%	5.0%	12.5%	-$1.27
1,230	6.15%	10%	8.5%	17.5%	-$3.96
3,200	5.90%	10%	14.0%*	25.0%	-$6.62

*Denotes only one observation behind the data.

Source: Paris, J. E., and D. L. Armstrong, *Economics Associated with Farm Size, Kern County California Cash Crop Farms.* Giannini Foundation Research Report No. 269, 1963, pp. 73–96.

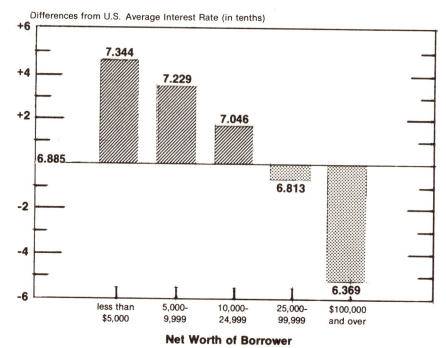

Differences from U.S. Average Interest Rate (in tenths)

Net Worth of Borrower

Source: Gene L. Swackhammer and Raymond J. Doll, "Financing Modern Agriculture: Banking's Problems and Challenges," Federal Reserve Bank of Kansas City, 1969.

FIGURE 2
Rate Variability by Borrower Net Worth
Production Loans (June 30, 1966)

They can more easily afford, for example, to raise cattle or develop an orchard which will not earn any money until the cattle or trees reach maturity. As long as the farm operates at a loss, the owner can reduce taxes on other professional or business income. When the farm begins to generate a profit, the owner can sell the operation. Any gain in the transaction is not taxed as regular income but as capital gains, which are given a more favorable tax treatment. In other words, agriculture is very attractive because it does not earn much current income; instead, most of the gains come in the form of appreciation of assets. The effectiveness of the tax laws in attracting wealthy investors is suggested by Internal Revenue Service data on reported farm losses. According to these figures, as nonfarm income rises, the reported farming losses become more frequent.[17]

Large corporations involved in farming are content to forego current income, preferring to take their profits in the form of capital gains from land appreciation. Tenneco Corporation, one of the largest conglomerates with interests in agriculture, is typical in this respect. Simon Askin, the company's executive vice president for agriculture and land development, expressed its position as follows: "We consider land as an inventory, but we are all for growing things on it while we wait for price appreciation or development."[18]

The "price appreciation" which Mr. Askin refers to has been very rewarding. The average acre of farm land in November 1975 sold for almost 2½ times its 1967 price.[19] Other figures for the same year give some idea of what this means in money terms; in 1975 the value of farm land increased by a total of 51 billion dollars,[20] while farmers realized a total net income of less than 29 billion dollars.[21] In other words, the profits earned in the form of agricultural real estate appreciation came near doubling farm earnings. These figures understate the potential gains from land speculation, however. Land values in general have doubled over the last five years.[22] The most successful speculators are able to convert agricultural land to more highly valued urban uses. For them, the increase in land values is truly spectacular.

Although rising land costs improve the appearance of the corporate balance sheet, they do little for the small farmer except increase the burden of property taxes. High land prices also add to the difficulty of beginning a career in farming.

Profits which result from tax laws, quantity discounts and land speculation have little to do with efficiency, even in the most narrow sense of the word. Tax laws, for example, encourage farmers not to use breeding livestock for as long as would be recommended on purely biological grounds.[23] The special advantages enjoyed by large farmers lead them to use more fertilizer, equipment, and pesticides than normal market conditions could justify.

At this point, we might recall our discussion of the mining of resources. The price of land is still sufficiently low that profit-maximizing farmers behave as if soil erosion and the loss of agricultural productivity is not a pressing problem. Reason would dictate that sooner or later agriculture would have to pay the penalty for its wasteful practices. In fact, in the topsy turvy world of supply and demand it will be rewarded for its waste. Once the natural cushion of stored up fertility is spent, the scarcity of food-producing resources will be felt. Of course, the price of food will rise, causing the market to place more value on the means of producing food.[24]

John H. Perkins, President of Continental Bank of Chicago, a major agribusiness force, expressed a vision of reality more sophisticated than the usual myopic view of supply and demand. Addressing an audience assembled for a meeting on the subject of Feeding the World's Hungry: The Challenge to Business, he said, "The incentive-minded business community has a way of seeing an opportunity lurking inside a shortage."[25]

Government policies which are theoretically designed to help farms in general, in fact, do more for the large farm. Government programs to

support farm prices have disproportionally benefited the large operations. Calculations by Phillip LeVeen of the Berkeley campus of the
University of California indicate that if price supports had been with-
drawn in 1971, the typical large farm would be earning about 3.75 times
as much as the typical small farm. With supports it earns 9 times as
much.[26]

Some of the most important government subsidies of large-scale agriculture come from the public research establishment. Even though many
of the scientists employed in agricultural research come from small farm
backgrounds, most seem to have lost touch with the small farmer. They
spend their time on such projects as methods of disposing of manure for
the benefit of feed lot operators. The small farmer has no need of such
research, since he can rely on the time-honored solution of fertilizing his
land with manure. For him it is an asset.[27] The machines the research
establishment develops have no place on the small farm. In one of the
most honest appraisals of the work of the Department of Agriculture ever
to come from a major departmental figure, Dr. Ned Bayley (then director
of the department's Office of Science and Education) posed the rhetorical
question, "What has agricultural research done for . . . [the small]
farmers?" His honest response was "very little," and he added that the
overall impact of agricultural research has, on the contrary, threatened
the survival of the small farm.[28] Although the Agricultural Act of 1961
adopted the policy of acting "to encourage, promote and strengthen" the
small farm, little has been accomplished in this area. In fact, one study of
family farm income discovered that inequality was highest in those states
where the most money was paid for agricultural research and extension.[29]
Quite naturally, the author concluded that the money was being spent in
a manner which did little to benefit the small farmer.

In spite of lip service in support of small-scale farming, the policy of
the government seems to move in the opposite direction. According to
Paul Sears, one of the most respected students of the costs of improper
treatment of the soil, the Department of Agriculture privately tells the
heads of the agricultural extension to encourage the large heavily financed and mechanized operations.[30]

Regardless of the artificially created disadvantages facing small farmers, many have held on to this day. According to the Department of
Agriculture, 95 percent of all farms may be classified as small farms on
which less than 1.5 man-years of labor are hired.[31] Although the other 5
percent produces 48 percent of farm output, the family farm still appears
to be a vital force.* Remember that many of these 5 percent are really
highly capital intensive operations worth hundreds of thousands of
dollars.

Using a slightly different classification in terms of the value of sales per

---

*The 95 percent figure is based on a study of 1969 Census Study.[32] Although many family
farms have gone out of business since then, I used the 1969 figure of share or farm output to
be consistent.

farm, the reasons for the strength of the small farm emerge. In the first place, small farms are less vulnerable to price fluctuations. In other words, they are less likely to go belly up when conditions take a turn for the worse. A 1965 study discovered that if farm prices fell by 33 percent, the average large farm would have to halt production, while a fall of 50 percent would be required to force small farms to discontinue.[33]*

Industrialists who sell to the small farmer are aware of the stability of that form of agriculture. For example, the farm implement dealers have had to establish lending institutions for the small farmers who cannot easily get cheap credit from the banks. Here is how the president of John Deere and Company described their credit operation:

> To us credit is a sales tool. We provide it because we must (because banks do not) . . . The paper we accept from our dealers carry [sic] higher rates than the banks charge for such paper, and our rates are as low as any in the industry. Even so, the amount of retail paper our company had on its hands last October 31 (1957), the end of our fiscal year, approximated one hundred million dollars, two hundred percent more than three years ago. Surely the limited availability of credit from other lower cost sources must be a factor in the situation.
>
> We do not attract this business by taking excessive risks. Our credit standards have been high . . . [and] our losses have been minor.[34]

You might think that Mr. Hewitt was just complaining because he, like the banks, prefers not to lend money to the small farmer, but Don Paarlberg, former Director of Agricultural Economics for the U.S. Department of Agriculture, confirming this observation, says:

> We know from our studies in the Department of Agriculture that the rates of foreclosure and delinquency are greater on big farm loans, for the large-scale farm units, than for smaller loans on family farms.[35]

A study of insolvent farmers in the San Joaquin Valley of California found that although only 7 percent of the farmers in the region owned more than 2,000 acres, 28 percent of the bankrupt farmers were in this category.[36] Evidence of the vulnerability of the large farm extends back as far as an 1889 study of Nebraska farmers' difficulties during the collapse of 1886 and 1887.[37]

Based on the expert opinion of Mr. Hewitt and Dr. Paarlberg, the large farm might seem to be a frail foundation for a stable agricultural system. The weakness of large-scale farming may turn out to be even more crucial than now appears to be the case. The government has abandoned the policy of supporting prices directly; instead, it intends to let the market determine the level of prices. It does promise to maintain a floor below which prices cannot fall, but in many cases this level is too low to offer much protection for farmers. The government recognizes that its new policy will lead to greater price instability; in fact; the *1975 Economic Report of the President* devotes considerable space to this problem.[38]

*LeVeen's figures on price supports uphold this view since they are not affected if the drop in price is caused by deteriorating market conditions.

How the large farms will fare under these conditions remains to be seen.

Even under good conditions, the large corporate farm, in spite of its favored treatment, does not have a very enviable record. According to the Department of Agriculture, "the typical farm corporation in 1970 had... business receipts of about $150,000 and showed a small net loss after paying salaries to its officers."[39] Some corporations fared worse than average. Gates Rubber Corporation, for example, whose spokesman was quoted above concerning his firm's willingness to lend a hand in clearing the land of superfluous farmers, found itself in the humiliating position of having to abandon its own agricultural operations. After years of the heady bigger-is-better syndrome, both government and business are coming to recognize what farmers have long known: the most effective fertilizer in the world is the shadow of the farmer on the land.

Although many corporate efforts in farming have ended in downright failure, and have been abandoned, major corporations have no intention of relinquishing control of agriculture. In fact, some corporations entered farming in the first place only because they wished to control the marketing of produce. Perhaps the most interesting case involved United Brands, most well known for its Chiquita Bananas (although its connections with the food industry were much more extensive). The corporation already had a well-developed food distribution system from its banana business. By taking advantage of existing facilities, it expected to realize substantial savings; the key to its plan was to market lettuce under the established brand name—Chiquita. For nine months, people in selected metropolitan areas were treated to commercials extolling the virtues of Chiquita lettuce. In payment for the service of wrapping the lettuce in cellophane and affixing a Chiquita label, the company expected to be able to raise the price supermarkets paid for lettuce by 50 percent. The plan failed, apparently only because of action by the Federal Trade Commission. According to the Commission, United Brands had no intention of developing a superior head of lettuce, or even of improving the yields in the lettuce fields; its plan was simply to "subdue" the short-run forces of supply and demand in order to acquire "some degree of control over the market and prices."[40]

United Brands' defense, framed by President Nixon's former law firm, argued:

Although there may be some nostalgic desire to see a market composed of many small growers, that structure cannot survive against a market buyer (chain stores) that is composed of fewer and fewer companies with larger and larger market shares.[41]

Compared to Tenneco, United Brands' involvement in the lettuce fields was mere child's play. Tenneco, originally known as Tennessee Gas Co., moved into agriculture in a big way with its purchase of the 350,000 acre Kern County Land Company in 1967. By 1969, Tenneco was a substantial producer of grapes, almonds, and several other very high

priced specialty crops which are lucrative enough to support a family on relatively few acres.[42]

These farms could be harvested with J. I. Case equipment, made by Tenneco. The machines could run on Tenneco fuel. The products could be packaged by another Tenneco division. Finally, they could be marketed by still another division of the company since Tenneco is the nation's largest marketer of fruits and vegetables. Tenneco literature proudly boasted of its role in agriculture "from seedling to supermarket." This slogan captured the dual sense of Tenneco's operations. It could be read to describe the flow of food from seedling to supermarket or the fate of Tenneco's agricultural land waiting to be developed into supermarkets or suburban developments. After all, we have already seen that for Tenneco, land was just "inventory."

While the type of operation run by Tenneco might seem to violate the antitrust provisions of the federal law books, the Department of Agriculture has chosen to encourage it because it "has come about through the free enterprise system of competition, and has brought about in our [the U.S. Department of Agriculture's] opinion the most efficient setup possible.[43] The department has no limitations whatsoever on the type of arrangements involved. In fact, the Assistant Agricultural Secretary, Robert Long, has urged more of this consolidation within the food industry to, in his curious phrase, "present a solid front to the consuming public."[44] To this end, he has advocated loosening of the antitrust laws rather than enforcing them.

In spite of the Department of Agriculture's beneficent vision of corporate power in agriculture, it does seem to create abuses. In one instance, Tenneco, according to testimony before a Senate subcommittee,[45] went to an independent firm which contracted with farmers to grow potatoes which were then processed into potato chips and other products. The firm paid a rent for the land and was responsible for much of the work in growing the crop. Since Tenneco was having trouble with its cotton production, it needed to find a new use for some of its land. Tenneco suggested to the company that it was interested in buying them out or going into a joint venture. On that basis, the Tenneco management gained access to the company's books, learning the names of its customers and the prices which the processors paid. Using this information, Tenneco was able to offer lower prices to some of the largest processors even though its supposed partner-to-be was paying Tenneco rent for 1,300 acres of potato fields to grow crops which it was intending to sell to the processors. The firm found itself undercut by Tenneco, which appeared to be selling potatoes below cost in order to capture the market. To make matters worse, the giant conglomerate insisted that the company contract with no other firm and that it should move its packing facilities to Tenneco's property in Bakersfield.

In spite of all its advantages, Tenneco is pulling back from corporate farming. A report issued by the company states:

Agriculture is a high-risk business and typically shows little if any profit, especially for the large corporations . . . There is no effective substitute for the small-to-medium-sized independent grower who lives on or near his farmlands, who . . . has a deep personal involvement in the outcome of his efforts.[46]

Tenneco has already sold major parts of its California lands because it realizes that the real profits from farming come from marketing and distribution, not production. The company has managed to contract with about 3,000 growers to market their fresh fruit, vegetables, almonds, dates, and raisins.[47] It has even succeeded in making purchasers of its land contract to market through Tenneco.[48]

Corporations such as Tenneco are not alone in adopting strategies for running agriculture from the marketplace without setting foot on the farms. More and more banks, processors, and distributors are learning in their own way how to control the farmer through subtle manipulations of the market. Like the old feudalism, the new feudalism is giving way to control by the market.

In addition to being subject to the dictates of contracting firms, farmers are controlled increasingly by the institutions they rely on for credit. The rise in farm debt has been accelerated by technological innovations, which are also partly to blame for the disadvantages smaller farmers experience in the market.

The tomato industry in California provides an illustration of how technology can affect the farmer's position. In 1962, about 4,000 California growers farmed 177,000 acres of tomatoes. A tomato harvester designed to process 150 acres was introduced for the benefit of a small percentage of the growers. At the time, the average tomato farm was only 44 acres. Only the largest growers could afford the $45,000 price tag. To pay for one of the tomato harvesters, a farmer with 44 acres of tomatoes needed more than $1,000 per acre. The investment would have been uneconomic even for a small farmer who happened to have that kind of cash on hand. Since then, machines designed for handling 350 acres have become commonplace.[49] Acreage planted in tomatoes had increased to 250,000 by 1973, but 3,400 of the farmers had disappeared.

Because the cost of the new farming technologies is increasing faster than farm income, keeping abreast of these developments, means for many farmers, going deeper and deeper in debt. For obvious reasons the small farmer has been more reluctant to take up every new technology which comes on the market. As a result, more than 60 percent of the smallest class of farmers have managed without any debt at all,[50] while among the largest classes of farms, about 80 percent are in debt.[51] In 1950, U.S. farmers as a whole could have paid off their debt with three fourths of their annual income; by 1974, farm debt was equivalent to almost three years' income.[52] Farm debt as a percentage of total corporate debt continues to rise.[53] *Business Week* predicts that over the decade ending in 1984, agriculture will need to borrow an additional $400 billion.[54]

The problem of debt is less pressing for a farmer who owns his land than for a potential farmer who has to purchase land as well as equip-

ment. The present cost of farming operations presents an all but insurmountable barrier to entry into agriculture. Current land values alone, on a one-man corn-soybeans farm in Indiana, exceed one half million dollars.[55].

Mechanization, debt and inflated land values are part of the same process. In fact, until recently, most appreciation in land values could be directly traced to the effects of mechanization.[56] For example, suppose that a tomato farmer owned 44 acres in 1962. Since tomato harvesters were designed for 150 acres, presumably he would profit from expanding his farm size. Other owners of tomato harvesters would join him in bidding up the price of farm land until much of the potential benefits from mechanization would be translated into higher prices for land for growing tomatoes.

The debt resulting from mechanization is more extreme because of the nature of the farm machinery industry, which is dominated by only a few firms.[57] The effects of this domination can be seen in the following comparison: In 1952 a 30 to 39 horsepower tractor cost the equivalent of 1,283 bushels of wheat or 3,291 bushels of corn.[58] A *New York Times* report of April, 1973 points out that the Soviet Union is marketing tractors comparable to U.S. equipment at half the cost.[59]

Farmers who borrow from the banks give up their independence bit by bit. Monfort of Colorado, Inc., one of the world's largest feelot operators, noted in its annual report that "the Company is prohibited from paying cash dividends and making certain types of investments without consent of the lenders."[60] Banks also often allow more favorable credit conditions if the borrower agrees to regular visits by bank officials.[61]

The banks also require extensive data from prospective borrowers.[62] This information is compared with the computerized histories of the other farmers who have borrowed money. If the farmer does not intend to farm in conformity with the "best commercial practices," the bank will not extend credit—a form of agricultural reclining. In effect, the banks tend to stifle agricultural practices which diverge from the typical corporate chemical models.[63] Some midwestern farmers, for example, are discovering that they can increase their profit by returning to the traditional pattern of raising both crops and livestock. Using the manure instead of fertilizer slowly builds up the organic content of the soil. Consequently, the trend of soil depletion is reversed. Banks frown on this method, perhaps because it tends to increase the self-sufficiency of the farmer. In Nebraska, Barry Commoner reports, banks are called "fence pullers" because they insist that farmers carrying loans plant the entire farm to corn.[64]

A report by the Department of Agriculture acknowledges "the leverage that the lender may have in imposing his recommendations on the borrower," but does not elaborate on the nightmarish extent of their control.[65] One of the most frightening examples was the case of Peter Divizich.[66]

The early history of Mr. Divizich reads like a wonderful American

success story. Beginning as a farm worker, he eventually gained owner-ship of 5,000 acres of land in the very fertile Central Valley of California. In 1966, a Bureau of Reclamation survey of 2,600 acres of the property estimated its value at $4.3 million. Since 1940, Mr. Divizich had borrowed funds from the Bank of America, the largest agricultural lender in the U.S. After a relatively bad year, Mr. Divizich decided to try his luck marketing grapes through the company which is now the marketing arm for Tenneco. One year's experience with Tenneco brought him to the brink of bankruptcy. The bank threatened to foreclose unless Tenneco was allowed to manage his farm as well as market his grapes. Under this plan, the farm lost more than $2 million after a single year. At this point, according to testimony before the U.S. Senate, the bank foreclosed; ignoring higher bidders, it bought the farm for far less than it was worth, only to resell at very favorable terms to Tenneco.

We have already seen that business has a vested interest in making good customers out of farmers. Bankers also know that their business would not fare very well in a nation of self-sufficient farmers or even self-sufficient communities. They have no reason to encourage farming practices which could do away with the need for borrowing. On the contrary, the more farmers adopt capital intensive techniques, the brisker the demand for the commodity banks sell—namely money. Banks also realize that they are dependent on the success of business in general. A general business failure means a general banking failure. Again, capital intensive techniques are in the banks' best interest.

Since banks are reluctant to extend as much credit as farmers want, they have had to turn elsewhere for much of their credit needs. Since the agribusiness firms which process or distribute farm products have an easier time borrowing money, they have become a major source of credit.[67] In return for an advance payment for delivery of the crop, the firm signs a contract which can specify not only the quantity and quality of the delivery, but how it is to be grown and methods of pest control.[68]

Former Secretary of Agriculture Earl Butz has advocated this sort of arrangement since the 1950's. His reasoning was based on the fact that the small farmer could not cope in the world of giant corporations. Butz, like Veblen, wished to rid the farmer of any lingering fantasies about a world of independent entrepreneurs.[69] Farmers had to adapt to the real world and the adaptation envisioned by Veblen was contract farming. As early as 1964, the Department of Agriculture reported that crops grown under contract with processors and distributors had reached 100 percent for sugar beets, castor beans, safflower and hops.[70] Today we would add to this list broilers, fluid milk, vegetable seeds, hybrid seed corn, and vegetables for canning and freezing.[71] All in all, about 20 percent of all farm output is grown under contracts.[72]

Butz was quite blunt about what this new type of farming meant. The farmer's function will be to "assemble packages of technology which have been produced by others on a custom basis" according to an article he wrote for the business publication, *Banking*.[73] One of the first in-

34. William A. Hewitt, excerpt from speech before Board of Governors, Federal Reserve System, *Financing Small Business* (1958), p. 364.

35. Don Paarlberg, "Future of the Family Farm," speech before the 55th Annual Conventionof the National Milk Producers' Convention, Bal Harbour, Florida (November 30, 1971).

36. Sylvia Lane and Charles V. Moore, "Analysis of Attributes of Insolvent Farmers in San Joaquin Valley Study," *California Agriculture* (February 1972), pp. 6-7.

37. W. F. Mappin, "Farm Mortgages and the Small Farmer," *Political Science Quarterly*, Vol. 4, No. 3 (September 1889), cited by Fred Shannon, *Farmer's Last Frontier, Agriculture 1860-1897* (New York: Farrar & Rinehart, 1945), p. 189.

38. *1975 Economic Report of the President, op. cit.*, pp. 173-83.

39. United States Dept. of Ag., *Fact Book of U.S. Agriculture*, Miscellaneous Publication No. 1063, Office of Communication, U.S. Dept. of Ag., March 1976.

40. Federal Trade Commission, "In the Matter of United Brands Company, Corporation," Docket No. 8835, Final Order, Majority Opinion and Concurring Opinion of May J. Thompson (14 May 1974).

41. Nick Kotz, "Corporate Giant Looks Like Grim Reaper to Farmer," *op. cit.*

42. "Personnel: One of the Basics of KLC," *Western Fruit Grower* (October 1969), p. 5.

43. Statement of J. Phil Campbell, Undersecretary, U.S. Department of Agriculture, before Antitrust Subcommittee No. 5 of the House Committee on Judiciary on HR 11654, *Family Farm Act* (Washington, D.C.: U.S. Government Printing Office, March 22 and 23, 1972), p. 28.

44. Cited in Jim Hightower, "Food, Farmers, Corporations, Earl Butz . . . .And You," reprinted in Subcommittee on Monopolies and Commercial Law of the Committee on the Judiciary, House of Representatives, 93d Congress, 1st Session, *Food Price Investigation* (June 27 and 28 and July 11, 12, 16, 17 and 19, 1973), p. 366.

45. Testimony of S. P. Lipoma, in Subcommittee on Migratory Labor of the Committee on Labor and Public Welfare of the United States Senate, *Farmworkers in Rural America, 1971-72*, 92d Congress, 1st and 2d Sessions (1971-1972), Part 3B, pp. 1217-19.

46. Tenneco Corporation, *Agricultural Report*, Houston (November 1975).

47. *Ibid.*

48. Philip M. Raup, "Nature and Extent of the Expansion of Corporations in American Agriculture," paper presented at a conference on "New Developments in the Organization and Technology of Agriculture in East and West," University of Kiel, Germany (18-19 November 1974), published as Staff Paper, Department of Agriculture and Applied Economics, University of Minnesota, Minneapolis (April 1975), pp. 75-78.

49. Barton and Friedlander, *op. cit.*

50. J. Bruce Hotel, Robert D. Reinsel and William D. Crowley, "Debt Status of U.S. Farm Operators, and Landlords by Economic Class, 1960, 1966, 1970," *Agricultural Finance Review*, Vol. 36 (April 1976), pp. 67-72.

51. *Ibid.*

52. Peter J. Barry and Donald R. Fraser, "Risk Management in Primary Agricultural Production: Methods, Distribution, Rewards, and Structural Implication," Texas Agricultural Experiment Station (n.d.).

53. Aaron G. Nelson, Warren F. Lee, and William G. Murray, *Agricultural Finance*, 6th ed. (Ames: Iowa State University Press, 1973).

54. Anon., "Agriculture's Need—$400 Billion—The Rural Banks Are No Longer Enough," *Business Week* (September 1975), p. 52.

55. Bayley, *op. cit.*

56. Robert W. Herdt and William W. Cochrane, "Farm Land Prices and Farm Technology Advance," *Journal of Farm Economics*, Vol. 58, No. 2 (May 1966), pp. 243-63.

57. See Council on Wage and Price Stability, "Report on Prices for Agricultural Machinery and Equipment," Washington, D.C. (May 1976).

58. Statement of James A. McHale, in Subcommittee on Migratory Labor of the Committee on Labor and Public Welfare, *Farmworkers in Rural America, 1971-1972*, 92d Congress, 1st and 2d Sessions (1971-1972), Part 4A, p. 2259.

59. See Theodore Shabad, "Soviet-Made Tractors Introduced Upstate," *New York Times* (April 24, 1973), p. 43. Another source places the cost of comparable Soviet tractors at 80 percent of U.S. prices. See Earl M. Rubenking, "The Soviet Tractor Industry: Progress and Problems," Joint Economic Committee of the Congress of the United States, *Soviet Economy in a New Perspective, A Compendium of Papers*, 94th Congress, 2d Session (October 14, 1976), p. 612.

60. Cited in Raup, "Nature and Extent . . . ," *op. cit.*, p. 21.

61. Marshall Harris, "Entrepreneurship in Agriculture," Agricultural Law Center, College of Law, University of Iowa, Iowa City, Monograph No. 12 (n.d.), p. 74.

62. Marshall Harris, "Entrepreneural Control in Farming," United States Department of Agriculture, Economic Research Service, ERS No. 542 (1974), p. 10.

63. George Ballis, statement in *Will the Family Survive in America?* Joint Hearing before the Select Committee on Small Farms and the Committee on Interior and Insular Affairs, United States Senate, 94th Congress, 1st Session, Part 1 (July 17 and 22, 1975), p. 58.

64. Barry Commoner, "Ruralamerica Interview," *Congressional Record* (September 24, 1976), pp. S16607-9.

65. Marshall Haris, "Entrepreneurial . . . . ," *op. cit.*, p. 125.

66. Testimony of Peter Divizich in Subcommittee on Migratory Labor of the Committee on Labor and Public Welfare of the United States Senate, *Farmworkers in Rural America, 1971-1972*, 92d Congress, 1st and 2d Sessions (1971-1972), pp. 1219-1224.

67. Marshall Harris, "Entrepreneurship . . . . ," *op. cit.*, p. 125.

68. Willard F. Mueller and Norman R. Collins, "Grower-Processor Integration in Fruit and Vegetable Marketing," *Journal of Farm Economics*, Vol. 39, No. 5, (December 1975), pp. 1471-86; and Anon., "The Farmer and His Farm," *The Farm Index* (April 1975).

69. Earl Butz, "The Social and Political Implications of Integration," *Proceedings of the 8th National Institute of Animal Agriculture*, Purdue University, (April 20-22, 1958), pp. 42-44.

70. William H. Scofield, "The Agribusiness Complex," presentation to the American Society of Farm Managers & Rural Appraisers (December 1, 1969), reprinted in Hearings Before the Subcommittee on Monopoly of the Select Committee on Small Business, United States Senate, 92d Congress, 1st and 2d Sessions, *The Role of the Giant Corporations in the American and World Economies*, Part 3B, *Corporate Secrecy: Agribusiness* (November 30 and December 1, 1971, and March 1 and 2, 1972), pp. 5068-71.

71. Leon Garoyan, "Is It Time for Contracts?" presented at the Summer Institute, American Institute of Cooperation, Kansas State University, Manhattan, Kansas (August 1974).

72. *Ibid.*

73. Earl Butz, "The Appraisal of Land-Grant Colleges," *Banking* (April 1962), p. 62.

74. Don Paarlberg, *American Farm Policy* (New York: John Wiley, 1964), p. 40.

75. Harrison Welford, "Poultry Peonage," from his *Sowing the Wind: The Politics of Food Safety and Agribusiness*, reprinted in Subcommittee on Monopoly of the Select Committee on Small Business of the U.S Senate, *Role of Giant Corporations*, Part 3A, *Corporate Secrecy: Agribusiness*, 92d Congress, 1st and 2d Sessions (1973), p. 3705.

76. Glen L. Johnson, in "The Modern Family Farm and Its Problems with Particular Reference to the U.S.A.," in Ugo Papi and Charles Nunn, eds., *Economic Problems in Agriculture in Industrial Societies*, (London: Macmillan, 1969), p. 247.

77. *Marcus v. Eastern Agricultural Association*, 32 N.J. 460, 161 A, 2d 247 (1960).

78. Anon., "SRS's Big Survey," *Agricultural Situation* (January/February 1976), pp. 2-4.

79. Lindley Finch, "Structural Changes in the Agricultural Industry: Their Meaning for American Business and World Food Production," in *Feeding the World's Hungry: The Challenge to Business*, Conference Sponsored by Continental Bank, (May 20, 1974), p. 108.

10

LARGE AND SMALL SCALE FARMING

We are far too prone to measure productivity in quantitative terms. We should also count the cost in loss of quality. The scrupulous accountancy of nature insists on balancing the books and if we enter a credit on one side, there is usually a debit on the other. Productivity, then, on the best farms will not be reckoned in ciphers, but on the complex and exacting scale of progress in husbandry.

—J. Tristamm Beresford, "The Farm as a Management Model"[1]

A small proprietor . . . who knows every part of his territory, who views it with all the affection which property, especially small property, naturally inspires, and who upon that account takes pleasure not only in cultivating but in adorning it, is generally of all improvers, the most industrious, the most intelligent, and the most successful.

—Adam Smith, *The Wealth of Nations*[2]

In 1969 the Stanford Research Institute published a study commissioned by the Department of Defense entitled "U.S. Agriculture, Potential Vulnerabilities."[3] The title did not refer to the likelihood of specifically agricultural problems such as the fungal attack on hybrid corn which occurred in the following year: instead, it concentrated on the difficulties associated with industrial breakdowns.

Between 1940 and 1970, dependence on mechanical power and machinery increased by 146 percent on U.S. farms. Chemicals, fertilizer, and pesticide use grew sevenfold.[4] The Department of Agriculture estimates that farmers purchased only 20 percent of the materials used in production in 1950.[5] By 1973, 65 percent were purchased.[6]

Dependence on the market is less for small farms, as may be seen from the breakdown of farm size and market dependence in Table 10-1. Farmers are categorized according to gross sales. The next columns show the percentage share of each farm class of Acres Grown, Cash Receipts,

Production Expenses, Pesticide Expenditures and Realized Net Income, for U.S. agriculture as a whole. The first point to notice is the difference between the shares of land (column 2) and realized net farm income. If large farmers need more than 1 percent of the land to produce 1 percent of the realized net farm income, we can infer that large farmers are not able to get as much production out of an acre of land as small farmers. On the basis of this table, we can see quite clearly that the larger the farm, the less efficient the operation in terms of making the land produce.

TABLE 10-1

Farm Size and Market Dependence, 1971

Gross Sales ($000's)	Percent of Total for U.S.				
	Acres Grown	Cash Receipts	Production Expenses	Pesticide Expenditures	Realized Net Income
0 – 2.5	6	2.7	3.7	2	7.0
2.5 – 5	5	3.0	3.2	2	4.6
5 – 10	7	5.9	5.6	5	7.9
10 – 20	14	11.0	10.1	11	14.5
20 – 40	22	20.0	18.4	22	24.6
40+	46	57.3	59.0	57	41.4

Sources: U.S.D.A. Economic Research Service, *Farm Income Situation*, FIS–222, July 1973, p. 71; and Helen T. Blake and Paul A. Andrilenas, "Farmers' Use of Pesticides in 1971," U.S.D.A., Economic Research Service, Ag. Econ. Report No. 296, Nov. 1975, p. 6.

On the other hand, by a similar criterion, the large farm appears to be capable of producing a greater value per acre of land when we compare the shares of cash receipts and total acreage. While this observation might be accurate, the figures in Table 10-1 overstate the performance of large farms.

Several reasons can be given for the favorable appearance of large scale farming when making the comparison between shares of total receipts and total acreage. To begin with, the statistics in Table 10-1 imply that size is the determinant of economic performance; and size is measured in gross sales. Obviously, gross sales are partly determined by the levels of managerial skill and resource endowment. Farms with careful management and productive soil will register larger gross sales and be classed as larger operations than farms without these advantages. As a result, farms with larger gross sales will tend to be able to produce more output per acre of land or per dollar spent on purchased inputs. The upshot of this argument is that some farms are large in terms of gross sales *because* they are efficient, even though the statistics might indicate that they are efficient because they are large. Careful statistical investigations which have tried to compensate for some of this bias have found that the appearance of efficiency in large-scale operations is significantly reduced.[7] We have no precise way of evaluating how important this factor is, but we must keep it in mind when reading that farms with sales of over $40,000 produce 57.3 percent of the harvest on 46 percent of the land.

A second reason for the large farmer's ability to get more receipts per acre can be explained in terms of economic advantages. For example, banks hesitate to lend money to small farmers for lucrative but risky crops like lettuce or potatoes.[8] The business publication, *Forbes Magazine* cites the example of Howard Fitzpatrick, the manager of the Blackfoot branch of the Idaho Bank and Trust. Fitzpatrick refuses to lend money to small potato growers. In his opinion, "There's no place in this [potato] business for the doughhead or the little guy."[9] Large farms also are able to get a higher price for their crop because they can do some of the processing on the farm or have more leverage in the market place. In the midwest, a typical 5,000-acre corn farm appears to be able to get about $.05 per bushel more than a 500-acre unit.[10]

Finally, the small farmer is more likely to use some of the land for growing crops for home consumption. These non-marketed crops will naturally reduce the cash receipts per acre, most noticeably in the case of the smallest farms. When we analyze U.S. agriculture using a more precise comparison between large and small farms, we find that productivity per acre declines as farms get bigger.[11]

The column for production expenses is very revealing. This column gives us a measure of how much the different farm classes depend on the market for purchased farm inputs. The figures indicate that small farmers buy fewer inputs per acre and per dollar of realized net income. For example, the smallest category used only 3.7 percent of the production expenses to harvest 6 percent of the land while earning 7 percent of the realized net farm income. In reality, the performance of the small farm on this score is better than it appears. In the first place, the small farmer, as we saw earlier, pays more money for the same inputs. Thus, while the small farmers might have incurred 3.7 percent of the total production expenses, they actually used a somewhat less percentage of inputs when we correct for the inflated prices they pay. A second distortion in the figures puts the large farmer in a more favorable light than might be justified by these figures. Recall our discussion of energy in the first chapter; at that time we discussed Department of Agriculture estimates of fuel use in agriculture for large and small farms. We made the point that the estimates of fuel use for small farms were overstated for tax purposes because some of the fuel attributed to farm use was not actually used for farming. If each farm family fudged an equal amount on their tax forms, the fuel cost per acre would be greater on small farms than large farms. Such manipulations of figures make the production expenses for small farmers look larger than they actually are.

Based on our interpretation of Table 10-1, the picture of a system of small scale farming which is far more efficient in terms of economizing on farm inputs.

To summarize, the small farm has the advantage of producing a greater net income per acre than the large farm. An added benefit of the small farm is its minimal consumption of purchased farm inputs. The small farm seems suited for an economy where resources are short and unemployment widespread since small farms can support more labor per acre while requiring fewer resources. In spite of these benefits, the Department of Agriculture has systematically ignored the problems of the small farmer.

The department's attitude is symbolized by a response to a General Accounting Office report questioning the department's neglect of the small farmer. The answer was framed by Assistant Secretary of Agriculture, Robert W. Long, who was previously the chief officer of the Bank of America in charge of agribusiness lending. Long argued that research designed to improve the small farm was of little avail; the small farm leads to a dead end. To support his case, Long referred to a departmental survey of the Ozarks area of Arkansas, Mississippi and Oklahoma which discovered that 20 percent of the household heads on these small farms are partially or totally disabled.[12]

Long's reasoning flies in the face of economic logic. If the small farm can make a totally disabled worker productive, we should take this state of affairs as evidence of the productivity of the small farm, not its backwardness. If a disabled farmer can produce a greater net income per acre with fewer resources than a healthy college trained farmer, what does this say about agriculture education?

To make this point stronger, we should mention that many of the small farmers devote only a small part of their time to agriculture. Many work at full time jobs over and above farming. More than half of the total income reported by farm families in 1970 came from work done away from the farm.[13] Although some of this money represents the profits and salaries of business and professional people who farm for speculative or tax purposes, most of this income does not.*

Our discussion of large and small farming should include a brief discussion of the implications of each system for food processing and distribution. As each region of the country specializes in a narrower range of products, the cost of distributing the food will necessarily rise. We have already alluded to the enormous energy cost of transporting food. In terms of money, the intercity truck and train transport of food cost more than $7 billion in 1974.[15] For fresh fruits and vegetables, shipping costs account for 10 percent and more of retail price.[16] In many cases, the cost is far more. The Committee on Agriculture and Forestry of the U.S. Senate reports than when a carton of California lettuce was selling at $1.25, the trucking rate to the east coast was $2.25.[17]

---

*Almost 60 percent of the total off-farm income is earned as salaries and wages while less than 15 percent is earned from outside business or properties.[14]

Besides the cost of shipping, the complicated pathways of distribution leave an incredible trail of wasted produce. An analysis of the movement of bell peppers in supermarkets revealed that more than 9 percent had to be discarded at the store. Another 3 percent went bad within 3 days after being taken out and chilled.[18] The situation with lettuce is even worse. Supermarkets trim off about one-third of the lettuce which is not culled.[19]

To limit the problem of spoilage, food marketers prefer to sell processed foods. Between the period 1925-29 and 1954-58, consumption of fresh fruit declined by 30 percent; while consumption of canned, frozen, and dried foods grew by 152 percent.[20] The consumption of fresh vegetables is also declining. It was about 20 percent higher in the period 1949–50.*[21]

Our food is not only frozen or canned, it is laced with innumerable preservatives which retard or camouflage the normal deterioration of food.

Further nutritional effects of large scale farming can be very profound. We can see in Table 2-1 that pesticide consumption tends to be larger on large scale farms, judging by the relationship between percentage of cash receipts and percentage of pesticide expenditures. The statistics for the largest category of farms might appear to contradict this last statement until we recall that the figures for pesticides are measured in costs. Since the large farmer pays less for chemicals, the contradiction disappears.

The nutritional consequences of large scale farming go further still. Because large farmers hire most of their labor, they prefer to specialize in crops which require little direct labor. Since fresh produce is generally more labor intensive, the large scale farmer will minimize the consumption of fresh produce. This tendency is evident in the California grape industry.

Until recently 150 table grape growers in the Coachella Valley farmed 13,000 acres of grapes. Today only 30 growers remain in grape production. The 120 former grape growers have converted their 7,000 acres to less labor intensive crops.[22] *Business Week* reports that what happened in the grape fields is relatively common; farmers are rapidly switching out of labor intensive crops. As a result, industry is furiously developing new synthetic foods to replace these natural products.[23]

We have no way of calculating to what extent the food distribution system developed as a direct result of the rise of modern farming technologies. Certainly, much of the transportation cost is traceable to the present organization of agriculture. When fruit is grown in one state and grain in another, transportation is essential to give a balanced diet to everyone. Some of the costs of packaging must be considered part of this same process. Of course, not all of the $11 billion spent for food packaging materials is essential for the food distribution system, but a substantial portion of it is.[24]

The potential for minimizing the cost of food distribution is suggested

*Mechanical harvesting is also generally simpler for processed fruits and vegetables.

by a Department of Agriculture study of farming within the highly urbanized Standard Metropolitan Statistical Areas which include most of the urbanized areas of the country.[25] About 70 percent of the U.S. population lives in these areas, which cover only 13 percent of the total land area of the country. In spite of a population density in excess of 3,100 people per square mile, the land in these urban areas produces almost 60 percent of the nation's vegetables and over 40 percent of the fruits and nuts. In 1969, 21 percent of all agricultural products was grown on these highly urbanized lands.

Instead of going directly to people living in the vicinity of the farm, these products enter into complex marketing chains moving from farmers to distributors to processors to wholesalers to stores—passages of hundreds or even thousands of miles. Simpler routes would result in substantial savings. The *Wall Street Journal* reports that produce sells for about 33 percent less at farmers' markets than in supermarkets.[26]

A few years ago, the idea of regional food self sufficiency might have been taken lightly, but today several state governments are actively pursuing that goal.[27]

The potential self sufficiency of urban areas could be greatly enhanced by home gardening. During the Second World War, about 40 percent of fresh vegetable production in the U.S. came from home gardens.[28] The savings from gardening can be substantial. A Cornell University study estimated that in 1975, when a bushel of peas cost $6 at a roadside stand, a home garden could produce the same amount for $1.17. The study estimated that a 4,800-square foot garden plot could grow an equivalent of $521 worth of food at supermarket prices. The total cost of the garden would be only $92; valuing the time spent in the garden at prevailing wage rates would bring the total cost of the garden up to $189, leaving a profit of $240 for the gardener.[29]

Besides saving on money, home gardening requires less energy and other resources. More importantly, home gardening can help in cutting some of the giant agribusiness corporations down to size.

Although few areas of the nation could grow all the foods available in the modern supermarket, the savings from a policy of regional self sufficiency could be enormous. For every dollar spent in the supermarket, only about $.42 goes to the farmer;[30] the rest goes to middlemen and the retailer.

Even if it is granted that small scale farming is more productive, uses fewer resources, and leads to a less costly food distribution system, the Department of Agriculture raises another objection. According to Earl Butz, the modern large scale farming practices have "tended to eliminate stoop labor . . . and much of the drudgery" of farming.[31]

We must grant the first part of Butz's claim. Mechanization is eliminating stoop labor. On the other hand, the new forms of farm labor in large scale agriculture are not necessarily very desirable. (Nor is the situation of the unemployed farm worker displaced by technology.) Labor on the modern farm is the third most dangerous occupation in the nation in

terms of industrial accidents.*[34] Continual exposure of farm labor to pesticides adds a burden that has yet to be fully evaluated.[35] Nor should we forget the hazards faced by nonfarm workers in manufacturing pesticides or fertilizer. The condition of labor cannot be expected to improve so long as agriculture is subjugated to corporate domination, since the large mechanized farm is designed merely to generate profits. On the other hand, life on a small farm deprived of culture, education, and an adequate income hardly seems a proper goal of society. Something new is needed.

THE FUTURE

In order to be exploited really in accordance with its nature, land requires different social relations.

—Karl Marx, *Theories of Surplus Value*[36]

The history of agriculture in the United States is not just a sequence of larger and larger machines; it concerns the complete restructuring of society according to the needs of business. For more than a century, government, business and the university threw their combined weight behind this restructuring. In place of families who grow their own food, we see farmers under the control of processors or banks, wives standing in supermarket lines and workers risking their lives in pesticide factories or fertilizer mines. Each has a prescribed role.

We work, we consume, we live our lives so that business may prosper. Human needs, truly human needs are forgotten. Where is the pride in spraying food with poisons? Where is the joy in a supermarket? Where is the sense of accomplishment in the tedious routine of the modern factory?

More and more the satisfaction of a job well done is enjoyed by the well-to-do. The ingenuity of the lawyer, the resourcefulness of the entrepreneur and the power of the corporate rulers shuffle the wealth back and forth, but they do nothing to raise a single grain of food.

Farming, like carpentry or music or any other skill, will suffer unless it can be enjoyed in a proper setting. The creation of a proper setting is the great challenge to modern society. Only when this challenge is met will we be able to speak unambiguously of efficiency in agriculture.

---

*The use of the word "eliminate" is curiously ambiguous for the normally blunt Mr. Butz. More than one out of every five farmworkers employed by giant farming corporations in California suffered a reported occupational illness or injury in 1971.[32] This rate is almost 3½ times the incidence in large scale industry[53] where reporting is much more comprehensive.

REFERENCES

1. J. Tristamm Beresford, "The Farm as a Management Model," Special University of London Lecture, College of Estate Management (February 1970), reprinted in *The Estates Gazette* (March 14, 1970).

2. Adam Smith, *The Nature and Causes of the Wealth of Nations,* Cannan ed., Modern Library (New York: Random House, 1937), p. 392.

3. Stephen L. Brown and Ulrich F. Pilz, "U.S. Agriculture, Potential Vulnerabilities," SRI Project MV-6250-052, Stanford Research Institute (January 1969).

4. Alex F. McCalla and Harold O. Carter, "Alternative Agricultural and Food Policy Directions for the U.S.: With Emphasis on a Market-Oriented Approach,: paper presented at the Policy Research Workshop on Public Agriculture and Food, Price and Income Policy Research, Washington, D.C. (January 15–16, 1976).

5. United States Department of Agriculture, Economic Research Service, "The Food and Fiber System—How It Works," Agricultural Information Bulletin No. 383 (March 1975), p. 4.

6. Anon., "Farm Suppliers, Mighty Link in the Marketing Chain," *The Farm Index* (February 1974), pp. 9–11.

7. Irving Hoch, "Returns to Scale in Farming: Further Evidence," *American Journal of Agricultural Economics,* Vol. 58, No. 4, Part 1 (November 1976), pp. 745–49.

8. Anon., "The Riskiest Game in Town," Forbes (June 15, 1975) and Federal Trade Commission, Docket No. 8835, *United Brands Co., Initial Decision* (March 19, 1973), p. 30.

9. "The Riskiest Game . . .," *op. cit.*

10. Kenneth R. Krause and Leonard R. Kyle, "Midwestern Corn Farms, Economic Status and the Potential for Large and Family-Sized Units," United States Department of Agriculture, Economic Research Service, Agricultural Economics Report No. 216 (November 1971), pp. 16–17.

11. See Ervin J. Long, "Land Reform in Underdeveloped Countries," *Land Economics,* Vol. 37 (May 1961), pp. 113–23; see especially the literature cited on p. 117.

12. Letter of April 24, 1975 reprinted in "Report to the Congress by the Comptroller of the U.S.: Some Problems Impeding Economic Improvement of Small Farm Operations: What the Department of Agriculture Could Do," (August 15, 1975).

13. Donald K. Larson, "Impact of Off-Farm Income on Farm Family Income Levels," *Agricultural Finance Review,* Vol. 36 (April 1976), pp. 7–11.

14. *Ibid.*

15. United States Department of Agriculture, *1975 Handbook of Agricultural Charts,* Agricultural Handbook No. 491, p. 30.

16. United States Department of Agriculture, Economic Research Service and Agricultural Marketing Service, "The Market Functions and Costs for Food Between America's Fields and Tables," prepared for the Subcommittee on Agricultural Production and Marketing of the Committee on Agriculture and Forestry, United States Senate, 94th Congress, 1st Session (March 25, 1975), p. 11.

17. Committee on Agriculture and Forestry, *The Immovable Feast,* Committee Print, 93d Congress, 2d Session (21 January 1974), p. 2.

18. M. J. Ceponis and J. E. Butterfield, "Market Losses in Florida Cucumbers and Bell Peppers in Metropolitan New York," *Plant Disease Reporter,* Vol. 58, No. 6 (June 1974), pp. 558–60.

19. "The Market Functions and Costs for Food . . .," *op. cit.*

20. Sarah Shaver Hughes, *Agricultural Surpluses and American Foreign Policy, 1952–1960,* Masters Thesis, History Department, University of Wisconsin (1964), p. 147.

21. Anon., "Craving for Vegetables," *The Farm Index* (October 1975)

22. Al Mullins, "The Economic Impact of the Migrant Worker in Northern California," *Northern California Economic Review* (Fall 1975), pp. 5-6.

23. Anon., "Making the Switch to Something Else," *Business Week* (September 14, 1974).

24. Terry L. Crawford and Andrew Weiser, "The Bill for Marketing Farm-Food Products," MTS-198, *Marketing and Transportation Situation,* United States Department of Agriculture, Economic Research Service (August 1975).

25. Robert Otte, "Farming in the City's Shadow: Urbanization of Land and Changes in Farm Output in Standard Metropolitan Statistical Areas, 1960-1970," United States Depart-

ment of Agriculture, Economic Research Service, Agricultural Economics Report No. 250 (February 1974).

26. Joann S. Lublin, "Farmer's Markets Sprout Inside the Cities as Buyers Save: Low Prices, Friendly Aura," *Wall Street Journal* (August 25, 1975), p. 1.

27. Jerome Goldstein, "Food Policies That Save Energy," *Environment Action* Bulletin, (April 1976).

28. Dean Pahl, "Gardening in Its Heyday," *Nutrition Action,* Vol. 2, No. 6 (October 1975), pp. 4-5.

29. Anon., "Digging in Against Inflation," *The Farm Index,* Vol. 15, No. 2 (February 1976), pp. 17-20.

30. *1975 Handbook Agricultural Charts, op. cit.,* p. 28.

31. Earl Butz, *Farmworkers in Rural America, 1971-1972,* Part 4B, Hearing before the Subcommittee on Migratory Labor of the Committee on Public Works, 92d Congress, 1st and 2d Sessions (June 20, 1972), p. 2566.

32. State of California, "Occupational Injuries and Illness Survey, California, 1974," Department of Industrial Relations, San Francisco (1974), p. 56.

33. *Ibid.*

34. Neal Smith, "The Third Most Dangerous Occupation," *Congressional Record* (September 17, 1969), pp. 25944–49.

35. Joel Swartz, "Poisoning Farm Workers," *Environment,* Vol. 17, No. 4 (June 1975), pp. 26–33.

36. Karl Marx, *Theories of Surplus Value,* (Moscow: Progress Publishers, 1971), Part 3, p. 301.

The Global Domain of Capital

. . . if capitalism could develop agriculture, . . . if it could raise the living standards of the masses, who in spite of the amazing technical progress are everywhere still half-starved and poverty-stricken, [the system could be salvaged]. But if capitalism did these things it would not be capitalism; for both uneven development and a semistarvation level of existence of the masses are fundamental and inevitable conditions and constitute premises of this mode of production.

—V. I. Lenin, "Imperialism,
the Highest Stage of Capitalism"

GROWING HUNGER
IN THE THIRD WORLD

Each rich nation amounts to a lifeboat full of comparatively rich people. The poor of the world are in other, much more crowded lifeboats. Continuously, so to speak, the poor fall out of their lifeboats and swim for a while, hoping to be admitted to a rich lifeboat, or in some other way to benefit from the "goodies" on board.

—Garrett Hardin[1]

How is U.S. agriculture responding to the needs of the world's hungry? To begin with a disproportionate amount of U.S. exports are used to satisfy the desires of the rich. About 25 percent of the value of U.S. exports are feed grains, not intended for human consumption.[2] Although most of the grains are shipped to wealthy nations, the Department of Agriculture is actively working with the United States Feed Grain Council to promote the consumption of these U.S. feed grains by livestock and poultry in countries such as the Philippines and Taiwan.[3] More directly, it has loaned the proceeds from the Food for Peace program to giant grain dealers to build feed mills. As a result, South Korea, for example, which had no livestock industry a decade ago, now imports 800,000 tons of feed grain annually.[4] The 12.5 million tons of soybeans exported by the U.S. would have been capable of supplying the protein requirements of more than one-half billion people, but most of it was fed to livestock, especially in Europe and Japan, which purchased two-thirds of all U.S. soybean exports. Since the poor do not enjoy the luxury of grain-fed animal products to a great extent, U.S. exports have little to do with fighting hunger.

A little more than one-third of our agricultural exports are sent to Africa, Latin America and Asia, excluding Japan.[5] In return, these nations devote much of their land to producing crops for the U.S., as we shall see. In 1971, the U.S. imported about $4 billion worth of agricultural products from Africa, Latin America and Asia, excluding Japan.[6]

By 1975, this amount had grown by 63 percent to more than $6 billion.[7] In the meantime, U.S. agricultural exports to these nations grew by almost 300 percent to about $8 billion.[8]

This rapid deterioration of the position of the Third World in agricultural trade helps to lend credence to the popular image of a world of lifeboats. Garrett Hardin, quoted at the beginning of this section, suggests that any attempt to assist the overflowing masses on the lifeboats of the Third World nations would be foolhardy; the more we feed them, the more they breed, thus multiplying their demand for food. Better to let each boat fend for itself. Those who can control their population will stay afloat; the others will sink.

In reality, the world most certainly is not made up of independent economies. While national governments do exert some control over their domestic production, no economy is totally independent of the rest of the world.

To look at the world as an aggregate of independent lifeboats, as Hardin suggests, is to make the same mistake as the American farmers whom Veblen criticized for seeing themselves as independent entrepreneurs. Just as within the domestic economy, the lives of farmers, workers and families are manipulated to make business more profitable; within the international economy, nations are relegated to performing specialized tasks to facilitate the development of the dominant economies.

Once we agree to look at the world more holistically, we begin to realize that the underdevelopment of the tropics and the development of the Atlantic nations are both aspects of the same process, which dates back to the sixteenth century when the European nations first began to control the economies of the peripheral lands.[9]

Initially, the colonial powers were content to extract valuable commodities from the existing economies in these exotic lands. Precious metals looted from India and Latin America flowed into Europe just when the money supply was proving to be a bottleneck to further economic growth. African slaves were an invaluable source of labor on plantations, which earned enormous profits.

Even spices, which may not seem terribly important in our world today, were vital because the emerging capitalist organization in Europe was concentrating people into cities. In lieu of an efficient food distribution system, spices were required to make the meat supply seem palatable after its long trip from farm to city. Profits from British re-export of tropical condiments were immensely important for importing essential industrial materials.[10]

The diet of the poor also depended on tropical condiments. Mantoux points out that when working class families were crowded into cities too confined for maintaining their cows, they substituted tea for milk.[11]* The urbanization of the period also depended on grain imported first from the Baltic lands, then the Americas and even India.[14]

---

*This change in diet was fostered by the British East India Company, since tea was their major product.[12] In the early nineteenth century, economists already recognized that the working class could afford tea only because the wages of the Chinese workers were so low.[13]

Gradually, as the industrial capacity of Europe began to exceed what the people could afford to consume, the colonial powers began to reorganize social relations in the peripheral lands to make the masses of people in the colonies better consumers of European exports.

This reorganization can be seen in much the same terms as the treatment of small farms discussed in the last chapter. As the President of the Manchester Chamber of Commerce informed a Parliamentary inquiry in 1840, "In India there is an immense extent of territory, and the population of it would consume British manufactures to a most enormous extent."[15] This gentleman put his finger on the difficulty in such an arrangement, forewarning the committee that "The whole question with respect to our Indian trade is whether they can pay us, by the products of their soil, for what we are prepared to send out as manufactures."[16] Two decades earlier, Malthus made a similar point in a more general way:[17]*

In the accounts of the year ended the 5th of January 1818, it appears that the exports of three articles alone in which machinery is used—cottons, woolen and hardware, including steel goods, etc. are valued at above 29 millions. And among the most prominent articles of the imports of the same year, we find coffee, indigo, sugar, tea, silks, tobacco, wines and cotton-wool, amounting in value all together to above 18 millions out of thirty! Now I would ask how we should have obtained these valuable imports, if the foreign markets for our cottons, woolens, and hardware had not been extended. . . ?

Although this question has plagued the developed nations in subsequent years, they went ahead with their plans to remake the colonial economies to add to the profits of industry and trade.

The key to the European strategy to rearrange social relations in the colonies was land. By abolishing traditional patterns of landholding, village society was immediately ruptured. As a result, the imperial powers could rearrange colonial society to suit their needs. Marx pointed out the hypocrisy of the imperial powers who made petty theft a capital offense while stealing entire states with "one stroke of the pen."[18] In some cases, colonists claimed the best land for themselves, banishing the native population to remote areas. In others, poll taxes or hut taxes were levied to coerce people into wage labor.[19] In almost all cases, these economies were at the mercy of the developed nations.

One partial exception was China. Although the colonial powers had long dreamed of capturing the vast Chinese market, they never quite succeeded in restructuring social relations. To be sure, the ports of China suffered from domination by foreigners, but the interior remained more or less intact. Even in the twentieth century, the average household in North China produced about 75 percent of all its meals; in East Central China, about 60 percent.[20] What goods were purchased came from a small

---

*Malthus is making the point in the text here that the use of machinery is required to extend the production of manufactured goods to pay for imports of raw materials. The underlying theme of the book is that the increase of manufacturing should not proceed too rapidly because of the potential threat of insufficient demand. As a result, the above citation may appear to be taken out of context when only the page is considered, but it fits in very well with the overall tenor of the book.

marketing area with an average population of 2,500 households.[21] Each peasant was acquainted with at least one member of each of these households.[22] As a result, market relations were not able to obliterate personal relations.

The strength of the Chinese village demonstrates the vitality of traditional society when landholdings are left unchanged. During the 1850s British textile manufacturers dispatched a commercial agent to assess their potential sales in China. He went up and down the land, sampling cloth, checking prices and sending samples back to England. After studying the samples and price lists sent from China, the manufacturers were unanimous in informing the agent that they could in no way send textiles to China at a competitive price, even if they were to get free transportation for their product. In spite of the modern techniques of the British textile industry, they could not match the efficiency of the Chinese village with its close integration of agriculture and industry.[23]

Because of the self-sufficiency of the Chinese village, the Emperor could boast in a letter to George III of England, "I set no value on objects strange and ingenious and have no use for your country's manufactures."[24] When all else failed, the British attempted to conquer the village by shipping opium into China. In response to the Chinese government's attempt to interfere with this business, the British declared war to protect the sanctity of free trade.

Even in those lands where the colonial powers succeeded in smashing traditional village society, they had to take pains to maintain the resulting state of underdevelopment. In 1751, the British Board of Trade issued instructions to the Government of Cape Castle, a small fort and trading settlement in what is now Ghana, demanding that the local population stop planting cotton. The message stated, "The introduction of culture and industry among the Negroes is contrary to the now established policy of this country, there is no saying where this might stop, and that it might extend to tobacco, sugar and every other commodity which we now take from our colonies."[25] In other words, the interests of the English would be better served if these people produced commodities as slaves in the Americas instead of working as free growers in Africa.

In South Africa, where wage labor was required for the mines, Africans showed an inconvenient ability to farm better than the whites. [26] Lest the workings of the market force white settlers to accept the undignified work in the mines while the blacks lived as self-employed farmers, laws were passed to keep the blacks off the land.[27] This arrangement increased the profits of the owners of the mines, since whites would have returned to Europe rather than accept the wage level of a black worker. Again, we find the conscious "development of underdevelopment."*

Besides destroying the traditional pattern of landholdings, the colonial powers systematically undermined indigenous industry. The English were forbidden to wear printed or dyed calicoes from India. A fine of £200 was levied on all persons found having or selling them. The majority of

---

*An expression coined by Andre Gunder Frank.[28]

Indian manufactures imported into England were brought there to be re-exported to the continent.[29] By 1814, the English sabotage of the Indian textile industry was so successful that one-half of all Indian imports were textiles from England.[30] Eventually, the interests of European manufactures succeeded in more or less determining the division of production between the Atlantic economies and the peripheral lands, "converting one part of the globe into a chiefly agricultural field . . . for supplying the other part which remains chiefly . . . industrial."[31] Even the benevolent John Stuart Mill saw the best chance for Indian development in a policy of promoting agricultural exports.[32]

Over the years, Western society has forgotten its deciding influence in the Third World. It prefers to accept the belief that the poverty of the so-called underdeveloped countries was due to the climate of the tropics, or racial inferiority or cultural backwardness, or even overpopulation; but the real cause was the exploitation of the poor. The evidence that poverty was a product of the search for profits is overwhelming. A typical example is England's use of India for cotton production during the Civil War, when supplies from the Southern states of the U.S. were disrupted. So much rice land was used for supplying the English textile mills that 1 million people starved to death in the district of Orissa alone.[33] In 1878, India saw the establishment of the famed parliamentary Indian Famine Commission, which told Parliament that the best response to the problem of famine was to let the market take its course. "[T]his, it is believed, will best subserve the interests of both Europe and India."[34] The British, who stole the lands and rigged the economy, even opposed giving preference to railroad cars moving toward famine-stricken areas;[35] such an action would violate the sacred laws of supply and demand. As a result of the intelligent application of these laws of supply and demand, the standard of living in India has gradually fallen from its peak during the rule of Akbar (1556–1605) to its present level.[36]

In practice, the laws of supply and demand worked in the Third World just as they did in the Atlantic economies: the workers supplied what capital demanded. The resulting reorganization of the world was so effective that whole nations such as Firestone's Liberia or United Fruit's Honduras became the private preserves of individual corporations whose naked self-interest took precedence over the needs of the people. One United Fruit manager, for example, wrote to a company lawyer in 1920:[37]

We must produce a disembowelment of the incipient economy of the country in order to increase and help our aims. We have to prolong its tragic, tormented, and revolutionary life; the wind must blow only on our sails and the water must only wet our keels.

Owing primarily to the policies of such corporate giants, between 1913 and 1953, exports of primary products from Africa and Latin America increased tenfold.[38] In spite of the massive demands imposed on the Third World economies, they managed to export grain as well as luxury crops until the Second World War[39] (see Table 11-1). In 1969, one of the most distinguished authorities on Third World economies, W. Arthur Lewis,

who was simultaneously President of the Caribbean Development Bank
and James Madison Professor of Political Economy at Princeton University, pointed out that the rate of growth in the tropics since World War II
exceeded the fastest growth rates which have ever occurred in Europe or
the U.S. How have these nations failed?[40]*

TABLE 11-1

The Changing Pattern and Balance* of World Grain Trade (1934-1975)

Region	1934-1938	1948-1952	1960	1966	1975
	million metric tons				
North America	+5	+23	+39	+59	+91
Latin America	+9	+ 1	0	+5	-3
Western Europe	-24	-22	-25	-27	-19
Eastern Europe & U.S.S.R.	+5	—	0	-4	-27
Africa	+1	0	-2	-7	-5
Asia	+2	-6	-17	-34	-43
Australia	+3	+3	+6	+8	+6

*Surplus and deficits do not always equal a net zero for a given year because of
errors in rounding.

Source: Department of Commerce.

To begin with, consider the amount of nonessential food grown for
sale wealthy nations. In 1976, U.S. alone imported almost $5 billion in
products such as tea, chocolate, and bananas, which can not be grown
easily in temperate climates.[42] Adding sugar imports, which were down
considerably in 1975, to this sum pushes the value of nonessential
agricultural products to about $6 billion.†[43]

The importance of these crops is often overlooked in spite of their
economic importance. Coffee, for example, with up to 7.9 billion pounds
sold or traded each year, is generally the second largest commodity in
world trade after petroleum.[44] The U.S. alone imported more than 2.6
billion pounds of green coffee in 1976.[45] Sugar imports in 1975 were
almost 4 million tons.[46] Included in the top nine sources of U.S. agricultural imports in 1975 we find Brazil, Dominican Republic, Mexico, The
Philippines, Colombia, Malaysia and Indonesia.[47] The only developed
nations among the list of the top 25 sources of U.S. agricultural imports
are Australia, Canada, Denmark, New Zealand, France, Italy, Spain and
Poland.[48]

*Lewis agrees with nineteenth-century economists in placing emphasis on the resource
base. He suggests that the principal weakness of the tropical countries was the lack of cheap
iron ores and coal.[41]

†Since sugar can be made from beets, it is not strictly a tropical crop, although cane
predominates in sugar imports.

The production of export crops in the Third World is usually justified in terms of the indirect farming we discussed in Part 2: If the amount of coffee a worker could produce in a year would exchange for more food than the worker could grow in that time, economic logic requires that worker specialize in the production of coffee.

In reality, production decisions are not made in that way at all. The choice is not between growing coffee or corn on the same land; more frequently, the peasant has to choose between working a tiny plot of land on a rocky hillside or accepting employment on the fertile lands of the plantation. To make sure that the wage rate remains near the subsistence level, large landholders often go so far as to hold extensive tracts of land idle; by limiting the alternative sources of income, this strategy helps to maintain a pool of unemployed and underemployed workers to bid down the wage rates.

A great deal of courage is required by any people which dares to challenge this strategy. In Guatemala, for example, the government decided to let peasants farm 400,000 acres of idle land held by United Fruit in Guatemala.[49] The amount paid to the company, $4 per acre, was equal to the value assessed for tax purposes.[50] After a successful public relations campaign by United Fruit, in 1954 the CIA dutifully overthrew the elected government of Guatemala.

After decades of exploitation, some of the established international plantation firms such as United Fruit are removing themselves from the actual production of cash crops.[51] Since the domestic market for most Third World export crops is not very extensive, Third World growers are dependent on the international agribusiness firms for marketing their crops. This dependence is magnified by the highly perishable or processed nature of tropical produce. Their strategic position in the marketing or distribution system allows the international agribusiness giants to extract just about as much profit as if they had participated in the actual growing. But while one generation of agribusiness firms withdraws from production, another enters the field elsewhere to produce fruits, vegetables and even flowers to be flown to the wealthy cities of Europe and America.

Not all cash cropping can be explained in terms of large-scale foreign enterprises. In many cases, tropical export crops are grown by small holders. Looking at the motives of these indigenous producers will give us some insight into the forces shaping Third World agriculture.

Recall from the Prologue that very little research goes into improving the production of food crops in the Third World. Even so, grain yields in industrial and developing countries were about equal during the period 1934–38.[52] After this period, yields began to diverge as a result of massive infusions of modern inputs such as fertilizer and hybrid seeds. Because of the nature of tropical soils, most of the technology developed for food production in temperate nations is useless, if not destructive, when applied in the Third World. On the other hand, the continued research and resulting improvement in cash crop yields leads to a gradual sinking of their prices. To take a relatively extreme example, the price of rubber in the period 1910-13 was more than eight times what it was in 1960-64.*[53]

Because years of exploitation have left indigenous populations too poor to be good customers even for staple foods, growers have had to expand production of luxury crops for the developed nations despite falling prices. Increased production has tended to depress prices still further.

The abysmal poverty of the majority of the people forces them to continue to accept work for lower wages than European or American workers are accustomed to earning. Because the buying power of the masses remains so limited, peasants have little incentive to grow food for the nonfarm worker in the city—thus the vicious circle of poverty is tightened.

To make matters worse, the peasant family functions in an international system which puts it at a disadvantage. After the Second World War, the U.S. was able to keep the value of its currency artificially high.[54] High exchange rates for the dollar, made possible in part because of the U.S.'s dominant position in the international financial system, reduced the amount which a nation could earn selling to the U.S. For example, because of high exchange rates for the dollar, a ton of coffee would trade for less wheat than would otherwise be the case.[55] Many Third World nations tried to improve their international trade situation by keeping their exchange rates higher. Since they have never had the financial power of the U.S., their success has been doubtful.

Because of the high cost of U.S. farm products in the international markets, the world refused to buy as much as the U.S. produced. Much of the resulting farm surplus was given away or sold under very favorable conditions. In effect, the U.S. subsidized the purchase of much of its farm exports.

For the Third World, this state of affairs was a mixed blessing at best. Exchange rates favorable to the U.S., together with increased productivity in the tropics, combined to make the Third World get less and less for their products. Still, a farmer's profits from growing export crops generally exceeded what could be earned by selling basic food crops to the domestic population. Production of local food needs was given further discouragement because of U.S. food surpluses.

The effect of the shipments of surplus grain was to depress the price, further discouraging the production of food.[56] Theoretically, the disposition of the "surplus grain" might have counterbalanced the effects of the overvalued exchange, but in practice the power of the U.S. to direct its food stocks to compliant countries has proved to be an effective weapon which the U.S. could apply at will. Countries who behaved in a way which suited the interests of the U.S. power structure would be "reward-

---

*The years 1910-14 fall within the four-year period which farm groups in the U.S. consider the last "normal" period of farm prices.

ed" with shipments of food at cut-rate prices. When India, for example, attempted to develop its own fertilizer industry during the drought of 1965 and 1966, the U.S. government gave notice that food shipments would henceforth be on a month-to-month basis. The New York Times editorialized about these pressures:

Call them "strings," call them "conditions," or whatever one likes, India has little choice but to agree to many of the terms that the U.S. . . . is putting on its aid. . . . for India simply has nowhere else to turn.[57]

Because of the massive power of the U.S., the Agency for International Development of the U.S. State Department was able to "encourage" the government of Colombia to "switch from wheat production."[58] "As a result," the Agency boasts, "Colombia now imports over 85% of its wheat requirement."[59] To pay for this wheat, Colombia exports coffee, sugar, bananas and tobacco to the U.S. In addition, Colombia has the distinction of being the largest supplier of cut flowers to the U.S.[60]

While flowers might not seem to be a high priority crop for nations with hungry people, they are very profitable, especially for European markets. In Colombia, for example, an acre of carnations is estimated to be worth 80 times more than an acre of wheat or corn,[61] because in affluent markets such as Belgium consumers spend almost 2 percent of their income for flowers.[62] Flowers are big business in Africa as well. DCK, a Danish horticulture firm, has purchased 10,000 acres in Kenya; it hopes to make that nation the major flower garden for Europe.[63] In effect, Africa is being converted into a farm for exporting luxury crops such as flowers, protein-rich legumes and even meat; in return, it has become a net importer of high carbohydrate foods such as grains.[64]

This new pattern of world agriculture has serious consequences for the poor in the Third World. Before the agricultural distribution systems of the world developed to the point where they could tap into the flow of lush produce from the tropics, fruits and vegetables were cheap enough that they were a normal part of the diet of the indigenous poor.* India, for example, is the world's largest producer of tropical fruits.[66] During the period April 1975/March 1976, exports of fresh fruit increased fivefold over the previous year.[67] Now that the poor have to compete with affluent Europeans and Americans for these nutritious foods, they can no longer afford them.[68]

The commercialization of the Third World, what we might term "developed underdevelopment," makes the poverty of the masses more severe. Peasants who were formerly self-sufficient are herded from the land into cities where they provide ultracheap labor. Consequently, the degree of income inequality is becoming more extreme. In Indonesia, the top 20 percent of the population earned 10 times as much as the poorest 20

*This phenomenon is not new. In his first article on an economic article, Marx described how the traditional practice of gathering berries in the forests of the Rhineland became a crime when berries became an article of commerce.[65]

percent in 1950; by 1963, the ratio had increased to 17 times.[69] Similar trends have been observed in Puerto Rico, Argentina, Mexico, Colombia, and Brazil.[70]

The changing distribution of income associated with "developed underdevelopment" increases the tendency for one class of people to bid food away from another in the domestic market. This problem is illustrated by a comparison between Burmese and Brazilian patterns of food consumption. In an extremely poor nation such as Burma, where small peasant farms predominate, hunger is relatively rare. If each Burmese family earned 10 percent more income, the nation as a whole would consume only 1 percent more rice and 3 percent more wheat.[71] If the average family felt a pressing need to increase the intake of staple foods, we would expect that a greater share of the increased income would be spent on rice or wheat. In Brazil, for example, a similar improvement in income would produce a 3 percent increase in rice consumption and a 4 percent in wheat.[72]

The poor Brazilian family is actually worse off than these data indicate. Since a disproportionate amount of the rise in income will go to the rich and middle classes who tend to spend less money on basic foods as their income improves, the poor in Brazil must spend a very high portion of their extra income to increase the national consumption of rice and wheat by 3 and 4 percent. The implication is that insufficient income is a more serious constraint to adequate diets in Brazil than in Burma.

This commercialization of world agriculture leads to the best of all possible worlds for employers. With the application of modern agricultural inputs which displaces labor, unemployment skyrockets. For example, in a nation where 80 percent of its workers are employed in agriculture and 20 percent in industry, a 10 percent reduction in the agricultural labor force casts 8 percent of the workers into unemployment. To absorb this many workers, the industrial labor force would have to grow by 40 percent. Yet the traditional agricultural technology in the Third World is so labor-intensive that the cost of the equipment required to replace a single worker is quite small.

In Java, for example, about 1 million people join the labor force each year; only 140,000 find jobs.[73] In that country, a simple rice huller is so cheap that about one job is lost for each $43 invested.[74] Because of the large number of people traditionally involved in the work of hulling rice, the widespread adoption of the new rice hulling methods has resulted in the elimination of 1.2 million jobs.

The translation of a relatively small investment into a substantial amount of unemployment in Third World agriculture allows the developed nations to manipulate the world labor supply by adjusting the flow of technology into those lands.* The consequences of this control are described in Figure 3.

---

*What follows in this section is a very simplified version of an extremely complex set of relationships. I believe that this treatment captures the essential features of the world system, but it necessarily ignores many of the finer points. To do real justice to this material would require an entire volume.

The right-hand arrow at the top of the diagram represents the introduction of the new labor-displacing technology. The resulting build-up of unemployment creates a precarious situation for Third World governments which are hemmed in from both sides. Unless conditions improve for the masses of unemployed workers, they will eventually turn to militant or even revolutionary behavior; but in order to get control over enough resources to improve conditions for the workers, these governments would have to challenge the privileges of the powerful elites. (Many governments in the Third World have proved too corrupt or too timid to do anything for the people.) Instead the governments arm themselves to withstand any revolutionary challenge and beg the developed nations for aid, as shown in the bottom line moving from the Third World to the Developed Capitalist nations.

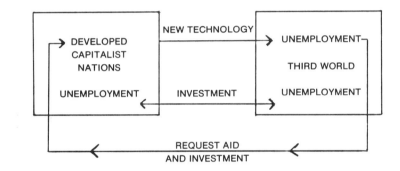

FIGURE 3
Technology and Unemployment

While aid projects may offer some short-run amelioration, the conditions which the "donors" extract have deleterious effects on the economic structure. The recipient nation must generally agree to give foreign investors the freedom to invest wherever and whenever they please. Frequently these nations are expected to go much further, promising special treatment such as restricting the power of labor, freedom from taxation for several years and lowering the value of their currency.[75]

The rationale for this policy grows out of the idea that new foreign investment creates new jobs. Western business interests willingly respond. In the first place, the investment may require a very small outlay of funds. As David Rockefeller explained at the 1966 annual meeting of the Chase Manhattan bank, ". . . the disguised but close association in the sphere of banking gives American banking immediate access to local deposits which are then channeled into financing American commercial activities."[76] Other firms minimize their initial investment by tapping local funds through bonds or partnerships.

In addition, Western firms are attracted by the opportunity to invest in lands where workers earn a few cents per hour and taxes are kept extremely low. The arrow to the right of "investment" indicates a relation to unemployment in Third World countries: the flow of investment creates unemployment because it is concentrated in technologies which employ relatively little labor. Mellor and Lele estimate that because of the move to more capital-intensive investment in India, industrial employment is only half of what it would be if investment had been used merely to expand the capital stock which existed in 1953.[77] In fact, the technology employed in the Third World is often more capital-intensive than comparable investments in the U.S.[78] In many cases, this capital-intensive technology replaces traditional jobs.

Perhaps more importantly, for every job produced by the influx of new investment, several old jobs are eliminated as rising Western influence manages to shape people's tastes. In the place of traditional patterns of consumption which created jobs for workers, people begin to consume Western-style goods produced by capital-intensive technologies.[79]

One study of Jogjakarta, Indonesia, where unemployment is extreme, found that the exports of that region were actually less labor-intensive than the imports. In effect, Jogjakarta was exporting jobs, because of its style of consumption and methods of production.[80] This Westernizing influence also siphons more capital off from productive investments into ventures which do little to develop the economic capacity of the nation. One report from Djakarta, Indonesia, reports two new soft drink factories, as well as a serious interest by potential investors in night clubs, bars, steambaths, massage parlours, restaurants, and bowling alleys instead of factories.[81]

The arrow to the left of "investment" in the diagram represents unemployment in the Western nations resulting from the transfer of factories from these countries to the Third World. According to Chip Levinson, an internation representative to the International Labor Organization, this process represents "a concerted effort . . . on the part of the multinationals to destroy unions in the Western world by going to low wage places."[82]

Low wage levels allow Third World agriculture to supply many labor-intensive crops to the U.S. market more cheaply than domestic farmers can in spite of the transportation advantage enjoyed by U.S. growers.[83] A pound of tomatoes, for example, costs almost three times as much to grow in Florida as in Mexico.[84] Third World nations, besides offering cheaper labor costs, have almost no restrictions on pesticide use. In Iran, additional advantages include a 10-year tax exemption, low interest loans of up to one-half of the total investment, the provision of irrigible land at low, long-term rentals, exemption of customs duties on imported machinery and raw materials, minimum price supports, free construction of access roads and irrigation canals, low prices for water and power, and low interest credits for agricultural exports.[85] A new wave of agricultural corporations is relocating in the Third World now that labor costs on U.S. farms are rising.[86]

The magnitude of U.S. agriculture in the Third World is suggested by the experience of Brazil. Since the military coup in 1964, U.S. investors have purchased about 80 million acres of farm land in some seven or eight agricultural states of Brazil in chunks of about 1 million acres.[87] For every acre of land planted with corn in the U.S. in 1974, these investors own more than one acre in Brazil.[88]

The subjugation of Third World agriculture completes the cycle of the domination of labor, because it gives capital the ability to direct the flow of labor from the countryside. When too much labor begins to move to the city, a suitable application of labor-intensive technology in the villages can keep workers in a holding pattern. Should labor be in short supply, the promotion of capital-intensive agriculture can speed up the flow of labor. The manipulation of this pool of cheap labor in the Third World suffices to keep in check the demands of workers in the developed nations as well. In effect, we have a global land policy, the scope of which exceeds the wildest dreams of Edward Gibbon Wakefield, whom we discussed earlier.*

This system is not without its weaknesses. To begin with, the effectiveness of the program depends on the difference in living standards between the developed and Third World nations. Making people dependent on markets for their food while their level of earnings is kept to a minimum places them in a very precarious position. When world prices move unfavorably, the result can be a disaster.† The suicidal nature of the role of the Third World nations in the global economy was hammered home in 1972 when world food prices began to skyrocket. Between 1971 and 1974, the value of U.S. food exports nearly trebled.‡ India, for example, paid almost nine times more for U.S. food in 1975 than in 1972,[94] while the volume of wheat which makes up the bulk of India's agricultural imports grew about 300 percent.[95]

Many countries are now beginning to reconsider their policy of indirect farming. Even Japan, one of the most agriculturally dependent nations in the world, is launching a program geared to increasing its food self-sufficiency after the failure of the U.S. corn harvest in 1970, a U.S. dock strike in 1971 and an embargo on U.S. soybean exports in 1973.[96] Although some nations are beginning to move away from reliance on

---

*The only real difference between Wakefield's plan and its modern counterpart is that instead of using immigration to soak up excess unemployment in England while limiting the amount of land available for settlement in the peripheral lands, the new technique throws people off the land within those nations to create the desired level of unemployment. This interpretation runs parallel to the literature on the political measures used to create unemployment within the developed nations.[89]

†The Japanese attempted to turn Taiwan into a sugar growing colony until the Rice Riots of 1918 led to a reversal of the policy.[90]

‡Theoretically, the 20 percent decline in the value of the dollar should have helped Third World nations who purchased food from the U.S.,[91] except that a fall in the value of the dollar coincided with a doubling and trebling in grain prices. Nobody has yet explained how a fall in world production of less than 4 percent could cause such an incredible price rise.[92] For many Third World countries which formerly paid less than the market price for grain, the effect was still more traumatic.[93]

indirect farming, most continue to rely on the capitalist network that is the main source of their economic difficulties. Unfortunately, the consequence of a continuation of the developed underdevelopment of the Third World will be more hunger and starvation.

REFERENCES

1. Garrett Hardin, "Living on a Lifeboat," *BioScience*, Vol. 24, No. 10 (October 1974), p. 561.

2. Sally E. Breedlove, "Farm Exports to Push U.S. Trade to Record Surplus for 1975," *Foreign Agriculture* (February 23, 1976).

3. Anon., "Cooperator Programs," *Foreign Agriculture*, Special Market Development Issue (May 26, 1975), p. 10.

4. Roger Burback and Pat Flynn, "U.S. Grain Arsenal," *NACLA's Latin American and Empire Report*, Vol. 9, No. 7 (October 1975), pp. 1-41.

5. United States Department of Agriculture, *Foreign Agriculture Trade of the United States* (May 1976).

6. United States Department of Agriculture, *Foreign Agriculture Trade of the United States* (April 1976).

7. *Ibid.*

8. United States Department of Agriculture, *Foreign Agriculture Trade of the United States* (May 1976).

9. Andre Gunder Frank, "The Development of Underdevelopment," *Monthly Review*, Vol. 18, No. 4, (1966), p. 17-31; and Immanuel Wallerstein, *The Modern World System, Capitalist Agriculture and the Origins of the European World-Economy in the Sixteenth Century* (New York: Academic Press, 1974)

10. P. Deane, *The First Industrial Revolution* (Cambridge, England: Cambridge University Press, 1967), p. 53.

11. Paul Mantoux, *The Industrial Revolution in the Eighteenth Century* (New York: Harper & Row, 1961), fn. p. 72 and pp. 179-80.

12. William J. Barber, *British Economic Thought and India, 1600-1858: A Study in the History of Development Economics* (New York: Oxford University Press, 1975), p. 95.

13. Nassau Senior, *Industrial Efficiency and Social Economy*, S. Leon Levy, ed. (New York: Henry Holt & Co., 1928), p. 231. Thomas Robert Malthus, *Essay on The Principle of Population*, 2d ed. (London: J. M. Dent & Sons, 1960): Vol. 2, p. 98.

14. Wallerstein, *op. cit.*; and William Appleman Williams, *The Roots of the Modern American Empire* (New York: Vintage, 1961), especially pp. 19, 22, and 304-6.

15. Cited in Michael Barrett Brown, *The Economics of Imperialism* (New York: Penguin Books, 1974), p. 118.

16. *Ibid.*

17. Thomas Robert Malthus, *Principles of Political Economy with a View to their Practical Application* (London: John Murray, 1820), reprinted in part in David Ricardo, *The Works of David Ricardo*, Piero Sraffa, ed. (Cambridge: Cambridge University Press, 1951), p. 359.

18. Karl Marx, "The Annexation of Oude," *New York Tribune*, May 28, 1858; reprinted in Shlomo Avineri, ed., *Karl Marx on Colonialism and Modernization* (Garden City: Doubleday Books, 1969), p. 288.

19. Hla Myint, *The Economics of Developing Countries* (New York: Praeger, 1964), p. 61.

20. G. William Skinner, "Marketing and Social Structure in Rural China, Part 2," *Journal of Asian Studies*, Vol. 24, No. 2 (February 1965), pp. 195-228.

21. G. William Skinner, "Marketing and Social Structure in Rural China, Part 1," *Journal of Asian Studies*, Vol. 24, No. 1 (November 1964), pp. 3-43.

22. *Ibid.*

23. Karl Marx, "Trade with China," reprinted in Schlomo Avineri, ed., *op. cit.*, pp. 370-75.

24. On the occassion of the Macartney Mission in 1793, cited in V. W. Bladen, *From Adam Smith to Maynard Keynes: The Heritage of Political Economy* (Toronto: Toronto University Press, 1974), p. 52.

25. Immanuel Wallerstein, "The Rise and Future Demise of the World Capitalist System, Concepts for Comparative Analysis," *Comparative Studies in Society and History*, Vol. 16, No. 4 (September 1974), pp. 387-415, citing A. Adu Boahen, *Tropics in West African History* (London: Longmans, 1966), p. 113.

26. Colin Bundy, "The Emergence and Decline of a South African Peasantry," *African Affairs*, Vol. 17, No. 285, (October 1972), pp. 269-388.

27. *Ibid.*

28. Andre Gunder Frank, *op. cit.*

29. Karl Marx, "The East India Company—Its History and Results," *New York Daily Tribune* (July 11, 1853); reprinted in Karl Marx, *Surveys From Exile*, David Fernbach, ed., (New York: Vintage, 1974), pp. 312-13.

30. Angus Maddison, *Class Structure and Economic Growth: India and Pakistan Since the Moghuls* (New York: Norton, 1971), p. 18, pp. 57-58.

31. Karl Marx, *Capital*, Vol. 1 (Chicago: Kerr, 1906), p. 493.

32. John Stuart Mill, *Principles of Political Economy*, Vol. 3 and 4 of his *Collected Works*, J. M. Robson, ed. (Toronto: Toronto University Press, 1962), Vol. 2, p. 174.

33. Karl Marx, *Capital*, Vol. 2 (New York: International Publishers, 1972), pp. 140-41.

34. John Hurd II, "Railways and the Expansion of Markets in India, 1861-1921," *Explorations in Economic History* (July 1975), p. 12, pp. 263-68, p. 263 fn.

35. *Ibid.*

36. Maddison, *op. cit.*, p. 18.

37. Richard J. Barnett and Ronald E. Muller, *Global Reach: The Power of Multinational Corporations* (New York: Simon & Schuster, 1974), p. 87.

38. Hla Myint, *op. cit.*

39. Lester Brown, *By Bread Alone* (New York: Praegar, 1974), p. 61.

40. W. Arthur Lewis, "Aspects of Tropical Trade," *Wicksell Lectures* (Stockholm: Almguist & Wicksell, 1969).

41. W. Arthur Lewis, "The Export Stimulus," pp. 13-45 in W. Arthur Lewis, ed., *Tropical Development: 1880-1913* (Evanston, Ill.: Northwestern University Press, 1970).

42. United States Department of Agriculture, *Foreign Agricultural Trade of the United States*, (April 1976), p. 391.

43. United States Department of Agriculture, *Foreign Agricultural Trade of the United States* (December 1976).

44. Richard O'Mara, "Coffee Freeze in Brazil," *The Elements* (October 1975). See also First National City Bank, "No Instant Solution for Coffee Prices," *Monthly Economic Letter* (August 1976).

45. *United States Department of Agriculture*, (February 1977).

46. *Ibid.*

47. *Ibid.*

48. *Ibid.*

49. John Gerassi, *The Great Fear in Latin America* (New York: Macmillan, 1963).

50. See Thomas P. McCann, *An American Company: The Tragedy of United Fruit* (New York: Crown, 1976), p. 49.

51. Anon., "United Brands May Have a Serious Suitor," *Business Week* (July 5, 1976), pp. 56–57.

52. D. Gale Johnson, "Politics and Hunger, U.S. Foreign Relations and Agricultural Trade" in *Feeding the World's Hungry: The Challenge to Business*, An International Conference sponsored by Continental Bank, Chicago (May 20, 1974), p. 23.

53. Lewis, *Aspects of Tropical Trade, op. cit.*

54. G. Edward Schuh, "The Exchange Rate and U.S. Agriculture," *American Journal of Agricultural Economics*, Vol. 56, No. 1 (February 1974), p. 1–13.

55. Thomas Grennes, "The Exchange Rate and U.S. Agriculture," Comment, *American Journal of Agricultural Economics*, Vol. 57, No. 1, (February 1975), pp. 134–35.

56. Franklin Fisher, "A Theoretical Analysis of the Impact of Food Surplus Disposal on Agricultural Production in Recipient Countries," *Journal of Farm Economics*, Vol. 45, (November 1963), pp. 863–75.

57. *New York Times*, April 28, 1966.

58. United States Senate, Committee on Agriculture and Forestry, Subcommittee on Foreign Agriculture Policy, *United States Foreign Agricultural Trade Policy* (March and April 1973), p. 160.

59. *Ibid.*

60. Henry O. Wagley, "U.S. Imports More Cut Flowers," *Foreign Agriculture*, Vol. 14, No. 5 (February 9, 1976).

61. Barnett and Muller, *op. cit.*, p. 182.

62. Anon., "Cloudy Future for Belgium's Flower Trade," *Foreign Agriculture* (October 13, 1975).

63. J. Freivalds, "Agro-Industry in Africa," *World Crops*, Vol. 25 (May 1973), pp. 124–26.

64. Ingrid Palmer, "Food and the New Agriculture Technology," United Nations Institute for Social Research, Report No. 72.9 (Geneva: 1972), p. 70.

65. Karl Marx, "Proceedings of the 6th Rhine Province Assembly, Third Article, Debates on the Law on Thefts of Wood," *Rheinische Zeitung*, No. 298 (October 25, 1842, Supplement), reprinted in Karl Marx and Frederick Engels, *Collected Works*, Vol. 1: Marx, 1835–43 (New York: International Publishers, 1975).

66. John B. Parker, Jr., "India Boosting Fruit and Vegetable Output for Export," *Foreign Agriculture*, Vol. 14, No. 38 (September 20, 1976). This same point is made by Karl Marx in his "Letter to Danielson, 10 April 1879," in Karl Marx and Frederick Engels, *Selected Correspondence*, Dona Torr, ed. (New York: International Publishers, 1942), pp. 359–60.

67. *Ibid.*

68. Daniel J. Balz, "Exporting Food Monopolies," *Progressive* (January 1975), pp. 18–19.

69. William C. Thiesenhausen, "Food & Population Growth," *Kkonomi Dan Keuangan Indonesia (Economy and Finance in Indonesia)*, Vol. 22 (September 1974), pp. 209–24.

70. *Ibid.*

71. Palmer, *op. cit.*, p. 11.

72. *Ibid.*

73. James Keddie, "The Mass Unemployment Explosion," *The Far Eastern Economic Review*, Vol. 85, No. 52 (December 31, 1973), p. 41.

74. William L. Collier, Jusuf Colter, Sinhardi, Robert d'A. Shaw, "A Comment," *Bulletin of Indonesian Economic Studies*, Vol. 9, No. 2 (July 1973), reprinted in Agricultural Development Council, Research and Training Network Reprint, *Choice of Technique in Rice Milling on Java* (September 1974).

75. Cheryl Payer, "The Debt Trap, the International Monetary Fund and the Third World," *Monthly Review* (1974), p. 177.

76. Eric and Charlotte Jacoby, *Man and Land: The Essential Revolution* (New York: Knopf, 1971), citing H. J. Abaya, *The Untold Story of the Philippines* (Quezon City, 1967).

77. John W. Mellor and Uma Lele, "The Interaction of Growth Strategy, Agriculture and Foreign Trade: The Case of India," in George S. Tolley and Peter A. Zadrozny, eds., *Trade, Agriculture and Development* (Cambridge, Mass: Ballinger, 1975), pp. 93–113.

78. Howard Pack, "The Employment-Output Trade-Off in the LDC's—A Microeconomic Approach," *Oxford Economic Papers*, Vol. 26, No. 3 (November 1974), pp. 388-404.

79. Bruce F. Johnston and Peter Kilby, *Agriculture and Structural Transformation: Economic Strategies in Late-Developing Countries* (New York: Oxford University Press, 1975, pp. 109-12 and 307-11. See also John W. Mellor and Uma J. Lele, "Growth Linkages of the New Foodgrain Technologies," USAID-Employment and Income Distribution Project, Cornell University, Department of Agricultural Economics, Occassional Paper No. 50 (May 1972).

80. See R. S. Montgomery and D. G. Sisler, "Labor Absorption in Jogjakarta, Indonesia: An Input-Output Approach," A. E. Res. 75-10 (Ithaca, New York: Cornell University, Department of Agricultural Economics, March 1976).

81. Payer, *op. cit.*, p. 87.

82. Don Marschall, "Multinationals: labor, business clash," *In These Times*, Vol. 1, No. 7 (January 5-11, 1977), p. 6.

83. Dale Hathaway, United States Senate, Commission on Agriculture and Forestry, Subcommittee on Foreign Policy, "Hearings on United States Foreign Agriculture Trade Policy" (March and April 1973), p. 281.

84. Ernest B. Smith, "Florida and Mexico's Share of the U.S. Fresh Winter Vegetable Market," *The Vegetable Situation*, TVS-199, United States Department of Agriculture, (February 1976).

85. M. H. Ghanamian, "New Approaches to Development in Iran," The Agribusiness Council, *Agricultural Initiative in the Third World: A Report of A Conference*, (Lexington, Mass: Lexington Books, 1975), pp. 125-31.

86. *The Farm Index*, Vol. 10, No. 10 (October 1974).

87. Ernest Feder, "The Penetrations of the Agricultures of the Underdeveloped Countries by the Industrial Nations and their Multinational Concerns," Occasional Paper No. 19 (Glasgow: Institute of Latin America Studies, University of Glasgow, 1975), p. 18.

88. U.S. Department of Agriculture, *Agricultural Statistics*, 1976, p. 31.

89. M. Kalecki, "Political Aspects of Full Employment," *Political Quarterly*, Vol. 14 (1943), pp. 322-31.

90. T. W. Schultz, "The Allocation of Resources to AS," in Wesley Fishel, ed., *Resource Allocation in Agriculture Research* (Minneapolis: University of Minnesota, 1971), p. 97.

91. Grennes, *op. cit.*

92. See D. Gale Johnson, "World Markets and Long Term Commodity Agreements," *Ag World*, Vol. 2, No. 8 (September 1976), pp. 1-3.

93. John B. Parker, Jr., "India May Buy Almost $1 Billion of U.S. Farm Products in 1975," *Foreign Agriculture*, Vol. 13, No. 10 (March 10, 1975).

94. United States Department of Agriculture, *Foreign Agriculture Trade of the United States* (May 1976) and *Agricultural Statistics*, 1975.

95. Bryant H. Wadsworth, "New Policies Could Spell Trouble for United States Farmer," *Foreign Agriculture*, Vol. 13, No. 40 (October 6, 1975). See also, Anon., "Mexico Gains in Drive to Meet its Food Needs," *Foreign Agriculture*, Vol. 14, No. 8 (May 3, 1976); from "Cotton to Food Crops," *Foreign Agriculture*, Vol. 14, No. 13 (March 29, 1976); and Robert Prinsky, "One Crop Economy—Ghana Moves to Stay No. 1 in Cocoa while Striving to Diversify," *Wall Street Journal* (May 14, 1976), p. 1.

12

THE ROOTS OF IMPOVERISHMENT: THE COLONIAL RELATIONSHIP

Parliament did not make Ireland, nor can Parliament make it anew to suit the golden vision of landless peasants or penniless agitators.

—*The Times* of London, 26 April 1864,
in response to a petition for tenant rights in Ireland.[1]

The whole agrarian history of Ireland is a series of confiscations of Irish land to be handed over to English settlers.

—Frederick Engels to Jenny Marx Longuet,
24 February 1881.[2]

The German philosopher Hegel once remarked that the only thing we have to learn from history is that it has nothing to teach us. He forgot to add, it is only because of our unwillingness to learn. Engels pointed out that Ireland may be regarded as the first English colony.[3] Considered in this light, the history of Ireland foreshadows contemporary efforts to remake traditional agriculture in the Third World.

In Ireland, the restructuring of agriculture was closely intertwined with the evolution of potato culture. This plant, apparently introduced by the close friend of Queen Elizabeth, Sir Walter Raleigh, around 1588, required less land and less labor than a grain-based diet.[4] These properties made the potato appear to be a viable defense against famine. This was recognized as early as 1662 by Robert Boyle, the great physicist who also owned large properties in Cork and Waterford.[5]

Although the potato had the potential to improve the lot of the people, in reality the benefits accrued to the landlords. In fact, the standard of living seems to have fallen in spite of rising yields. By 1727, Jonathan Swift could write about "the miserable dress and diet and dwelling of the people, the families of farmers who pay great rents living in filth and nastiness upon buttermilk and potatoes, not a shoe or stocking to their feet, or a house so convenient as an English hogsty to receive them.[6]

About 50 years later, Arthur Young described the state of the diet during the cold months with the words, "all winter long, only potatoes and salt."[7] By the time potato production had reached its highpoint in 1844, an occasional glass of milk had become a luxury for the poor.[8] Instead of milk and grain, a daily average of 8 to 12 pounds of potatoes per capita provided the bulk of the nutrition for Irish adults.[9] The Irish held out as long as they could, until the potato blight wiped out the mainstay of their diet. As a result, within 10 years two million Irish starved, two million emigrated and the other four million were left in their customary destitution.[10]

The potato was able to dominate agriculture in Ireland, because that country was a colony run for the profit of the English. The land was owned by large landholders, predominantly English, who wished to use it as "mere pastureland which provides English markets with meat and wool at the cheapest prices."[11]

The Irish cottars, who inhabited the land, were forced to adopt potato culture for two reasons. Firstly, they could not afford enough land to grow a sufficient supply of grain to keep them alive; only the potato could support them on such small parcels. Secondly, the potato offered the peasant a degree of protection from the ravages of war. Because the plants were grown beneath the surface of the earth, the trampling of the cavalry did not totally destroy the crop and the army did not easily confiscate it; but most of all, the Irish workers planted potatoes because no other choice was available to them. Industrial work was essentially foreclosed to them.

All major industries were extinguished under English rule[12] except linen manufacture and, as Karl Marx once noted, the construction of coffins.[13] The lack of nonagricultural occupations was exacerbated by the structure of agriculture. Vast tracts of land were used for grazing livestock and raising grain for export to England. Large crops of flax were also exported to England indirectly in the form of linen. Much land owned by the English lay unused. An estimated 1.4 million acres of idle land were capable of being used for cultivation; another 2.3 million acres were suitable for pasture.[14]

Competition for the remaining land was extreme. According to one report written for the Prime Minister, "the only protection against want, the only means by which a man could procure food for his family, was by getting and retaining possession of a portion of land."[15] Needy tenants bid against one another until rents absorbed all but a tiny portion of the harvest. Only by restricting their families to a potato-based diet could the tenants hope to get on from one year to the next.

The miserable economic status of the tenant was described by Karl Marx as one in which the "needy Irish tenant belongs to the soil, while the soil belongs to the English lord."[16]

Concern with the wretched lot of the Irish peasant was not unique to Marx. Even as conventional an economist as John Stuart Mill devoted an entire chapter to the subject, in his *Principles of Political Economy*.[17]

The basis of the Irish problem must be traced to the control of the economy by the English, whose greed overrode even the most minimal standards of human decency. During the reign of Queen Elizabeth, the English, in Marx's words, attempted to "exterminate" the Irish in order to plant the land with loyal English settlers.[18] By 1692, such plans were discarded;[19] the benefits from control of Ireland had to be based on control of the Irish. The agricultural system which grew up around the potato was an important tool for maintaining this control. Ireland became "an agricultural district of England, marked off by a wide channel from the country to which it yields corn, wool, cattle, industrial and military recruits."[20]

The harvest of Irish workers was especially important because they provided an effective restraint on the demands of English workers. As early as 1690, the English economist and friend of Cromwell, William Petty, suggested the wholesale transfer of the bulk of the Irish population to England as a method of providing employers with a cheap labor force.[21] Although his plan was never put into effect, the annual emigration of Irish workers served the same purpose. The willingness of the Irish to accept brutally low wages thwarted the attempt of English workers to earn more money. In addition, the use of Irish labor divided the English working class into two hostile camps whose mutual dislike undermined the capacity for concerted action.[22] In view of this situation, Marx wrote to Engels that "The English working class will never achieve anything before it has gotten rid of Ireland."[23].

In conclusion, the evolution of potato culture was an early part of that grander process: The construction of a new capitalist world system such as we discussed in the section on Third World economies. As Engels wrote:[24]

England was to become the "workshop of the world"; all other countries were to become for England what Ireland already was—markets for her manufactured goods, supplying her in return with raw materials and food. England, the great manufacturing centre of an agricultural world, with an ever-increasing number of corn and cotton-growing Irelands revolving around her, the industrial sun. What a glorious prospect!

The glory of this celestial system dazzled its makers, so much so that they forgot the lowly origins of this "agricultural world," the soil that Marx termed an "original source of all wealth"[25] from which springs forth the corn, cotton, potatoes and workers which are the vital factors in this modern industrial solar system.

Marx believed that neglect of the soil was responsible for the potato blight.[26]* Others stress that the Irish unwittingly selected plants which were susceptible to the disease.[28] In any case, British colonial rule offered the Irish cottar neither the incentive nor the opportunity to develop a

---

*Some later research has borne out Marx's judgment about soil fertility and plant health.[27]

healthy, sustainable agriculture. Potato monoculture took its toll. Marx was correct in his judgment: the potato blight was a product of British rule.[29]

When the disease struck in 1845, the stupidity of the existing form of social organization became transparent. Here was Ireland, in the midst of a devastating famine which eliminated millions of people from the face of the earth. The land was blessed with an abundant harvest of wheat, but the poor could not afford to buy it.[30] In fact, they did not even have the mills for grinding flour or ovens for breaking bread.*[31]

Although the British made some half-hearted efforts at relief, the prevailing attitude was expressed by Charles Trevelyan, the permanent head of the Treasury. Trade, according to Trevelyan, would be "paralyzed" if the government, by providing free food, interfered with the legitimate profit of private enterprise. The Chancellor of his department, Charles Wood, took pains to assure the House of Commons that every effort would be made to maintain "as much liberty as possible" in the grain trade.[32]

In spite of all the needless suffering, Robert Boyle was essentially correct: the potato crop, a crop ideally suited to the Irish climate, should have made life better for the Irish. Only the irrationality of the system of social organization negated that potential.

For the Irish poor, the difference between technical and social improvement was obvious. About the same time Arthur Young was surveying rural Ireland, the noted English economist, Nassau Senior, was questioning Irish school children to gauge the depth of their comprehension of economic affairs. What would happen if each worker sprouted an extra pair of arms, he asked. The children all agreed that everyone would become poorer. The children understood that only the possessing classes would reap the benefits from the enhanced capacity of the workers. Production would not be doubled by the extra arms; employment would more nearly be halved.

The bewildered Senior noted in his journal, "This must be the obvious opinion, for I have everywhere met with it."[33]

Malthus perceptively understood that the potato was the economic equivalent of an extra pair of arms. In his words:

> The cultivation of the potatoe, and its adoption as the general food of the lower classes of people in Ireland, has rendered the land and labour necessary to maintain a family, unusually small, compared with most of the countries of Europe. The consequence of this facility of production, unaccompanied by such a train of fortunate circumstances as would give it full effect in the increase of wealth, is a state of things resembling, in many respects, countries less advanced in civilization and improvement.[34]

---

*Of course, wheat can be eaten without baking. It can be boiled or sprouted just as well, but dietary patterns are usually rooted in the overall pattern of social relations.

Malthus went on to specify what he meant by "less advanced." To his credit, he began with unemployment. "Ireland," he wrote, "possesses... a much greater population than it can employ."[35]*

Although the English economists recognized the widespread existence of poverty in Ireland, they understood its cause less keenly than the Irish school children, or even Malthus. In their eyes, the Irish themselves were to blame for their sorry state of affairs; their lack of respect for private property and their periodic outbursts of insurrectionary activity frightened off the investment which might have otherwise rescued the Irish economy.[38]† The only economist of note to challenge this theory, Colonel Robert Torrens, pointed out that Ireland lacked the means of production to effectively compete with English industry.[40] Investment would necessarily be constrained to agriculture, where capital would tend to replace labor. In short, the usual recommendations of the economists would intensify the suffering of the people, since the workers displaced by new investment would have no alternative sources of employment.[41] Upon hearing Torrens' speech, the astounded future Prime Minister of England, Sir Robert Peel, snapped back that if political economy showed that the free functioning of the market did not necessarily work to the benefit of the people, his faith in that science would be "greatly shaken."[42] So much for the objective workings of political economy!

*Malthus must be faulted on two counts in his evaluation of Ireland. Firstly, he considers the potato to be "the single cause which has produced the effects that excite our astonishment."[36] Secondly, as Ricardo pointed out, Ireland could have employed more people under different social conditions.[37]

†Bernard Semmel has shown that the British economists' faith in the beneficence of the market in international economic relations was a convenient fiction held at the time when the British industrial superiority was so great that free trade was equivalent to an institutionalization of the British domination of world trade.[39]

REFERENCES

1. *The Times of London* (April 26, 1864) in response to a petition for tenant rights in Ireland.

2. Frederick Engels to Jenny Marx Longuet (February 24, 1881) reprinted in Karl Marx and Frederick Engels, *Ireland and the Irish Question, A Collection of Writings*, R. Dixon, ed. (New York: International Publishers, 1972), pp. 326–29.

3. "Letter to Karl Marx" (May 23, 1856) in Karl Marx and Frederick Engels, *Selected Correspondence*, Dona Torr, ed. (New York: International Publishers, 1942), pp. 92–95.

4. Redcliffe N. Salaman, "The Influence of the Potato on the Course of Irish History," The Tenth Finaly Memorial Lecture Delivered at University College, Dublin (Dublin: Richview Press, 1943), p. 3.

5. Redcliffe N. Salaman, *The History and Social Influence of the Potato* (Cambridge: Cambridge University Press, 1949), p. 228.

6. Salaman, "The Influence of the Potato on the Course of Irish History," *op. cit.*, p. 5.

7. L. M. Cullen, *An Economic History of Ireland Since 1660* (London: B. T. Batsford Ltd., 1972).

8. *Ibid.*, p. 25.

9. L. M. Cullen, "Irish History Without the Potato," *Past and Present*, No. 40 (1968), pp. 72-83.

10. Salaman, *The History and Social Influence of the Potato, op. cit.*; and Cullen, *op. cit.*, p. 132. Again, Cullen minimizes the problem.

11. Karl Marx, "Letter to Meyer and Vogt, April 9, 1870," in Karl Marx and Frederick Engels, *Selected Correspondence*, Dona Torr, ed. (New York: International Publishers, 1942), pp. 281-82.

12. Salaman, *The History and Social Influence of the Potato, op. cit.*, p. 18; and Karl Marx, "Indian Question—Irish Tenant Right," *The New York Daily Tribune* [date], reprinted in Marx and Engels, *Ireland and the Irish Question, op. cit.*, p. 61 and "Outline," *op. cit.*, pp. 131-32.

13. Karl Marx, "Record of a Speech on the Irish Question Delivered to the German Workers International Association in London on December 16, 1867," reprinted in Marx and Engels, *Ireland and the Irish Question, op. cit.*, pp. 140-42. See also Adam Smith, *An Inquiry into the Nature and Causes of the Wealth of Nations*, Cannan editon (New York: Modern Library, 1937), p. 231.

14. R. D. Collison Black, *Economic Thought and The Irish Question*, 1817-1870 (Cambridge: Cambridge University Press, 1960), p. 179.

15. *Ibid.*, p. 8.

16. Karl Marx, "Indian Question—Irish Tenant Right," reprinted in Marx and Engels, *Ireland and the Irish Question, op. cit.*, p. 62.

17. John Stuart Mill, *Principles of Political Economy*, reprinted as Vols. II and III of his *Collected Works*, John M. Robson, ed. (London: Routledge and Kegan Paul, 1965), Book 2, Chapter 10.

18. Karl Marx, "Outline of a Report on the Irish Question to the Communist Educational Association of German Workers in London," in Marx and Engels, *Ireland and the Irish Question, op. cit.*, p. 127.

19. *Ibid.*, p. 129.

20. Karl Marx, *Capital*, Vol. 1 (Chicago: Charles H. Karr, 1906), p. 771.

21. William Petty, *Political Arithmetick*, reprinted in Vol. 1 of his *Economic Writings*, Charles Henry Hull, ed. (New York: Kelly, 1963), pp. 285-90.

22. Karl Marx, "Confidential Communication," reprinted in Marx and Engels, *Ireland and the Irish Question, op. cit.*, p. 162.

23. Karl Marx, "Letter to Frederick Engels, December 10, 1869," in Marx and Engels, *Selected Correspondence, op. cit.*, pp. 281-82.

24. Frederick Engels, "Preface to the English Edition of *The Condition of the Working-Class in England*," reprinted in Marx and Engels, *Ireland and the Irish Question, op. cit.*, pp. 345-46.

25. Karl Marx, *Capital, op. cit.*, p. 556.

26. Karl Marx, "Record of a Speech on the Irish Question Delivered to the German Workers' Educational Association in London on December 16, 1867," and "Notes for an Undelivered Speech on Ireland," reprinted in Marx and Engels, *Ireland and the Irish Question, op. cit.*, pp. 141 and 123.

27. Albert Howard, *An Agricultural Testament* (New York: Oxford University Press, 1941), pp. 165-68.

28. Donald Ugent, "The Potato," *Science*, Vol. 170, No. 3963 (December 11, 1970), pp. 1161-66. See also John S. Niederhausen and William S. Cobb, "The Late Blight of Potatoes," *Scientific American* (May 1959); and E. C. Stackman, Richard Bradfield and Paul

C. Mangelsdorf, *Campaigns Against Hunger* (Cambridge, Mass.: M.I.T. Press, 1967), p. 112.

29. Karl Marx, "Record of a Speech on the Irish Question Delivered to the German Workers' Educational Association in London on December 16, 1867," in Marx and Engels, *Ireland and the Irish Question, op. cit.*, p. 141.

30. Redcliffe N. Salaman, "The Influence of the Potato on the Course of Irish History," *op. cit.*, p. 26.

31. Jane Jacobs, *The Economy of Cities* (New York: Random House, 1969), p. 10.

32. This paragraph very closely follows John Kenneth Galbraith, *The Age of Uncertainty (Boston: Houghton Mifflin, 1977), p. 38.*

33. *Nassau Senior, Industrial Efficiency and Social Economy*, S. Leon Levy, ed. (New York: Henry Holt Co., 1928), p. 107.

34. Thomas Robert Malthus, *Principles of Population Considered with a View to their Practical Application* (London: John Murray, 1820) reprinted in part in David Ricardo, *The Works of David Ricardo*, Piero Sraffa, ed. (Cambridge: Cambridge University Press, 1951), pp. 344–45.

35. *Ibid.*

36. Thomas Robert Malthus, "Newenham and others on the State of Ireland," *Edinburgh Review* (July 1808) reprinted in Thomas Robert Malthus, *Occasional Papers of T. R. Malthus*, Bernard Semmel, ed. (New York: Burt Franklin, 1963), p. 36.

37. David Ricardo, *Notes on Malthus*, Vol. 2 of *The Works of David Ricardo*, Piero Sraffa, ed. (Cambridge: Cambridge University Press, 1951), pp. 344–45. Ricardo's assessment of the actual social conditions affecting Ireland was very shallow in this passage although he had earlier written to James Mill that "the difficulties of the Government proceed from an unwillingness to make timely concessions to the people. Reform is the most efficacious prevention of Revolution, and may in my opinion be at all times safely conceded." David Ricardo, "Letter to James Mill" in David Ricardo, *The Works of David Ricardo*, Vol. 8, *Letters 1819-1821* (Cambridge: Cambridge University Press, 1952), p. 49.

38. David Ricardo, Letter to Trower (January 25, 1822), reprinted in David Ricardo, *The Works and Correspondence of David Ricardo*, Piero Sraffa, ed., vol. 9 (Cambridge: Cambridge University Press, 1952), p. 153; Nassau Senior, "Ireland," *Edinburgh Review*, Vol. 89 (January 1840), p. 189; and Erskin McKinley, "The Problem of 'Underdevelopment' in the English Classical School," *Quarterly Journal of Economics*, Vol. 69, No. 2 (May 1955), pp. 244–45 especially.

39. Bernard Semmel, *The Rise of Free Trade Imperialism* (Cambridge: Cambridge University Press, 1970).

40. Colonel Robert Torrens, Speech in the House of Commons, *Hansard*, 3d Series, Vol. 17, Col. 416, cited in Black, *op. cit.* (February 8, 1833), p. 139.

41. *Ibid.*

42. Sir Robert Peel, *Hansard, op. cit.*, in Black, *op. cit.*, p. 139.

13

SACRED COWS AND BUM STEERS

Why the cow was selected for apotheosis is obvious to me. The cow was, in India, the best companion. Not only did she give milk, but she also made agriculture possible.

—Mahatma Gandhi

Food production in the Third World continues to improve,[1] but the benefits from this improvement are enjoyed by a small group of people within the Third World. The increase of livestock in these nations is symbolic of the affluence of the few compared with the poverty of the majority. In Asia, the amount of feed-grains consumed has increased more than fourfold in the last fifteen years.* This increase has been most pronounced in nations such as South Korea that toe the U.S. line most doggedly.[2]

Although the problem of world hunger is likely to intensify with the spread of the U.S. feedlot system, Western observers have chosen the traditional system of cattle raising in India as a symbol of the blind adherence to inefficient and irrational ways. Actually, each system of cattle raising is a rational adaptation to a particular set of social relations.† In the U.S. the struggle for profit shaped the cattle industry; in India, where precapitalistic social relations prevailed, an entirely different method of raising livestock has evolved.

*Excluding Japan, where the increase has been threefold, the Middle East which is lumped together with North Africa in the Department of Agriculture's data, and China.

†Sometimes the claim of rationality appears to grant too much credit to the Western system. In contemporary Europe, for example, the dairy industry is protected by the government. As a result, the Common Market countries have accumulated a surplus of nonfat dry milk enormous enough to produce three billion gallons of skimmed milk.[3] In an effort to rid itself of this surplus, the European Community is forcing the livestock industry to use this milk as feed. As a result, European cattle are now being fed milk to produce milk. Although the U.S. is furious with this plan, which will cut into the $2 billion market in Europe for U.S. soybeans, this country does not make particularly good use of its own milk products. The U.S. is not without problems in its own pattern of milk utilization. Not only does the U.S. dump milk, but it uses two and one-half times more milk for nonfood purposes than all the people in the Third World consume.[4]

By considering the difference between the behavior imposed by traditional social relations and the new set being foisted on the Third World, we can estimate the consequences of the importation of capitalist agriculture. For this reason, we now turn to the sacred cow of India.

The treatment of the cow in India appears to Western agriculture experts to be totally irrational. They point out that India, according to estimates of the U.S. Department of Agriculture in July 1975, had 240.5 million cattle and buffalo, more than any other nation; yet Indian cattle supply only a small amount of meat. We have been told for a half-century that India is poor because she refuses to slaughter her cows.[5]* One Western economist recommends that India slaughter thirty million female cattle; the remaining herd would be capable of converting the same feed supply into more milk, meat, and dung; in addition, the hides would be of superior quality.[8] While such a course would perhaps be "technically" correct, it totally ignores the social relations inherent in Indian agriculture. The bulk of the cattle are not owned by a theoretical national entity; they are the property of poor peasants. If their cattle were slaughtered, could they afford to buy or rent the services which their cattle now supply for almost no cost? Field studies report that peasants who have to rent animals for plowing are at a serious disadvantage because they are not ensured of timely access to the animals in a monsoon-based agriculture in which timing is all-important.[9] Another important question is whether the cattle would be maintained in feedlots or dairies to supply the affluent or whether the poor would be assured of a share of the benefits.

Instinctively Gandhi put his faith in traditional patterns of production rather than risk putting any additional burdens on the poor. He never forgot the lesson taught by the English textile industry; cheaper commodities or machines which seem to be more efficient can tear apart the social fabric. Consequently, he clung to his spinning wheel to remind the people of the pitfalls of what is usually considered sound economic reasoning. For him, it[10]

. . . represents to me the hope of the hope of the masses. [G]inning, carding, warping, sizing, dyeing, and weaving. . . kept the village carpenter and the blacksmith busy. With [its decline] went the other village industries, such as the oil press. Nothing took the place of these industries.

Gandhi obstinately opposed modernizing India because his political blinders limited his vision to a choice between allowing the Western nations to bind India more closely into a world market or holding on to the old ways.

With respect to cattle, the old ways represent an intricate system of social relations. A poor peasant can maintain a cow for almost no cost

---

*By the same logic, one could ask why Brazil—which has a relatively modern slaughtering industry, even in its impoverished and backward regions—continues to be poor.[6] One study of northeastern Brazil discovered that 75 percent of the population suffered from caloric deficiencies.[7]

whatsoever. In fact, if it should cease to lactate or to produce offspring, the cow can be freed to roam at will. Should it stray onto the small plot of a poor peasant, it will certainly be chased away in an instant. The rich, who have less time to concern themselves with any particular plot of land, are more likely to suffer the consequences of the hunger of the stray cow. Should the cow recover its productivity, the owner is free to claim it again.[11] Like most welfare systems, this one is fraught with inefficiencies, but it may well serve a useful purpose so long as the poor have no other options.*

The cow redistributes income in another way. Cattle are most likely to die during times of famine or stress, just when the malnourished most need protein.[12] The death of a cow is a windfall for the untouchables for whom carrion is a major source of protein.[13] Thus, during good times a portion of the economy's meager surplus of vegetable matter is "invested" in these cattle, so that "withdrawals" can be made during time of need.[14] As slaughter becomes more commonplace, this source of nutrition falls beyond the reach of the poor.

The abolition of the taboo on cattle slaughter will also upset production relations. Peasants depend upon their cattle as a source of collateral in borrowing money. Since the culling of thirty million cattle would leave many peasants without collateral, their existence in agriculture would become even more tenuous. More importantly, the cattle in India are not just raised to produce beef and dairy products. They produce fertilizer, fuel and leather.[15]† Besides working as a tractor and truck for the peasant family, cattle are able to produce their own replacements. The cow has the remarkable ability to perform all these tasks without consuming any protein whatsoever.[18] The cow can obtain the bulk of its diet from nonedible organic matter; it can even consume large amounts of paper or wood with favorable results.[19] In short, the cow's operating costs are extremely low considering its manifold capabilities.‡

The cow also cycles mineral in its dung, maintaining the fertility of the land. Many peasants believe that drawing a plow with a tractor harms yields. Some quantitative data seems to back up this preference,[21] perhaps because the bullock creates a more shallow cultivation.[22]**

Western studies of the Indian cattle system fail to take account of the value of the resiliency of Indian cattle. At the time of this writing, dairy farmers in the state of Victoria in Australia have slaughtered over 40,000

---

*Among the inefficiencies we would have to include crops trampled or eaten by cows, as well as the suffering of the cows who starve before finding sustenance.

†Among an African tribe, the Nuer, cattle by-products include shields, thongs, tools, plaster, dressing for wounds, ashes for mouthwash and tooth powder, and urine used for washing, making cheese and dressing skins.[16] In the U.S., the by-products from cows include shampoos, glue, animal feed, ornaments, glycerine, lubricants, leather, and fertilizer.[17] The simple rules of economics become too complex for unambiguous results when joint products such as these exist.

‡Even when cattle are raised on irrigated lands where their costs are highest, animal power in Asia appears to be cheaper than tractors.[20]

**The new high-yielding varieties of seeds seem to benefit from a deeper plowing.[23]

cattle as a result of drought conditions.[24] Industry spokesmen predict that as many as 200,000 cattle may eventually have to be killed.[25] Indian cattle are not immune to such drought conditions, but they are more resistant than the more highly-bred Western animals. In fact, the cattle industry in the arid regions of the U.S. was considerably strengthened by the introduction of hardy Indian stock. Indian cattle are also better able to build up herd size after the periodic losses from rinderpest;[26] in addition, they are less susceptible to contagious disease.

To compensate for the lack of resistance of U.S. cattle, they are fed large amounts of antibiotics. Eventually, indiscriminate use of these chemicals becomes self-defeating, because strains of pathogens evolve which are resistant to the antibiotics. As a result, human populations as well as cattle herds are threatened because many diseases, apparently including even leukemia, can be transmitted from cattle to humans.[27]

All these considerations are ignored because Western selection methods concentrate on yields. This process is being intensified by a computerized scheme developed by the Department of Agriculture.[28] Because of the narrow vision of efficiency inherent in this program, too little attention is being paid to its unintended consequences.

In the first place, the national scope of the program helps to create a uniform genetic structure in the dairy herds, raising the danger of the same type of problem which attacked hybrid corn in 1970.[29] Widespread use of artificial insemination makes the dangers of genetic uniformity even more threatening. Some bulls sire over 20,000 daughters.[30] In one particular case, a single twelve-year-old bull which is estimated to have sired a female descendant in one of every three dairy herds is still producing at a rate of 10,000 offspring per year.[31]* The emergence of firms specializing in producing calves for the dairy industry suggests a strong parallel with the corn industry.

This breeding program is taking on worldwide dimensions. The U.S. exports more than 22,000 breeding cattle annually,[33] as well as semen. Many of these cattle are breeding stock exported in specially outfitted 747 and DC-10 planes to nations such as Iran, Ecuador, and Argentina.[34] Even India is beginning to "modernize" its dairy herds.[35]

The nutritional effect of introducing U.S. practices may well be negative. Between 1955 and 1975, the percentage of Holstein cattle in U.S. herds has risen from 66 to 80.[36] Although production per cow is improving, protein and fat content are falling. Because of the lower fat content, soluble vitamins A, D, E, and K are reduced.[37]

A further consequence of the selection for maximum production per cow has been the favoring of cattle which consume the most nutrients. Since cattle can process more nutrients per day by consuming grain

---

*This bull, named Astronaut, suggests the problem with narrowing the genetic pool. Since his sire did not have a good pedigree, he was originally sold by default at a public auction. Now that the value of these "inferior" genes is recognized, the bull is worth an estimated $5 million.[32]

instead of roughage, the breeding program makes food more scarce for the poor.[38]* In India, the major constituent of animal feed is straw which is unfit for human consumption.

The quality of the air where I live suffers terribly because farmers can find no better use for their straw than to burn it. Not only is rice straw wasted in the U.S., the Department of Agriculture reports that as much as four to six tons of unused forage per acre are left from the corn crop aftermath in the north central states.[40] In addition, in the high plains of Texas, as much as two million tons of sorgham roughage is not used.[41]

Our range land, which makes up 25 percent of the total land area of the U.S., is not being used effectively. A 1972 survey of more than one thousand farmers revealed that they were using only about two-thirds of their capacity for producing hay and forage.[42] In addition, very little research has been put into improving rangeland.[43]†

Finally, the cow's ability to convert inedible waste products into food is not exploited. We have already referred to the favorable results when paper or wood are used for feed. If all the organic waste products in the U.S. were used for cattle feed, they could support a herd three times as large as the existing cattle population.[44] In fact, one industry source reports that feeder cattle do better on dry processed garbage than on conventional feed.[45]

What reason does the cattle industry have for feeding such high quality food to animals? One explanation concerns transportation costs. The complex distribution network requires that cattle may have to be transported as many as thirteen times during their lifetime, according to an industry trade journal.[46] Transportation stress alone results in great losses reaching as much as 6.5 percent of the weight of the animal.[47]

More importantly, the profits of the livestock industry depend, to a large extent, on the speed with which the product can be turned over. Because grain-fed animals are ready for market in less than half the time required for range-fed animals (seventeen months compared to three years), profits would be more than twice as high in the feedlot industry, other things being equal.[48]‡ Of course, costs of production are higher in the feedlots, but not so much higher that they eat up the extra profits resulting from the quicker turnover. The influence of turnover time is less obvious in the dairy industry than in the feedlots, but it is just as important. The average turnover time in the dairy industry depends upon the proportions of the cost of production spent for materials which repay their cost over a long period compared to those which repay themselves

---

*The cows selected for their ability to consume grain tend to be more susceptible to a serious metabolic disease, ketosis.[39]

†During draught conditions such as the Western range lands are currently suffering, the difference between the carrying capacity and the herd size could be expected to narrow.

‡The first economist to point out the influence of turnover time in livestock production was Marx, who compared the slow turnover time of Indian cattle with improved British stock.[49] Thomas Hodgskin had earlier theorized that the slow turnover time in agriculture as a whole puts it at a disadvantage compared to other industries.[50]

rapidly. The animal belongs in the former category and the feed in the latter. Thus, if a dairy producing one hundred gallons per day can reduce the number of animals it keeps by feeding them more grain, the average turnover time will be shorter.

Here is a nation which feeds in excess of ten times more grain and thirty times more legumes to livestock than to people, irresponsibly exporting its magnificent technology to hungry nations.[51] A comparison of energy values points up the wastefulness of this technology. Studies show that the Indian cattle require a little more than six calories of food to produce one calorie of useful output, either as milk, work or fertilizer,[52] while in the U.S., fifty calories of food are required to produce one calorie of range-fed beef, ignoring the energy costs of slaughter, transportation and marketing.[53]

A more inclusive comparison of Indian and American systems of livestock management is very difficult to develop because of the diverse functions of cattle that exist in the two economies. Comparison can be simplified by measuring each system against what we would expect to find in a society which cooperatively plans its economic behavior. In such a society, each possible activity would be evaluated in terms of how well it could use the productive base to improve the life of the people. Decisions would not be affected by turnover rate. Instead, the cost of an industry would be measured by the flow of resources required to maintain its productive capacity intact.[54] A premium would be placed on those processes which could economize on resources. Accordingly, the cow would most likely be given an important role in converting inedible waste products into useful goods and services.

The Indian system has evolved a pattern of animal husbandry which shares some of these characteristics. It has made an art out of maintaining cattle with as few resources as possible, while converting a very high proportion of the animal's metabolic activity into useful goods and services. Yet the Indian system falls short of what we would find in a rational economy. The system is held together by a system of beliefs which hinders the development of the people. It does little or nothing to incorporate the potential of science to improve on traditional methods. Most importantly, it is an integral part of a precapitalistic set of social relations which siphons off much of the productive capacity of the people for the benefit of India's ruling class, as well as imperialistic forces outside of India.

Some Western experts are no doubt correct to point out that a redistribution of the land would allow India to produce more with the same resources.[55] In addition, consolidation of small farms into cooperative or collective enterprises could reduce the number of cattle required in India. As mentioned earlier, fewer cattle might be capable of converting the same resources into a greater supply of goods and services. These potential improvements will be nothing more than dreams until a more rational set of social relations is developed in India.

The U.S. cattle system depends upon an entirely different sort of logic.

It is predicated on production for profit. Instead of determining the method of raising cattle on the fewest possible resources, the U.S., lacking a rationally planned economy, has developed the wasteful feedlot system, with its dependence on high yields, quick turnover, and an elaborate distribution network. Many factors have influenced the growth of the feedlot system—not least the structure of the tax laws—but fundamentally it is the social relations of the market which have shaped the U.S. cattle industry.

The uncertainty of an unplanned economy gives further encouragement to the feedlot industry. No one can know what the state of the economy will be by the time the cattle reach maturity. Venturing a guess about the future of the cattle industry seventeen months later is risky enough, but looking ahead three years—the time it takes range-fed beef to mature—is almost impossible. In a capitalistic economy, the danger of being caught off guard increases the risk for investors in tying their funds up in enterprises which take a longer time to repay the investment.[56] As a result, feedlots become more attractive.

Western experts are quick to point out the failings of the Indian system; but are their recommendations in the best interests of the people? Do they have a plan for lifting the poor from poverty, or will they be content to just tear away the few shreds of production left to the poor? Do they have a plan for the progress of society, or do they represent the interests of those who expect to profit at the expense of society as a whole?

In evaluating the answers to these questions we must not let ourselves fall into the trap of seeing the abundance of free-ranging Indian cattle as a mere reflection of the idiosyncrasies of the Hindu faith. In 1776, Adam Smith described the "ancient practice" of treating cattle as the "spontaneous growth" of the land.[57] He specifically referred to the Colonies, where cattle were half starved.[58] In the middle of the nineteenth century, agricultural publications in the U.S. could describe the "very pitiable sight of [the] cattle and sheep" because of the farmers' inclination to "keep too much stock."[59] Others wrote that this observation held only during the winter; "they invariably look fat and sleek in summer."[60]

In the ante-bellum South of the U.S., we find the same characteristic of the Indian system. Eugene Genovese writes of the "abundance of livestock and an inadequate supply of meat and work animals."[61] Contemporary agricultural writers repeatedly called attention to the situation. For instance, the Reverend G. Lewis complained in 1854 that Georgia cattle were ". . . objects of pity, not to be fed upon but to be fed. Left to shift for themselves all winter, their bones look and stare at you."[62] During the Civil War, Confederate troops complained that the animals supplying them with beef had to be held upright for shooting.[63]

We are not likely to ascribe the low standards of animal husbandry in the U.S. to an irrational religious faith. Like India, the South had strong economic motives for maintaining "sacred cows." It was predominantly rural without the more concentrated markets that might have encouraged the intensive pursuit of animal husbandry.[64] The improvement of cattle breeds and the development of adequate transportation facilities to transport the cattle to market involved heavy investments of capital, which the South as well as India lacked.[65]

Once we see livestock systems as rational adaptations to economic conditions, we need not be surprised that pastoral societies around the world from Africa[66] to the Yakut reindeer herders behave in a fashion similar to the Indian farmer. In all these cases, animals are the major constituent of the capital stock.* These people refrain from slaughter or restrict it to ceremonial occasions in order to protect their capital from being consumed. Predictably, attempts to transplant Western ranching schemes to Africa have generally tended to undermine existing social and economic relations without yielding benefits to the population as a whole.[68]†

Even the English came to recognize the importance of the traditional system of cattle raising. During World War II, when imports of Burmese rice were cut off at the same time that armed forces were consuming more beef, the Bengalis began to slaughter animals.[70] With the breakdown of the traditional prohibitions of slaughter, direct military intervention was required to protect the stocks of animals needed for plowing, milking and breeding. In effect, the colonial government was called upon to enforce the religious beliefs of the local population.

Now that the immediate pressures of warfare are over, Western experts are advocating measures which go much further than the mere destruction of the capital stock of traditional agriculturalists; they are actively sponsoring new methods of farming which will tear up traditional agriculture by its roots. Observers of Third World agriculture express surprise at the human costs of the restructuring of agriculture. A little reflection on history will demonstrate that irresponsibly tampering with traditional agricultural systems can undermine the basis of life itself.

---

*In this sense we can classify the traditional Indian peasant as a pastoralist. Concerning the importance of cattle for the Indian peasant, Marx cited an English document which said, "While the peasant farmer starves, his cattle thrive. . . . The prescriptions of superstition, which appear cruel to the individual, are constructive for the community; and the preservation of the labouring cattle secures the power of cultivation, and the future sources of life and wealth."[67]

†The introduction of animals for agricultural traction power in Africa, however, seems to have a great deal of promise.[69]

REFERENCES

1. United States Department of Agriculture, Economic Research Service, *World Economic Conditions in Relation to Agricultural Trade* (June 10, 1976), p. 16.

2. John B. Parker, "The Developing Nations of Asia: A Growing Market," *Foreign Agriculture* (April 9, 1973); and Anon., "Feed Needs Seen Increasing in Southeast Asia Nations," *Foreign Agriculture*, Vol. 14, No. 16 (April 9, 1976).

3. Lloyd J. Fleck, "EC Product Surpluses May Worsen During 1976," *Foreign Agriculture*, Vol. 14, No. 17 (April 26, 1976).

4. Lyle P. Schertz, "Economics of Protein Improvement Programs in the Lower Income Countries," United States Department of Agriculture, Foreign Economic Development Report No. 11 (July 1976), p. 7.

5. Elsie Weil, "Hungry Lands Learning American Farm Methods," *New York Times* (June 13, 1926).

6. R. L. Beukenkamp, "Northeast Brazil Still Lags Behind Rest of Country," *Foreign Agriculture*, Vol. 19, No. 30 (July 26, 1976), pp. 10-11.

7. *Food Consumption in Brazil: Family Budget Survey in the Early 1960's* (Rio de Janeiro: Geitulio Vargas Foundation, November 1970).

8. Alan Heston, "An Approach to the Sacred Cow of India," *Current Anthropology*, Vol. 12, No. 2 (April 1971), p. 191-97. See also, S. N. Mishra, "Cattle Meat and Economic Welfare," *Kyklos*, Vol. 19, Fasc. 1, (1966).

9. Marvin Harris, "The Cultural Ecology of India's Sacred Cattle," *Current Anthropology*, Vol. 7, No. 1 (February 1966), p. 53.

10. Gandhi, *The Harijan* (April 1940), cited by O. P. Kalra, *Agricultural Policy in India* (Bombay: Popular Prakashan Press, 1973), pp. 29-30.

11. Harris, *op. cit.*, p. 58.

12. Alexander Alland, Jr., *Adaptation in Cultural Evolution: An Approach to Medical Anthropology* (New York: Columbia University Press, 1970), pp. 76-77: "The habit of many primitive peoples of eating protein during times of stress (funerals, war parties, etc.) may be related to an adaptation in which antibody production is mobilized during times of greatest need and stress. Roy Rappaport has suggested such an adaptive mechanism for the Maring of New Guinea." See Roy Rappaport, *Pigs for Ancestors* (New Haven: Yale University Press, 1969).

13. Joan Mechner, "Comment on Heston," *Current Anthropology*, Vol. 12, No. 2, (April 1971), pp. 202-4. Also, Kusim Nair, *Blossoms in the Dust: The Human Factor in Economic Development* (New York: Frederick Praeger, 1967). She says that in one survey of the district of Basti in Eastern Uttar Pradesh, the National Council of Economic Research found that "eating of carrion is common. Almost a fifth of the population is compelled to resort to these abnormal practices," citing National Council of Applied Economic Research, *Rehabilitation and Development of Basti District* (New Delhi: Asia Publishing House, 1967), p. 9.

14. Kent V. Flannery, "The Origins and Ecological Effects of Early Domestication in Iran and the Near East," in Peter J. Ucko and G. W. Dimbleby, eds., *The Domestication of Plants and Animals* (Chicago: Aldine, 1969), pp. 73-100. The author suggests on p. 74 that we can think of marginal cattle as "protein banks."

15. "The annual amount [of dung] used as fuel in India is estimated to be equivalent of 35,000,000 to 131,000,000 tons of coal." Dwain W. Parrack, "An Approach to the Bioenergetics of Rural West Bengal" in Andrew P. Vayda, ed., *Environment and Cultural Behavior* (New York: Natural History Press, 1969), p. 38.

16. B. A. L. Cranstone, "Animal Husbandry: The Evidence from Ethnology" in Peter J. Ucko and G. W. Dimbelby, eds., *op. cit.*, pp. 251-52.

17. Anon., "More than Meat," *The Farm Index*, Vol. 14, No. 12 (December 1975).

18. Artturi I. Virtanen, "Milk Production of Cows on Protein Free Food," *Science*, Vol. 153 (September 30, 1966), p. 1603-4.

19. As much as 50 percent of Holstein diets have been successfully replaced with paper and in some cases paper diets have resulted in higher beef to fat ratios and 20 percent faster weight gain. See Paul Meinhardt, "Cattle As An Economic Base For An Abundance of Beef Without Using Human Foodstuffs," *Feedstuffs*, Vol. 43, No. 27 (July 3, 1971), p. 18-20; and L. B. Daniels and J. R. Campbell, "Paper—A Cheap Source of Energy for the Cow?" *Hoard's Dairyman*, Vol. 115, No. 20 (October 1970), p. 1092. Also, Anon., "Cattle Gain Well on Wood Pulp," *Agricultural Situation*, Vol. 58, No. 12 (December 1974), p. 13.

20. Swadesh R. Bose and Edwin H. Clark II, "The Cost of Draft Animal Power in West Pakistan," *Pakistan Development Review*, Vol. 9, No. 3 (Autumn 1969), p. 189.

See also K. N. Raj, "Investment in Livestock in Agrarian Economies: An Analysis of Some Issues Concerning 'Sacred Cows' and 'Surplus Cattle.'" *Indian Economic Review*, Vol. 4 (New Series), No. 2 (October 1969), pp. 53-85, and the consequent critique: V. M. Dandedar, "Cow Dung Models," *Economic and Political Weekly*, Vol. 4, No. 31 (August 2, 1969), pp. 1267-71.

21. Om Prakash Sharma, "Bullock Plough vs. Tractor" in *The Cow in Our Economy*, J. C. Kumarappa *et al.* (Varanasi: Bhargva Bhushan Press, 1957), pp. 18-20.

22. Albert and Gabrielle L. C. Howard, *The Development of Agriculture in India* (Oxford: Oxford University Press, 1927), pp. 47-48.

23. Edward J. Clay, "Equity and Social Productivity Effects of a Package of Social Institutions: Tractors, Tubewells, and High-Yielding Varieties," *Indian Journal of Agricultural Economics*, Vol. 30, No. 4 (October–December 1975), pp. 74-87.

24. Anon., "Drought Hits Cattle in South Australia," *Foreign Agriculture*, Vol. 19, No. 26 (June 28, 1976).

25. *Ibid.*

26. *Michael Horowitz, "Comment on Heston," Current Anthropology*, Vol. 12, No. 2 (April 1971), pp. 201-2.

27. Anon., "Transmission of Bovine Leukemia," *Agriculture Research*, Vol. 24, No. 9 (March 1976), p. 15.

28. Robert M. Shapito and Pamela Hardt, "The Impact of Computer Technology, A Case Study: The Dairy Industry, Meta Information Applications," Wellfleet, Mass., draft (November 22, 1975) and "Problems in the Dairy Industry" (May 20, 1975).

29. See Part II, "The Industrialization of Corn."

30. Shapito and Hardt, "The Impact of Computer Technology . . . ," *op. cit.*

31. George Getschow, "A 12-Year Old Has 10,000 Offspring—What a Lot of Bull," *Wall Street Journal* (July 27, 1976), p. 1.

32. *Ibid.*

33. Anon., "An Inside Look at Livestock Exporting," *Foreign Agriculture*, Vol. 19, No. 27 (July 5, 1975) and "U.S. Cattle Take to the Air as Foreign Demand Accelerates," *Foreign Agriculture*, Vol. 13, No. 43 (October 27, 1975).

34. Anon., "Seminar Tackles Problems in Shipping Livestock, Meat," *Foreign Agriculture*, Vol. 19, No. 26 (June 28, 1976); and "Foreign Cattle Sell by the Hundreds at Central America's EXPICA '76 Show," *Foreign Agriculture*, Vol. 12, No. 25 (June 21, 1976).

35. Ivan E. Johnson, "India Seeks Improved Yields in Dairy, Poultry Industries," *Foreign Agriculture*, Vol. 13, No. 34 (August 25, 1975).

36. Hardt and Shapito, "Problems in the Dairy Industry," *op. cit.*

37. *Ibid.*

38. *Ibid.*

39. *Ibid.*

40. Anon., "Forage Future," *Agriculture Situation*, Vol. 58, No. 10 (November 1974), pp. 6-7.

41. *Ibid.*

42. "Forage Future," *op. cit.*

43. Anon., "Using Less Grain to Fatten Cattle," *Business Week* (December 14, 1974), pp. 72-75.

44. Paul Meinhardt, "Cattle as an Economic Base for an Ecological Loop: Using Only Organic Wastes and Marginal Lands It May Now Be Feasible to Produce an Abundance of Beef without Using Human Foodstuffs," *Feedstuffs*, Vol. 43, No. 27 (July 3, 1971), pp. 18-20.

45. Meinhardt, *op. cit.*, citing "Beefcattle Feeding Garbage," *Feedstuffs* (October 21, 1970), p. 29.

46. Meinhardt, *op. cit.*

47. *Ibid.*

48. Anon., "Using Less Grain to Fatten Cattle," *op. cit.*, pp. 72-75. 72-75.

49. Marx, *Capital*, Vol. 2, *op. cit.*, p. 237.

50. Thomas Hodgskin, *Popular Political Economy* (London, 1827), p. 147.

51. David Pimentel, "Energy and Land Constraints in Food Production," *Science*, Vol. 190 (November 1975), pp. 754-61.

52. Stuart Oden'hal, "Energetics of Indian Cattle in Their Environment," *Human Ecology*, Vol. 1, No. 1 (1972), pp. 3-22.

53. William Lockeretz, "Agricultural Resources Consumed in Beef Production," CBNA-AE-3 (St. Louis: Center for the Biology of Natural System, Washington University, June 1975).

54. See for example, Peter Dorner and Don Kanel, "The Economic Case for Land Reform: Employment, Income Distribution and Productivity," University of Wisconsin, Land Tenure Center Reprint No. 74.

55. Elmar Wolfstetter, "Surplus Labour, Synchronised Labour Costs and Marx's Labour," *Economic Journal*, Vol. 83, No. 331 (September 1973), pp. 787-809.

56. Michael Perelman, "Natural Resources and Agriculture Under Capitalism: Karl Marx's Economic Model," *American Journal of Agricultural Economics*, Vol. 57, No. 4 (November 1975), pp. 701-4.

57. Adam Smith, *An Inquiry into the Nature and Causes of the Wealth of Nations*, Cannan, ed. (New York: Modern Library, 1937), pp. 232 and 186.

58. *Ibid.*, p. 232.

59. Clarence Danhof, *Change in Agriculture: The Northern United States, 1820-1870* (Cambridge, Mass.: Harvard University Press, 1969), p. 160 citing *The Genesee Farmer* (1840).

60. *Ibid.*, fn. p. 160, citing *Rural New Yorker* (1854).

61. Eugene D. Genovese, *The Political Economy of Slavery* (New York: Vintage, 1967), p. 143.

62. *Ibid.*, p. 116.

63. *Ibid.*

64. *Ibid.*

65. *Ibid.*, p. 112.

66. Cranstone, *op. cit.*, p. 215; and Rada and Neville Dyson-Hudson, "Subsistence Herding in Uganda," *Science American*, Vol. 220 (February 1969).

67. Marx, *Capital*, Vol. 2, *op. cit.*, p. 327.

68. Eduardo Cruz do Carvalho, "'Traditional' and 'Modern' Patterns of Cattle Raising in Southwestern Angola: A Critical Evaluation of Change from Pastoralism to Ranching," *The Journal of Developing Areas*, Vol. 8, No. 2 (January 1974), pp. 199-226; also Eduardo and Jorge Viera de Silva in Granz-Wilhelm Heimes, ed., *The Cuene Region: Ecological Analysis of an African Agropastoral System in Social Change in Angola* (Munich: Weltform Verlag, 1973), pp. 145-92; and Rada and Neville Dyson-Hudson, "Subsistance Herding in Uganda," *op. cit.* 1968), pp. 35-38; and Wesley F. Buchele, "No More Starving Billions: The Role of Agriculture Engineering in Economic Development," an Inaugural Lecture delivered at the University of Ghana, May 9, 1969 (Legon, Accra: Ghana Universities Press, 1969).

70. Marvin Harris, "The Cultural Ecology of India's Sacred Cattle," *Current Anthropology*, Vol. 12, No. 2 (April 1971), pp. 201-2.

14

THE GREEN REVOLUTION

AMERICAN AGRICULTURE IN THE THIRD WORLD

The end of the fight is a tombstone white
With the name of the late deceased
And the epitaph drear: A fool lies here
Who tried to hustle the East.

—Rudyard Kipling

Since the seventeenth century, the wealth of India has poured into Western lands. Economists in Britain, the birthplace of the discipline, have held a direct responsibility for the status of India; in fact, all the major figures in Britain were engaged in work related to the administration of India, with the sole exception of Adam Smith, whose application for a position was rejected.[1]* For some, the subcontinent was a laboratory for testing their pet schemes of social organization. Through successful application in Asia, these ideas were sure to win acceptance in England.†[4]

The Indian laboratory seemed to sink in importance as the strength of the British empire subsided. With the success of the revolution in China, Western interest in it was renewed. India was supposed to prove, once and for all, that the "democratic" institutions of the West were more benefi-

---

*Both James and John Stuart Mill were employed by the East India Company as full-time officials. Malthus was a professor at the company's college for training administrators. David Ricardo was a member of the East India Court of Proprietors. The tradition of involvement in Indian affairs continued well into the time of Keynes, whose first job was with the India Office in 1905.[2] Mill, at least had some nagging doubts, it seems, about the benificence of his employers. In the letter he wrote to Ricardo about the sorry state of Ireland, after discussing the subject of Ireland and the temptation of one government to abuse its powers over another land, his thoughts turn to the East India Company. "But could this go further than the Oligarchy of the East India company goes . . . ?" he asks. Then he abruptly cuts off the letter with: "But I must now conclude, and go to talk about Zemindars [the large landholders installed by the British] from the ryots [peasants]."[3]

†Acceptance depended upon the degree to which England benefited from the backward state of the colonies and the ease with which institutional changes could be made in the colonies.

cial for the Third World than those of Communist China.[5] With the passage of time, economic comparisons between China and India became less flattering to the latter. To help remedy this situation, a plan was developed to revolutionize agriculture in Asia.

The main ingredient in the new Indian experiment was to be the development of new plants, specifically bred to further the type of capital-intensive grain production desired by Western interests.* William S. Gaud, head of the State Department's Agency for International Development, reflected the official excitement over the new technology by dubbing it the Green Revolution.[6]† Optimism reached such a pitch that agricultural economists began to fret about the expected world grain surpluses.[8]

The highpoint of optimism was reached in 1970, the same year in which disaster wrecked the hybrid corn harvest in U.S. That year the Nobel Peace Prize was awarded to Norman Borlaug, a plant scientist working out of the Rockefeller Foundation-financed Center for the Improvement of Corn and Wheat (CIMMYT) in Mexico for his work in developing new technology. The spirit of the award was captured by Ms. Aase Lionaes, who chaired the Nobel Prize Committee, when she said, "In short, we do not any longer have to be pessimistic about the economic future of the developing nations."[9]

At first glance, the fanfare surrounding the award seemed justified. Borlaug and his associates had managed to breed new short-stemmed varieties of wheat capable of producing two or three times as much per acre as traditional varieties. Over and above its apparent potential for increasing food production, the Green Revolution had social and economic implications every bit as far-reaching as the potato culture in Ireland.

The social and political implications of the Green Revolution were suggested by its beginnings in 1939 when Mexico expropriated Rockefeller's Standard Oil interests.[10] At the same time, the Nazis appeared to be making inroads into Latin America. Given the uncertain climate in Latin America, Secretary of Agriculture Henry A. Wallace suggested that an intensive agricultural research program might produce political dividends in Mexico. By 1951, the program had produced results. Borlaug and his associates had developed a rust-resistant variety of wheat which was exceptionally well suited to the newly irrigated lands of Mexico's northwestern deserts.

The innovations in plant breeding which won acclaim for Norman Borlaug and his associates are less unique than has been supposed. Mankind has been successfully breeding plants for centuries. As early as

---

*Exports are frequently produced by capital-intensive methods in the Third World. Food crops, especially those for consumption on the farm, are typically grown with more traditional technology.

†The Term was first used in 1940 at the suggestion of Peter Maurin at the School of Living, founded by Ralph Borsodi in 1940, to describe a decentralized system of agriculture. Later the term was adopted by *The Catholic Worker*. David Mitrany[7] used it to describe radical peasant movements in Eastern Europe.

the eleventh century, a Sung emperor introduced a rapid-maturing rice from Indochina which could be harvested in only 100 days instead of the usual 180.[11] By the 1830's the Chinese had developed rice which matured within 35 days after transplanting.[12] In fact, short-stemmed varieties, which form the basis of the Green Revolution, have been in use in the Orient for centuries.[13]

Nor was the breeding of resistant varieties new. What made Borlaug's work seem revolutionary was its potential to modernize agriculture in a relatively poor nation such as Mexico. On closer examination, the apparent success in Mexico is seen to be illusory.

In 1917, the same year the Bolsheviks came to power in Russia, Mexico experienced her own revolution. The new government drafted a constitution empowering the state to carry out an extensive policy of land reform. Large estates were to be broken up into small plots called *ejidos*.[14] The ejido could neither be bought nor sold nor rented. In practice, this land reform had barely touched northwestern Mexico, the area in which the use of the new wheat was concentrated.

The Cardenas government (1934–40) stepped up the pace of land reform. It also moved to collectivize the *ejidos*, as well as give them access to water and credit. At the same time, Cardenas let expropriated landlords keep the best land for themselves. After 1940, the Mexican government gave far more support to large agribusiness interests.

While the large private farmers were banding together cooperatively to purchase farm inputs at discounts of 35 to 40 percent, the National Ejido Credit Bank treated the *ejidos* as captive clients. Whenever the bank wished to sell, it delivered quantities of materials to the *ejidos* regardless of whether or not they were ordered. To recover some of the expense, the *ejidos* frequently sold the chemicals and seeds at a substantial loss to dealers who resold them to private farmers.[15] In addition, inferior goods were often dumped on the *ejidos*. An unidentified white powder, for example, was known to have been delivered in the place of fertilizer. Seeds which were known to be dangerously susceptible to rust were issued to the *ejidos*. To make matters worse, materials often arrived too late to be used effectively.[16] Finally, the Ejido Bank purchased crops from the peasants at substantially less than the market price.[17]

In spite of the disadvantages under which the *ejidos* were forced to operate, critics of land reform persist in pointing to Mexico as an example of the negative consequences of redistributing the land.[18] In terms of their disadvantages, the performance of the *ejidos* has in fact been impressive. Yields in 1960 on the *ejidos* were not substantially different from those of private farms with more than 12 acres,[19] even though the *ejidos* generally occupied inferior land and had access to substantially smaller amounts of agricultural chemicals than the statistics indicate.

The combined effect of agricultural modernization and the absence of land reform in northwestern Mexico has been a systematic deterioration in the economic status of the peasantry. Even the Rockefeller personnel now admit that the work in Mexico did little to aid the poor.[20] Rather, the new seeds benefited wealthy farmers whose holdings were large, even by U.S. standards.[21]

For years, the government constantly has worked for the interests of the large private farmers instead of the workers of the *ejidos*. The expensive irrigation projects, the overvalued exchange rates and official favoritism all worked for the benefit of the private farmers. As a result, yields on private farms are now improving much faster than on the *ejidos*. If we see this tendency as proof of the failure of ejidal farming, then we must recognize that this failure is political, not technical.

In light of the Mexican experience, the transfer of the new technology did not promise much hope for the mass of small farmers who make up the bulk of the population of the Third World. The future direction of Green Revolution reflected its inauspicious beginnings. In 1960 when the Ford Foundation, with the approval of the Indian government, initiated its Intensive Agricultural Districts Program with the expressed purpose of modernizing agriculture, the seventeen districts selected were seen as being the most adaptable to agricultural modernization. These regions were, in fact, largely "already prosperous, productive areas" and enjoyed satisfactory water control.[22] The Green Revolution was to be concentrated there—government moneys and personnel were to be funnelled into those districts which were the least in need of help.

By the next year the Ford and Rockefeller Foundations had joined forces to establish the International Rice Research Institute (IRRI) in the Philippines. This new institution, together with CIMMYT, set out to produce a high-yielding variety of rice comparable to the Mexican wheat.

The new wheat and rice seeds were expected to undermine traditional forms of agriculture in Asia. Both varieties could outproduce traditional plants only if they were accompanied by adequate complements of fertilizer, pesticides and irrigation. Traditional farmers could not afford to pay for these expensive materials unless they abandoned their attempts at self-sufficiency and participated more actively in the market economy. According to the planners of the Green Revolution, those who opted for the high-yielding varieties would be compensated for their pains because the new seeds had superior technical characteristics.

The new seeds would remake social relations in a single stroke, fragmenting relatively self-sufficient villages into individual farmers and workers engaged in production for world markets. Asia would become an appendage to world capitalism as traditional imperialist relations give way to a new form of imperialism in which Third World economies were subjected to the forces of the world market instead of the political decisions of the capitalist nations.*

---

*The political use of plant breeding did not begin with Borlaug. In 1951, for example, H. H. Love, a professor of plant breeding at Cornell with a long history of foreign involvements, wrote from Thailand, where he was advising the government:[23]

We do not know when we will be back in Ithaca, but we may be a year or longer. Joe Stalin may have the answer for us . . . . our agricultural program for Thailand is being enlarged and we have a very extensive project on rice breeding planned.

Major spokesmen for the Green Revolution were quite open about the role of the new technology in remaking social relations in the Third World. Lester Brown, then the leading advocate of the Green Revolution within the Department of Agriculture, said:[24]

As the mold of tradition is broken, farmers become more susceptible to change in other areas. . . . The economic and political relationship between farmers and the rest of the economy begins to change fundamentally. Using purchased inputs, and marketing additional production, the peasant farmers are drawn into the mainstream of modern economic life. At the same time, the industrial sector turns more and more to the countryside as a market, not only for farm supplies, but for consumer goods as well.

Arthur Moser, then President of the Agricultural Development Council, founded by John D. Rockefeller III, used even blunter language in his handbook for remaking social relations in the Third World.[25] Moser explains that farmers in the Third World often hesitate in breaking with the traditions of cooperation and mutual aid.[26] Although he recognizes that these traditions offer protection against catastrophies,* Moser calls for their elimination because they hinder the introduction of social relations of the market.[27] He compares such traditions to the pull of gravity which holds people down. In a sense he is correct. At the same time, these traditions may be of crucial importance to a people as a whole. China is a case in point. The government was able to call on the tradition of mutual aid to bring the people together in building the nation's economy.

To accelerate the elimination of such traditions, Moser recommends influencing wives and children to encourage them to demand more consumer goods.[28]† With the introduction of new capitalist social relations, agriculture will be dominated by a new group of middle-class farmers whose behavior will conform to the interests of the capitalist nations.** In the words of Martin Kriegsberg, the U.S. Department of Agriculture's Director of Planning and Evaluation in the Foreign Economic Development Service, these wealthy farmers will "serve . . . . as countervailing power to radical labor groups."[32]

---

*The monetary value of the privilege of letting a cow stray, for example, or the right to eat its carrion may not be high by U.S. standards, but it may represent the difference between starvation and survival.

†Moser's program echoes the earlier words of Malthus cited in the "Roots of U.S. Agriculture": "It is the want of *necessaries* which mainly stimulates the laboring classes to produce luxuries." As the production of necessities becomes less demanding, taste for luxuries must be instilled in people. In Malthus' words, "if the facility of getting food creates habits of indolence, this indolence may make him prefer the luxury of doing little or nothing to the luxury of possessing conveniences and comforts."[29] Later, he applied his theory to Ireland noting that "the taste of the Irish peasant for articles of this description is yet to be formed. His wants are few, and these wants he is in the habit of supplying principally at home."[30]

**This logic requires that televisions and motorbikes be treated, not as luxuries, but as "very necessary incentives to farmers to increase their output . . . so that they can buy them."[31]

By the time Norman Borlaug won the Nobel Peace Prize, the Green Revolution seemed to be taking hold, especially where traditional social relations were weakest. The new seeds were particularly successful in the Punjab, where the British had distributed land to Indians who fought as soldiers in the Imperial cause. By 1970, about 8 percent of the area planted to rice in the capitalist Third World and 17 percent of the area planted to wheat was sown with the new varieties,[33] although in certain locales the transformation was almost total.*

The adoption of the seeds has dramatic effects. A *New York Times* report described a Massey Ferguson tractor dealership which had accumulated so many orders that it would require 12 years before they could all be filled at the present rate of delivery.[35] The same article described a wealthy farmer, Mahinderpal Singh, who had utility poles installed on the edge of his field so that he could run his tractor by remote control in the future.

Although Mr. Singh's optimism might have been a bit extreme, life was becoming much more comfortable for the well-to-do farmers. Indian farmers who could afford the 10,000 to 12,000 rupees which are required to outfit a 7 to 10 acre holding could benefit from cheap credit and discount prices for fertilizer, pesticides and other inputs designed to accompany the seeds. All these incentives siphoned off money from the meager government treasury. Public funds were further depleted by the government policy of paying high prices to support the price of grain.[36]† In the four countries where high yielding wheat is most common— Mexico, India, Pakistan and Turkey—the wholesale price of wheat ranges from 1½ to 2 times the price of Australian wheat shipped to the United Kingdom, even though the Australian wheat is of superior quality.[38]‡

High price supports favor the large farmer. In Indonesia, for example, small farmers must sell their crops at a lower price at harvest time to pay off their debts, then purchase their food on the market during the year.[39]** Many other small farmers purchase food because they do not have the resources to supply themselves with enough grain. An estimated 33 percent of all farmers in Indonesia, India and Pakistan are net

---

*In the nations of India and West Pakistan, 37 percent and 46 percent of the sown wheat acreage was planted to the new varieties, and in the Philippines 43 percent of the sown rice land.[34] Within specific communities, the proportion was far higher.

†One study suggests an unfortunate consequence of higher food prices: If higher food prices result in higher wages (i.e., if consumers do not absorb the *total* burden of higher food prices), then the cost of labor can be expected to increase relative to the cost of capital goods. As a result, employers will have a greater incentive to adopt less labor intensive technologies.[37] This effect should be kept in mind below when we discuss the effects of the Green Revolution on employment.

‡Consumers complain about the tastes and milling properties of the new varieties. Later we shall discuss their nutritional qualities.

**Poor farmers in Indonesia cannot afford adequate storage facilities to maintain a year round supply of grain.[40] In all likelihood, the investment in storage would repay itself in a few years if the peasants could borrow the funds required at a moderate rate of interest.

purchasers of grain.[41] In one village survey of North India in 1969, only 14 percent of the peasants in the area managed to feed themselves and their families for 10 to 12 months of the year.[42] Even if the farm family does not purchase food, it will not benefit much from price supports if, as a small producer, it consumes most of its harvest.

Price supports do far more to augment the income of the large farm, which markets most of its produce.[43] Even though they make up the bulk of the total, small farmers receive only about 10 percent of all the money spent to support high crop prices.[44] In addition, small farmers generally have neither the collateral nor the connections to assure them of adequate access to credit and the other necessary inputs.[45]

The lack of access to cheap credit makes the small farmer vulnerable to the consequences of an occasional crop failure. One bad year could doom a small farmer to an indefinite period of unemployment or an uncertain future as a wage laborer. As a result, the small farmer adopts technologies to minimize risk rather than to maximize profits.[46] Small farmers have further reason to resist adopting the new varieties, because they are much less predictable and require several times as much expense* as traditional varieties.

Small farms also have difficulty in obtaining the irrigation which is an essential component of the new technology. Many farms are too small to afford the expense of a tube well,[48] and public wells, as well as roads, are strategically located in the interest of the wealthy and influential.[49] Similarly, the small farm benefits little from discount prices on farm inputs, since it relies on labor more than purchased inputs. For example, small farm operators making compost will not save as much as a result of reduced rates for fertilizer[50] as the larger firm which relies on the market for manufactured fertilizer.[51]† In Indonesia, statistics indicate that only about 25 percent of the farmers, benefit from the Green Revolution.[52]

Although the new technology may not have helped the small farmer much, in India as well as the Philippines profits per acre doubled for those larger farmers who could take advantage of the full economic potential of the new seeds.[53] After the introduction of the new seeds in the 1960's, military officers, civil servants, doctors, lawyers and businessmen in the Punjab joined the scramble for land with the intention of enjoying tax-free profits from agriculture.[54] Land values soared as much as 500 percent.[55] An IRRI study of several Philippine villages reports comparable and even more spectacular rises in land values between 1965 and 1972.[56]

Traditional social relations could not withstand the mad rush for profits. In the Punjab, rents in many cases rose from the illegal but normal 50 percent of the harvest, to as much as 70 percent.[57] In other cases, the traditional rights of peasants were brushed aside. One IRRI study

---

*IRRI estimates that the cash costs of farming with the new rice seeds in the Philippines are 11 times greater than when traditional varieties are used.[47]

†LeVeen's calculations mentioned in the last chapter estimated these same sorts of tendencies in U.S. agriculture.

describes the current state of tenants as "more like permanent servants than independent farmers."[58] Elsewhere, the break with tradition is completed with an eviction notice.*

Even conservative estimates by the Pakistan Planning Commission show that by 1985 4 million Pakistanis in the Punjab would be affected by evictions.[60] One Indian was so anxious to free himself of his "excess" laborers that he actually burned them in kerosene.[61]

The social dislocations of the new technology are intensified by the low prices for labor-saving agricultural inputs. A World Bank study estimates that for each tractor purchased in Pakistan, between 7.5 and 11.8 full-time jobs are lost.[62]† According to the same study, after the purchase of a tractor the average farm size increased by 240 percent within three years, mostly through the eviction of tenants.[64]

Besides replacing farm workers, the introduction of the tractor further adds to the problem of unemployment by displacing artisans who produce and repair traditional farm implements. Although some new jobs are created in conjunction with the new machines, tractorization results in a net loss of off-farm jobs.[65] Even if the number of jobs in farming and farm services had remained constant, overall unemployment would still increase because a greater proportion of these jobs would be located in the cities where patterns of consumption favor fewer labor-intensive goods.[66]‡

Proponents of the Green Revolution argue that the tractor betters the lot of the poor. The speed of the machine minimizes the time required for farm tasks, allowing the farmer to complete two harvests a year instead of one. As a result, the demand for labor increases.[68] In some cases this claim holds, although in most cases double cropping does not seem to have sufficed to maintain the demand for labor. According to the World Bank study of Pakistan, employment per cultivated acre declined about 40 percent.[69]

Part of the difficulty in assessing the employment effects of the Green Revolution must be blamed on a careless use of the concept "the demand for labor," which must refer to both the number of workers and the

---

*Indira Rajamaran provides statistics on the changing mix of poverty in the Punjab.[59] In 1960-61, 47.1 percent of all the rural households below the poverty line were headed by cultivators; a decade later only 31.5 percent. Households headed by agricultural laborers accounted for only 22.5 percent in 1960-61; after ten years, the proportion had risen to 40.5 percent.

†Farmers in Pakistan have to sell about one-half as much wheat to pay for a tractor as farmers in most other nations.[63]

‡Some writers point to a higher wage rate since the beginning of the Green Revolution. Keith Griffin, one of the most careful observers of the Green Revolution, cautions the unsuspecting to be leery of such numbers:

> In the Philippines, Pakistan, and possibly India, technical change has been associated with falling real wages. Cash outlay may be higher but payments in kind and customary rights have been abolished. Peasants can no longer obtain fodder for their animals from the landlord's fields, and when combines are used, no fodder is to be had. Fuel is no longer part of the wage payment. No longer do workers get interest free loans from employers.[67]

duration of employment. The new technology seems to increase the demand for temporary labor during peak seasons while reducing the need for full-time workers.[70]*

As a result, the underutilization of the agricultural labor force becomes more extreme. In Pakistan, for example, an estimated 30 to 40 percent of the total available hours of labor are wasted because of unemployment or underemployment.[72] In Sri Lanka, formerly known as Ceylon, 83 percent of all the youth aged 15-24 were reported to be out of work.[73]

Where can the unemployed turn? The traditional social relations which previously helped to protect them from destitution have been dissolved by the new technology. The government cannot afford to aid them financially until it becomes willing to tax the wealthy landowners instead of subsidizing them. Just the cost of maintaining the price of wheat in Pakistan, for example, was estimated at $100 million per year.[74] As a result of this distorted fiscal structure, influential planners conclude that provision of housing, health and social welfare programs is not economic and must be resisted.[75] Instead, all too many Third World governments attempt to provide these services indirectly by subsidizing the rich who, theoretically, invest the funds to create jobs. The resulting wages are supposed to eliminate the need for any substantial assistance from the government. Unfortunately, this chain of economic consequences breaks down. The wealthy tend to squander their funds on luxurious living, while those workers who do find employment earn a wage barely sufficient to provide for their needs.

Besides the destruction of traditional patterns of social relations, the Green Revolution is seriously disrupting traditional patterns of nutrition. Food which had previously been consumed by people on the farm is now sold in urban markets. Between the middle sixties and early seventies, grain sales in the Indian Punjab grew almost twice as rapidly as food production, because of the fall in consumption on the farm.[76]

With the advent of the Green Revolution, not only has grain become more difficult for the poor to purchase, but the quality has declined. Two officials of the U.S. Department of Agriculture confirmed that whenever they tested for protein content, the new seeds proved inferior.[77] A later Department of Agriculture study suggests how agricultural practices characteristic of the Green Revolution affect protein quality.[78] With the new wheat, applications of commercial fertilizer seem to increase the amount of protein while lowering its quality.[79] How these two factors offset each other is unclear. Irrigation, which is a prerequisite of the new varieties, also seems to contribute to lower protein content.[80] Higher densities of planting which are made possible by herbicides also tend to decrease the protein content.[81]

The nutritional value of grain is crucial in Asia; for example, 60 percent of the protein intake comes from cereals.[82] In India, the decline in

---

*The new varieties use slightly more female labor and much less male labor in Indonesia.[71]

protein content of grains is made all the more serious because of a stagnating production of the legumes which provide from 18 to 25 percent of all the protein consumed.[83]* These highly nutritious crops, which contain up to four times as much protein as grain, are less attractive to grow when compared to the highly subsidized grains; consequently,[84]† the per capita production of legumes dropped by 38 percent between 1961 and 1972.

Although India has more than enough food to feed itself,[89] survival is an open question for the more than 200 million people who live in abject poverty (defined by the government of India's minimum consumption level). A 1960–61 survey of the rural population in India found that the poorest 5 percent of the population consumed about .6 pounds of cereals per day and little else, while the richest 5 percent consumed 2 pounds of cereal as well as a substantial amount of other foods.[90] With widening income disparity, many farmers shifted out of the production of basic foods to produce dairy products and other luxury products for the growing population of well-to-do consumers.[91] Such is the way in which benefits of technical improvements are meted out when farming is directed to profit instead of people.

Lester Brown, Arthur Moser and other leading lights of the Green Revolution have prescribed a duplication of the pattern of U.S. experience agriculture for the Third World. They forget that the social relations developed along the U.S. road to capitalism took 200 years. Even at this measured pace, the casualties were enormous. Progress in the U.S. was carried on the backs of slaves and working people who never enjoyed its fruits and at the expense of Native Americans whose land was stolen. Progress in the U.S. was bought cheaply from millions of workers whose products sped us along the road to plenty.

To imagine that this road is open to the Third World is either foolish or hypocritical.‡ To try to push nations along this path is to set up a jet-age

---

*Measured in terms of the ratio of lysine to total protein.

†We should note here that the total amount of legumes produced has remained at a relatively constant level.[85] The decline in production per capita reflects the rise in population rather than a decrease in legume production, although in some places legume production has virtually disappeared,[86] while in other areas the introduction of more rapidly maturing wheat varieties frees the land for a sufficient time to grow a second crop of soybeans. An estimated 10 million acres of soybeans can be credited to these short-duration wheat varieties.[87] Finally, we might add that the shift to grains might be rational if caloric deficiencies are more pressing than shortages of protein, as some writers suggest,[88] although to make such a suggestion requires faith in the proposition that the state of nutrition necessarily improves when an improved supply of food is available. This faith is hard to maintain in the face of evidence to the contrary.

‡Japan is frequently mentioned as an example of the potential of the U.S. approach. This case is hard to make because of the peculiar nature of Japan. In the first place, Japan was an imperial nation in its own right. Secondly, the history of capitalistic social relations dates back to the Meiji restoration in 1867. Because of this gradual development spanning more than 100 years, the Japanese were able to abandon the old forms of social relations very slowly. The duty of an employer to keep workers on the job even when the immediate economic conditions may not justify the outlay of wages is only now beginning to be

juggernaut hurtling towards disaster. We have already mentioned the increasing disparity of incomes in the "developing nations." (And even in the U.S. we are told that we cannot afford to care for the poor.) To push the Third World nations down this road, while explicitly destroying the traditional mechanisms which give a minimum of protection, meanwhile providing no alternatives to those most affected, requires a rare degree of inhumanity.

THE FAILURE OF THE GREEN REVOLUTION

[W]hoever could make two ears of corn or two blades of grass to grow upon a spot of ground where only one grew before, would deserve better of mankind, and do more essential service to his country than the whole race of politicians put together.

—Johnathan Swift, *Gulliver's Travels*[93]

In these colleges the professors contrive new rules and methods of agriculture and building, and new instruments and tools for all trades and manufactures, whereby, as they undertake, one man shall do the work of ten; a palace may be built in a week, of materials so durable as to last for ever without repairing. All the fruits of the earth shall come to maturity at whatever season we think fit to choose, and increase an hundred fold more than they do at present, with innumerable other happy proposals. The only inconvenience is, that none of these projects are yet brought to perfection, and in the mean time, the whole country lies miserably waste, the houses in ruins, and the people without food or clothes. By all which, instead of being discouraged, they are fifty times more violently bent upon prosecuting their schemes, driven equally on by hope and despair. . . .

—Jonathan Swift, *Gulliver's Travels*[94]

Advocates of the Green Revolution shrug off the suffering resulting from the new technology; all progress entails some human costs. In their eyes, the higher yields of the new seeds are sure to make life better for all, but how much does the Green Revolution actually improve yields?

In experimental fields, the new seeds can produce two and even three times as much as traditional varieties, but private farmers do far less well with the new seeds. How much worse they do is difficult to ascertain.

We can be sure that in countries such as India, production of wheat and rice did spurt forward after the new varieties were introduced. In part, this represented a trend of improving yields which had begun before the Green Revolution.[95] Some of the improvement can be credited to a very favorable turn in the weather during the first years of the Green Revolution. The cultivation of previously idle land contributed to the totals.

---

ignored. These traditions made for much more social cohesion than would have been possible otherwise. Thirdly, the Japanese have never really relied on the market. The government and the few large corporations which dominate the economy work so closely that U.S. business interests often refer to them as Japan, Inc. Finally, the progress of Japan is overstated because of a systematic understatement of the level of production before 1867.[92]

The survey of the impact of mechanization on farm size, mentioned in the last section, found that of the 240 percent increase in farm size, 22 percent of the expansion, an amount equivalent to about 50 percent of the original farm size, resulted from the cultivation of land which had been left idle during the past season.[96] Finally, remember that the subsidization of the Green Revolution encouraged farmers to substitute wheat and rice for other crops.

Even after allowing for the influence of weather and the extra land planted to the new seeds, the Green Revolution did increase the average yields of wheat and rice in the Third World. Unfortunately, further increases will be much more difficult to obtain because the amount of land which is presently suitable for the new technology is limited.

In Pakistan, for example, farmers expanded their plantings of the new wheat after its good performance in the 1967–68 season. Many farmers planted the new seeds on more marginal land. One study by ESSO Pakistan, Ltd., found that yields on these suboptimal lands were so low that they dragged the national average down by 20 percent.[97] Another study of the Punjab found that only 16.9 percent of the area could profitably support the new seeds. On the rest of the land, native varieties would produce a greater return;[98] yet defenders of the Green Revolution generally identify the Punjab, perhaps more than any other place in the world, as an area in which the Green Revolution is succeeding.*

The shortage of prime lands in Asia can be partially compensated for by irrigation.† At the time when the Green Revolution was introduced, Asia had a backlog of inexpensive projects planned that were capable of expanding the supply of irrigation at a comparatively low cost. In 1961, the India Planning Commission estimated that about 25 percent of the available irrigation potential was being wasted in India.[102] A. M. Klurso, in his 1968 Presidential Address to the Annual Conference of the Indian Society of Agricultural Economics, reported that the irrigation ministers estimated a figure of 4 to 5 million acres of land which could be irrigated if only the farmers built small channels to link their land up with the main arteries of water.[103]

In addition, many of the irrigation facilities could be substantially improved, especially in the south where channel and field losses are estimated to be 62 percent.[104] Tapping unused irrigation potential has been a major source of the increased production in India. Between 1964–65 and 1970–71, about 29 percent of the growth in the output of food grains in India is attributed to increased irrigation,[105] but the mere construction of irrigation facilities is not sufficient to ensure adequate production.

---

*The success of the Punjab can be traced to its particular situation. The extensive irrigation system built by the English has been followed by a widespread adoption of tube wells. Today 70 percent of the land is irrigated, compared to 41.8 percent for the next most irrigated states, making the establishment of the Green Revolution much simpler there than elsewhere.[99] Traditional social relations which have never been strong in the Punjab are further weakened by the opportunities to make higher profits through irrigated farming.[100]

†Irrigation is probably a better investment than most industrial activities.[101]

When water is not properly managed, the productive capacity of the soil can be destroyed. If the water table rises too far, the resulting waterlogging or salination of the soil can prevent plant growth. Although this problem has long plagued Pakistani agriculture, the recent widespread adoption of the tube well has made waterlogging and salinization a national disaster. In the absence of a rational method for planning the intelligent use of resources, an estimated 6 million acres, 30 percent of the annual cultivated area of the Indus Plain, have been seriously affected.[106] To minimize this damage, in 1973 the government of Pakistan committed itself to spending one-half billion dollars in a period of 10 years.[107]

Even if the problem of water control were solved, extensive pumping would result in the eventual depletion of underground water reserves. Since India, like many Third World nations, has no framework to regulate the use of ground water, a continued mining of the underground reservoirs could lead to a drying up of the Green Revolution or serious social disruptions over water rights.[108]

Marvin Harris reports on another serious problem of water management. According to Harris, the increasing use of irrigation in India has been of sufficient magnitude to seriously reduce the flow of major rivers.[109] Consequently, hydroelectric generation has been impaired.

Shortages of electricity production have affected industry, resulting in cutbacks in fertilizer plants.[110] Because of India's heavy reliance on hydroelectric power, in other words, efforts to provide the irrigation necessary for an expansion of the Green Revolution threaten to destroy the soil, deplete the supply of fossil groundwater, and disrupt generation of electricity unless these efforts are accompanied by proper social planning.* Social planning, however, means more than a document from the government printing office. Even state ownership is no guarantee of constructive results.

State-run tube wells, for example, are notoriously inefficient in India because of the relationship between manager and client. Since Indian public officials are often motivated by graft, corruption and favoritism instead of by consideration of the public welfare,† the state-owned tube wells fail to serve the small farmer adequately.[114]

In those areas where irrigation facilities have made the Green Revolution profitable, large stretches of land are planted to the highly uniform seeds which form the basis of the new technology. This situation is ideal for the buildup and spread of plant pests and diseases such as those which struck the U.S. corn harvest in 1970 and the Irish potato crop in the 1840's.

---

*An archaic system of international relations further complicates water management. Since many major rivers flow between nation states, frequent disputes arise over the rights to the water. At the time of this writing, for example, military tensions are growing between India and Bangladesh over the diversion of water from the Ganges.[111]

†The U.S. Department of Agriculture estimates that India could conceivably double the amount of lands under irrigation,[112] but this goal would be very costly without the mobilization of massive numbers of the unemployed. This strategy would require a new system of social relations. Only China has really succeeded in developing its irrigation potential. Presently, China accounts for 40 percent of the world's irrigated area; India, only 14 percent.[113]

Just as the Irish system of potato culture inadvertently selected plants which were susceptible to the potato blight,[115] the architects of the Green Revolution unwittingly developed varieties with very undesirable characteristics.[116]

In the Philippines, a hybrid called IR-8, one of the new rice varieties, was hit by a disease called tungro. Most farmers then switched to a new variety called IR-20, which was resistant to tungro but which was hit by a grassy stunt virus and carried brown leafhopper insects. So, many farmers switched to a new variety called 1561 which resists the virus and the bugs, but 1561 is not fully resistant to tungro. Now the scientists have come up with IR-26, which is resistant to almost all Philippine diseases and insects but is vulnerable to damage from strong winds during flowering.[117] In Indonesia, the leafhopper problem destroyed the rice crop on one-half million acres of rice land in 1974–75. The government blamed the problem on the peasants for not informing it in time.[118] ·

On the north coast of Central Java, after a three-year string of crop losses, 25 percent of the land was sold to people who lived outside the villages.[119] In a nation with as serious an unemployment problem as Indonesia, a widespread displacement of people from the land would have serious social repercussions.

The danger of large-scale crop losses to pests, diseases or weather was far less under traditional agriculture.* Each village would select varieties which are adapted to its own resources and social relations. Within each village and even within each field, a wide variety of plants would be sown.[120] In a dry year one type might excel, although another strain might outproduce it in a wet year. This diversity afforded the peasant a biological insurance policy.

Traditional farmers in Indonesia planted at least 600 varieties of rice, and twice that number in Bangladesh.[121] In addition to minimizing the risk of a severe national crop disaster, the wide array of traditional varieties contained valuable genetic information. In northeast India, for example, researchers discovered varieties of rice resistant to stem borers, gall midges, leafhoppers, rice blast disease, rice tungro virus.[122] This area of the nation was selected, because it contained a very diverse mix of ethnic groups each of which had a different set of social relations. As a result, they could be expected to select for different properties in their rice. With the conquest of the land by a homogenious capitalistic agriculture, most of these plant types will be lost.

When a plant disease or an insect strikes a genetically uniform crop such as hybrid corn or the new varieties of rice, plant breeders typically look to traditional varieties for resistant genes to breed back into the seeds.† Modernizing agriculture destroys the natural habitat of the traditional seed varieties. Only those strains which can be stored in seed banks can be salvaged. Even these storage facilities are not infallible. In one

---

*This statement must be qualified for drought-induced crop losses. To the extent that the Green Revolution is accompanied by new irrigation, the new technology can reduce risk.

†Today, plant breeders are coming to rely more on the artificial manipulation of genes induced by radiation or chemicals.[123]

case, the failure of three refrigerator compressors resulted in the loss of a major Peruvian collection of corn germ plasm. In another, some irreplaceable corn collections were lost during the reorganization of a seed bank in Mexico.[124]

Feeding a growing population requires the conscious selection of genetic material and the consequent loss of much that might prove invaluable under unforeseen circumstances. Increased production also involves the selection of higher-yielding varieties. The decisions about the type of genetic material to discard are not just technical decisions. They are rooted in the structure of the economy.

W. David Hopper described the ordering of priorities in traditional Indian plant breeding:

> The dreadful famines of the late nineteenth century, and the brush with famine conditions at several intervals of the nineteenth century, led to a dominant concern with a need to produce crop varieties that were disease, insect and drought resistant. . . . Research was not the only aspect of twentieth century agricultural development dominated by the need for stability. Irrigation projects were designed and built to distribute water over as many acres as possible to assure a harvest in years of drought. State plant protection services were established to act when the threat of insect attacks reached a level that presaged severe crop loss. . .[125]*

The plant breeding work on which the Green Revolution depended displayed an appalling lack of sensitivity to the extraordinary genetic variety of traditional agriculture. Bengali farmers were taught to plant the short-stemmed new varieties in the river deltas without realizing that the traditional long-stemmed plants were better adapted to the erratic water levels in the deltas than the new varieties, which could not survive when the water rose higher than normal in 1973 and 1974.[127] In the latter year 80 percent of the summer rice crop as well as seedlings for the winter were destroyed.[128]

In the Philippines, farmers partially controlled weeds by harrowing 16 days after sowing. The traditional varieties were undisturbed; the new varieties went the way of the weeds.[129]

One factor which strongly influences plant breeding in capitalist economies is the willingness to fall back on chemicals, because of the high profits associated with pesticide production and the pressure for quick profits which is endemic to capitalism. Consequently, less attention is given to maintaining a resistant seed stock than we would expect in a rationally planned society.†

The Green Revolution is especially reliant on huge doses of chemical biocides. As a result of continuous spraying, the IRRI test plots where the

---

*The work of the Indian plant breeders may not be typical, even for Asia. High yielding varieties of wheat and rice were developed in Japan, Taiwan, Indonesia, Malaya and Ceylon. Interestingly enough, the Western experts seem to give little credit to this work which preceded or paralleled their own. The social ramifications of these varieties have not been made as explicit as those developed in Western-sponsored institutions.[126]

†This lack of information about health risks may prove to be a harbinger of modernization. In the U.S., one out of every four workers is exposed to toxic substances. For the most part, these people are uninformed about the possible health risks.[130]

new seeds are developed are so infested with insects that failure to spray at certain periods of the year would result in a complete crop failure.[131] Given the lack of adequate monitoring of pesticide use in the United States, one can only imagine what sort of protection is afforded the people in the Third World. In Indonesia, for example, pesticides killed off the fish in the paddies, leaving the people without a major source of protein in their traditional diet. Although it was alleged that the fish kill had been caused by the same outlawed chemical which had previously killed millions of fish in the Rhine, the government never investigated the charge.[132] Another study of farmers who adopted the new seeds in a Filipino village found that they were happy with the new technology although they felt dizzy while working in the fields.[133] One wonders if these people were informed that pesticides had any effects other than dizziness.

Suppose for the moment we forget about the difficulties which have just been discussed: what would be the consequences of the unanimous adoption of the Green Revolution in the Third World? Folke Dovring, an agricultural economist at the University of Illinois, attempted to answer this question with a simple numerical experiment.[134] Using 1970 census data when farm input prices were far less, Dovring calculated that if Indian agriculture were to spend as much for fuel as U.S. agriculture, fuel costs would total 4 to 5 percent of India's 1970 National Product.* If the Indians also paid as much as U.S. farmers for depreciation and repairs of farm machinery, these costs together with the cost of fuel would total more than 10 percent of India's 1970 National Product.

Since India's population is 2.5 times as large as the U.S. population, fuel and machinery costs would actually be equivalent to 25 percent of the 1970 Indian National Product, assuming that the costs per Indian were equivalent to comparable U.S. costs per capita. With the new technology, we can expect the use of other sophisticated inputs. Fertilizer and pump sets alone are expected to consume well over 3 percent of India's domestic product.

If Indian farms were to adopt the type of technology used in the U.S., where $1 worth of purchased inputs produces only about $3 worth of food,[136] the nation would require almost 17 times as much farm inputs. The difficulty in paying for these expensive capital-intensive inputs can be overcome through economic growth which increases the capacity to purchase or produce these materials; but for the vast majority of farmers cost remains a major obstacle. The new rice, for example, requires double the expense of traditional varieties.[137] In nations where interest can run as high as 15 percent per week,[138]† obtaining the funds necessary to adopt

---

*As a matter of fact, one recent survey indicates that mechanized Indian farms actually use more energy per acre than U.S. farms.[135]

†The crushing burden of debt at 15 percent per week is not exceptional. Hari P. Sharma provides an excellent discussion of the problems with the Green Revolution.[139] Sharma, who is not likely to minimize the impositions of users, puts the interest rate at 24 percent.[140] On the other hand, interest in prerevolutionary China ran as high as 30 percent per month.[141] In any case, the real burden of debt is not measured by the rate of interest, but on

the new technology can prove extremely costly.

Dovring points out that Indian farmers consume only about 1 percent of the national income in the form of purchased agricultural inputs.[144] In comparison, farmers in the more developed lands have historically consumed about 3 percent of the national income in the form of agricultural inputs.[145] In practice, this means that only $1 worth of farm inputs is required for over $50 worth of farm products. Since this statistic is a composite which includes more capital-intensive operations, traditional farms are characterized by a ratio well in excess of 50:1.

The 50:1 ratio is an average for all farms. Small farms in the less developed countries, just as in the U.S., have the ability to outperform larger ones in terms of output per unit of purchased inputs. This capacity is illustrated by Table 3-1, in which the smallest farms provide the base comparison. Among the Javanese farms represented here, the large operations use about 22 percent more fertilizers and pesticides per hectare than the smallest farms; yet they produce only 78 percent as much. (Notice also that the amount of labor does not differ significantly with farm size).

Today, only a handful of nations plant more than 25 percent of their total acreage of wheat and rice with the new varieties.[146]* The spread of the Green Revolution is checked by peasants who abandon the new technology because of its expense. A contributing editor for the house organ of the Rockefeller Foundation, Robert Critchfield, for example, writes of joining forces with a young Indonesian agriculture graduate to persuade the young man's father to adopt the new technology.[148] Critchfield even lent the family $30 to purchase chemical fertilizer and insecticides. A year later, the farmer had reverted to his old methods. Two surveys in the Philippines found that 50 percent of those who ceased using the new seeds cited the higher expense as the reason.[149] A U.S. Department of Agriculture report concludes that although many people assume that the increased sales from the new varieties are sufficient to offset the costs, "there is little solid evidence on this point."[150] Besides the higher costs of production per acre, the yields of the new varieties are highly irregular.[151]

As a result of such difficulties, the Green Revolution seems to have lost its momentum. In the Philippines, the government has resorted to an advertising campaign complete with catchy songs, jingles, and cartoons, designed by J. Walter Thompson, to infuse new energy into the flagging Green Revolution.[152]

---

its human effects. Hinton describes the death of a peasant subsequent to the repayment of a loan of $1.50,[142] and the plight of another peasant who had to indenture his boy for 7 years to pay off a $4 debt.[143] Of course, the higher profits from the new technology might be more than sufficient to repay the costs of the materials plus interest, but the profits are not guaranteed. Because of the risk involved in the new technology, cost remains an effective barrier to adoption for many farmers.

*About 38 percent of the wheat and 26 percent of the rice in the less developed countries of the Near East and Asia is grown from the new seeds.[147] The acreage involved is a smaller proportion of the total, because of the higher yield of the new varieties.

TABLE 14-1

Technology and Yields on Owner—Operated Farms
Subang District, West Java, Wet Season, 1969-70

Farm size (rank: smallest to largest)	Number of Farms	Family labor per hectare, average of 3 seasons (index)	Hired labor per hectare (index)	Fertilizers plus pesticides per hectare (index)	Yield (index)
1	6	100	100	100	100
2	26	43	94	89	104
3	10	25	114	116	105
4	13	30	111	116	85
5	3	17	92	122	78

Source: Agro-Economic Survey, *Analisa Usaha Tani Pedi Sawah Dan Talanaga Beras Ditiga Kabupaten Di Djawa Barat,* 1971, Appendix tables 1c, 1d, 12a, 12b, 12c, 15e, as compiled in Keith Griffin, *The Political Economy of Agrarian Change: An Essay on the Green Revolution* (Cambridge: Harvard University Press, 1974), p. 44.

The Indonesian government went much further in its attempt to promote the Green Revolution. It contracted with several international chemical companies who agreed to encourage farmers to adopt the new technology.[153] In return, the government agreed to pay these firms $20 for each acre of land which they succeeded in having planted to the new seeds.[154] The results were disastrous. The program was riddled with corruption. Needed farm inputs failed to arrive.[155] As mentioned previously, the insecticides killed the fish which provided the major portion of the protein for the people.[156] Finally, a major famine occurred.[157]

Most of the failures of the Green Revolution could have been anticipated. No mere technical change could be expected to transform the slums and villages of the Third World into the comfortable affluence of middle-class America, any more than the potato was able to enrich the mass of the Irish peasantry. In fact, reliance on the market is far more likely to change the basis of technical progress into a social calamity than to replace the basis of social calamities with technical progress.[158]

The advocates of the Green Revolution refused to see the obvious; instead they buried their heads in the barren sands of economic theory. Not content with what they found there, the Ford Foundation financed a leave for Theodore W. Schultz, enabling him to write his *Transforming Traditional Agriculture,* which was published in 1964. This book represented a revolution in the way economists viewed the process of economic development. A highly respected survey of economic development literature, coauthored by the present head of the Agricultural Development Council, concurs in this judgement.[159] Because of the use made of this book by proponents of the Green Revolution it is worth examining.

On a rather slender basis, Schultz concludes that peasants are extremely efficient profit-maximizing farmers who produce as much as is possible with the existing technology.* As evidence, Schultz cites a rise in the price of cotton which led to an increase in production in the Punjab;[162] but this example proves only that *some* farmers display profit-maximizing behavior; the behavior of the masses of small farmers toiling on their tiny plots of land is not necessarily visible in the statistics of aggregate production. If, on the other hand, Schultz only meant to argue that peasant communities might contain a sufficient number of profit-maximizing peasants for the establishment of capitalistic agriculture, then he was displaying a keen sense of the workings of the Green Revolution, along with a discrete silence on the subject of its effects on the not-so-capitalistically inclined segment of the population.

Schultz's analysis of Mexican agriculture lends support to this interpretation. Although he recognizes that the small communal farms in Mexico fared poorly during the process of modernization, he does not suggest any strong concern over the likelihood of this problem repeating itself in the rest of the Third World. For Schultz, the key to agricultural progress is to give the farmers access to better technology.

Resources and social relations do not figure in his analysis. Since 1932, he had been arguing that land and other resources were not an important determinant of agricultural production.[163] His rejection of the usual preoccupation with natural resources in agriculture apparently grew out of his experience in the Corn Belt, where cheap fertilizer compensated for the declining fertility of the soil.† Schultz forgot that fertilizer is inexpensive only as long as the monopoly power of the seller is not too great, and resources consumed in production are cheap. More importantly, by focussing on fertilizer production, which is perhaps the simplest example of manufacturing a resource substitute, Schultz diverted the attention of economists from other more difficult questions of resource scarcity. Schultz even argued that endowments of land and other resources were not crucial in agricultural production.[164]

His mistake was fatal to any attempt at understanding Asia, where resource scarcities are very pressing; in his view, all that Asia needed was access to modern technology. The market would take care of everything else. No wonder the sponsors of the Green Revolution did not anticipate the problems of shortages.

Schultz's analysis reflects the naivete of the promoters of the Green Revolution who were caught completely by surprise when the new

---

*Schultz bases his work mostly on two studies of peasant agriculture.[160] Both studies limit the scope of the analysis to a particular class of people. In the village of Panajechel, Guatemala, the author studied only the Indians although they were confined to about one-third of the land, much of which was extremely marginal. In the other study, Senapur, India, the author, W. David Hopper, who later became chief of agricultural economics for the Rockefeller Foundation in India, goes no further than the high-caste land-holding class.[161]

†We will ignore the problem of the declining quality of corn at this point.

technology led to social upheavals. If land and resources are not important, why should anyone worry about who owns land and who does not? In short, the relations of production must be inconsequential; only technology matters.

In spite of its reputation for hard realism, business got caught up in the Schultzian fantasy of economic development. Sales of agricultural technology meant not only profit; sales meant progress and prosperity leading to more sales and still more profits. Businessmen were delighted with this self-congratulatory vision of the world. They must have thrilled to hear the Secretary of Agriculture, speaking in 1968 before the Chicago Council on Foreign Relations, tell them:

The impact of these new grains—which double, triple, and even quadruple yield—goes beyond crop yields. They alter basic farm practices; they increase the demand for fertilizer, pesticides, tillage machinery, pumps, engines, wells, and for such things as transistor radios and motorbikes, by farmers able for the first time to buy them with profits from increased production. They can become powerful engines of change in national economies in the less-developed countries.[166]

Such breezy optimism is hard to find today. With the advent of the "energy crisis," farmers in India had to stand in line for days waiting for five gallons of diesel fuel for running their tractors.[167] J. G. Harrar, President Emeritus of the Rockefeller Foundation, explained to the Centennial Meeting of the American Chemical Society that "cheap energy has been the keystone to productivity, and agriculture, an enormous consumer of power is no exception."[168] Another representative of the Rockefeller Foundation estimated that, in Asia alone, about 75 to 90 billion pounds of rice are dependent on Middle East petroleum supplies.[169]

Today, even the original sponsors of the Green Revolution admit their mistakes. Henry Romney, Director of Information for the Rockefeller Foundation, confesses that "much of the criticism of the last few years has been accepted. The crises have turned us around."[170] The Rockefeller Foundation,[171] IRRI,[172] and the United States Department of Agriculture[173] now repudiate the cruder reliance on expensive capital-intensive technology which originally made the Green Revolution seem like a cornucopia of profits for Western corporations. Even IRRI is now hard at work breeding insect-resistant rice.[174]

REFERENCES

1. William J. Barber, *British Economic Thought and India, A Study in the History of Development Economics* (Oxford: Clarendon Press, 1975).

2. *Ibid.*

3. James Mill, "Letter to David Ricardo, August 14, 1819," in David Ricardo, *The Works of David Ricardo*, Vol. 8, *Letters, 1819–1821*, Piero Sraffa, ed. (Cambridge: Cambridge University Press, 1952), p. 53.

4. *Ibid.*, p. 160; and Eric Stokes, *The English Utilitarians* (Oxford: Oxford University Press, 1959), p. 178.

5. Wilfred Malenbaum, "India and China: Contrasts in Development Performance," *American Economic Review*, Vol. 49, No. 3 (June 1959), pp. 284-309. See also, Akhter Hameed Khan, "Rural Development: Lessons from China," *Land Tenure Center Newsletter*, of the Land Tenure Center, University of Wisconsin, No. 53 (July-September 1976), pp. 12-14. This paper describes the author's progressive disillusionment with the Indian model.

6. William Gaud, Administrator of the Agency for International Development, first used the term to describe what the press now calls the "Green Revolution" in his address before the Society for International Development, "The Green Revolution: Accomplishments and Apprehensions" (Washington, D.C.: 1968).

7. David Mitrany, *Marx Against the Peasant*, (Chapel Hill: University of North Carolina Press, 1951), pp. 118-45.

8. Ester Boserup, "Surpluses in the Third World—Who Needs Them?," *Ceres—The FAO Review*, Vol. 1, No. 5 (September/October 1968), p. 19.

9. *New York Times* (October 22, 1970), p. 1.

10. Harry M. Cleaver, Jr., The Contradictions of the Green Revolution, *Monthly Review*, Vol. 24, No. 12 (June 1972), pp. 80-111.

11. Ping-Ti Ho, *Studies in the Population of China, 1368-1953*, (Cambridge, Mass.: Harvard University Press, 1959), p. 174.

12. *Ibid.*

13. See Dana G. Dalrymple, "Development and Spread of High-Yielding Varieties of Wheat and Rice in the Less Developed Nations," United States Department of Agriculture, Economic Research Service Foreign Agricultural Economic Report No. 95, 5th ed. (August 1976).

14. Ed McCaughan and Peter Baird, "Harvest of Anger: Agro-Imperialism in Mexico's Northwest," *NACLA's Latin American and Empire Report*, Vol. 10, No. 6 (July-August 1976), pp. 1-30.

15. Cynthia Hewitt de Alcantara, "The 'Green Revolution' as History: the Mexican Experience," in Ernest Feder, ed., *Gewalt und Ausbeutung: Latein-amerikas Landwirtschaft* (Hamburg: Hoffman und Campe, 1973), pp. 473-95.

16. *Ibid.*

17. McCaughan and Baird, *op. cit.*

18. See Eduardo L. Venezian and William F. Gamble, *The Agricultural Development of Mexico: It's Structure and Growth Since 1950* (New York: Praeger, 1969), pp. 52-54.

19. Edwin J. Wellinghausen, "The Agriculture of Mexico," *Scientific American*, Vol. 235, No. 3 (September 1976), pp. 128-53.

20. Cynthia Hewitt de Alcantara, "Green Revolution," *Elements* (June 9, 1975), extracted from "Modernization without Development: Patterns of Agriculture Policy and Rural Change in the Birthplace of the Green Revolution," UN Research Institute for Social Development (Geneva, November 1974).

21. Folke Dovring, "Land Reform in Mexico," *Land Economics*, Vol. 46, No. 3 (August 1970), pp. 264-74.

22. John W. Mellor, *The New Economics of Growth: A Strategy for India and the Developing World* (Ithaca: Cornell University Press, 1976), p. 43.

23. Cited by Rick Dorner, "The Development of Agribusiness in Thailand," *Bulletin of Concerned Asian Scholars* Vol. 6, No. 1 (January/March 1974), pp. 8-15.

24. Lester Brown, *Seeds of Change: the Green Revolution and Development in the 1970's* (New York: Praeger, 1970), p. 10.

25. Arthur Moser, *Getting Agriculture Moving: Essentials for Development and Modernization*, (New York: Frederick A. Praeger, 1966).

26. *Ibid.*, p. 35.

27. *Ibid.*, p. 36.

28. *Ibid.*, p. 34. Mr. Coffin, a Deputy Administrator of the State Department's Agency for International Development while the new varieties were being introduced, testified to Congress that "U.S. assistance to the agricultural sector of the developing countries is therefore, to an exceptional degree, significant in the influence it has in the ideological

contest." Cited in Susan George, *How the Other Half Dies: The Real Reasons for World Hunger* (Montclair, N.J.: Allanheld, Osmun & Co., 1977), p. 50.

29. Thomas Robert Malthus, *Principles of Political Economy with a View to Their Practical Application* (London: John Murray, 1820); reprinted in part in David Ricardo, *Works of David Ricardo*, Vol. 2, *Notes on Malthus*, Piero Sraffa, ed. (Cambridge: Cambridge University Press, 1951), p. 337.

30. *Ibid.*, p. 349.

31. Delane E. Welsh, "Agricultural Problems in Thailand," *Bankogkok Bank, Monthly Review*, Vol. 12, No. 3 (March 1971) cited in Dorner, *op. cit.*, p. 13.

32. Martin Kriegsburg, "Developing Nations—The Political Implications of the War on Hunger," *Journal of the Albert Einstein Medical Center*, Vol. 18 (Spring 1970), pp. 25-30.

33. Cleaver, *op. cit.*, pp.80-111.

34. *Ibid.*, pp. 86-87.

35. Joseph Lelyveld, "Green Revolution Transforming Indian Agriculture, But It Has A Long Way to go," *New York Times* (May 28, 1969), p. 12.

36. Wolf Ladejinsky, "Ironies of India's Green Revolution," *Foreign Affairs* (July 1970), p. 763.

37. Paul J. Isenman and H. W. Singer, "Food Aid: Disincentive Effects and Their Policy Implications," *Economic Development and Cultural Change*, Vol. 25, No. 2 (January 1977).

38. D. Gale Johnson, *World Agriculture in Disarray* (London: Fontana, 1973), p. 244.

39. Rudolf Sinaga and William L. Collier, "Social and Regional Implications of Agricultural Development Policy," *Prisma: Indonesian Journal of Social and Economic Affairs*, Vol. 84, No. 2 (December 1975), pp. 24-35.

40. Comptroller General of the United States, *Hungry Nations Need to Reduce Food Losses Caused By Storage, Spillage, And Spoilage*, 76-65 (Washington, D.C., 1976), p. 5.

41. Keith Griffin, *The Political Economy of Agrarian Change: An Essay on the Green Revolution* (Cambridge: Harvard University Press, 1974), p. 109.

42. Susan George, *How the Other Half Dies: The Real Reasons for World Hunger* (Montclair, N.J.: Allanheld, Osmun, 1977), p. 21.

43. John Mellor, "The Functions of Agriculture Prices in Economic Development," *Industrial Journal of Agriculture Economics*, Vol. 23, No. 1 (Jan/March 1968).

44. Walter P. Falcon, The Green Revolution: Generations of Problems, *American Journal of Agricultural Economics*, Vol. 52, No. 5 (1970), pp. 698-710.

45. M. Schluter and John W. Meller, "New Seed Varieties and the Small Farm," *Economic and Political Weekly*, Vol. 7, No. 13 (March 25, 1972), pp. A31-A38. See also International Rice Research Institute (hereafter referred to IRRI) "Changes in Rice Farming in Selected Areas of Asia" (Los Banos, Philippines, 1975), pp. 117, and 319; and Clive Bell, "The Acquisition of Agricultural Technology: Its Determinants and Effects," *Journal of Development Studies*, Vol. 9, No. 1 (October 1972), p. 252.

46. Michael G. G. Schluter and Timothy D. Mount, "Management Objectives of the Peasant Farmer: An Analysis of Risk Aversion in the Choice of Cropping Patter," Surat District, India, Occasional Paper No. 78, Employment and Income Project, Department of Agricultural Economics, Cornell University (Ithaca, October 1974); and Robert Tempest Masson, "Utility Functions with Jump Discontinuities: Some Evidence and Implications from Peasant Agriculture," *Economic Inquiry*, Vol. 12, No. 4 (December 1974), pp. 559-66.

47. Clifton Whatron, "The Green Revolution: Cornucopia or Pandora's Box," *Foreign Affairs* (April 1969).

48. See, for instance, IRRI, p. 319.

49. Arjun Makhijani with Alan Poole, *Energy and Agriculture in the Third World: A Report to the Energy Policy Project of the Ford Foundation* (Cambridge, Mass.: Ballinger, 1975), p. 24.

50. Dana Dalrymple, "Fertilizer Subsidies," *Development Digest*, Vol. 14, No. 1 (January 1976), pp. 113-24.

51. IRRI *op. cit.* Shows small farmers rely more on compost, p. 53.

52. Sinaga and Collier, *op. cit.*

53. Cleaver, *op. cit.*, p. 93. See also IRRI, *op. cit.*, pp. 38, 68, and 87.

54. Ladejinsky *op. cit.*, p. 762.

55. *Ibid.*, p. 760.

56. Tito E. Contado and Roger A. Jaime, "Baybay, Lete," in IRRI, pp. 285–301.

57. Ladejinsky, *op. cit.*, p. 760. Also IRRI, *op. cit.*, p. 65.

58. IRRI, *op. cit.*, pp. 65–66.

59. Indira Rajaramen, "Poverty, Inequity and Economic Growth: Rural Punjab, 1960–1970/1," *The Journal of Development Studies*, Vol. 14, No. 4 (July 1975), pp. 278–90.

60. Arthur McEwan, "Contradictions of Capitalist Development in Pakistan," *Pakistan Forum* (October/November 1970), pp. 8–9. A report commissioned by the Massey-Ferguson Corporation, entitled "The Pace and Form of Farm Mechanization in the Developing Countries" uses a "very cautious estimate" of 2½ million jobs lost in Latin America as of 1972 resulting from agricultural mechanization. Cited in George, *op. cit.*, p. 77.

61. Lasse and Lisa Berg, *Face to Face: Fascism and Revolution in India*, (Berkeley: Ramparts Press, 1971), picture facing p. 54 and text on p. 55.

62. John P. McInerney and Graham F. Donaldson, "The Consequences of Farm Tractors in Pakistan," Bank Staff Working Paper No. 210, International Bank for Reconstruction and Development (February 1975).

63. K. M. Azam, "The Future of the Green Revolution in West Pakistan: A Choice of Strategy." See also, Carl H. Gotsch, "Tractor Mechanization and Rural Development in Pakistan," *International Labor Review*, Vol. 107, No. 2 (February 1973), pp. 133–66.

64. McInerney and Donaldson, *op. cit.*

65. Bruce F. Johnston and Peter Kilby, *Agriculture and Structural Transformation, Economic Strategies in Late-Developing Countries* (New York: Oxford University Press, 1975), pp. 380–81.

66. John W. Mellor and Uma Lele, "Growth Linkages of the New Foodgrain Technologies," *Indian Journal of Agriculture Economics*, Vol. 28, No. 1 (January/March 1973).

67. Griffin, *op. cit.*, p. 65. See also pp. 31–33.

68. S. S. Johl. "Mechanization, Labor Use and Productivity in Agriculture," Economics and Sociology Paper No. 23, Studies in Agriculture, Capital and Technology, Department of Agricultural Economics and Rural Sociology, Ohio State University (Columbus, 1971). In part, the loss of jobs resulting from mechanization is obscured because the larger farms which can afford to mechanize also have access to the capital which is required for more labor-intensive cropping patterns. On this point, see Shakuntla Mehra, "Some Aspects of Labour Use in Indian Agriculture," Occasional Paper No. 88, Technical Change in Agricultural Project, Department of Agricultural Economics, Cornell University (Ithaca, June 1976).

69. McInerney and Donaldson, *op. cit.*

70. I. J. Singh and Richard H. Day, "Microeconomic Chronicle of the G.R.," Studies in Agriculture, Capital and Technology, Economics and Sociology, Occasional Paper No. 69, Department of Economics, Ohio State University (Columbus, n.d.) See also Amartya Sen, *Employment Technology and Development* (Oxford: Clarendon Press, 1975), p. 155.

71. R. D. Montgomery and D. G. Sisler, "Labor Absorption in Jogjakarta, Indonesia: An Input-Output Study," A.E. Res. 75-10, Cornell University (Ithaca, March 1976), p. 61.

72. Naved Hamid, "Alternative Development Strategies, *Monthly Review*, Vol. 26, No. 5 (October 1974), p. 48.

73. T. T. Poleman, "Employment, Population and Food: The New Hierarchy of Development Problems," *Food Research Institute Studies in Agricultural Economics, Trade and Development*, Vol. 11, No. 2 (1972), pp. 11–26.

74. Falcon, *op. cit.*, p. 702.

75. Muhbubal Haq, *The Strategy of Economic Planning: A Case of Pakistan* (Lahore: Oxford University Press, 1963), p. 35.

76. Mohindar S. Mudahar, "Dynamic Analysis of Direct and Indirect Implications of Technology Change in Agriculture," The Case of Punjab, India, Occasional Paper No. 79, Department of Agricultural Economics, Cornell University (Ithaca, December 1974), p. 21.

77. Aaron M. Altuschul and Daniel Rosenfield, "Protein Supplementation: Satisfying Man's Food Needs," United States Department of Agriculture, Foreign Economic Development Service No. 3, reprinted from *Progress: The Unilever Quarterly*, Vol. 54, No. 305 (March 1970), p. 76. See also Jonathan Hollman, "Ecological Approaches to Agricultural Development," in Anthony Vann and Paul Rogers, eds., *Human Ecology and World Development* (London: Plenum Press, 1974), pp. 93–108, which estimates 10–25 percent less protein in new varieties.

78. Dana G. Dalrymple, "The Green Revolution and Protein Levels in Grain," Draft No. 2, United States Department of Agriculture, Economic Research Service, International Development Center (May 5, 1972).

79. *Ibid.*

80. *Ibid.*

81. *Ibid.*

82. Randolph Barker, "The Evolutionary Nature of the New Rice Technology," *Food, Research Institute Studies in Agricultural Economics, Trade, and Development*, Vol. 10, No. 2 (1971), p. 126.

83. Alan Berg, *The Nutrition Factor: Its Role in National Development* (Washington D.C.: The Brookings Institution, 1973), pp. 58–59.

84. *Ibid.* See also editorial in *Nature*, Vol. 236 (March 3, 1972); and IRRI, op. cit., p. 133.

85. Ingrid Palmer, "Food and the New Agricultural Technology," United Nations Institute for Social Development, Report No. 72.9 (Geneva, 1972), p. 19.

86. Berg, *op. cit.*, p. 58.

87. Uma Lele, "The Green Revolution, Income Distribution and Nutrition," Occasional Paper No. 48, Department of Agricultural Economics, Cornell University Employment and Income Distribution Project (September 1971).

88. *Ibid.*

89. James D. Gavan and John A. Dixon, "India: A Perspective on the Food Situation," *Science*, Vol. 188, No. 4188 (May 9, 1975), p. 546.

90. Lele, *op. cit.*

91. Lewis Simons, "The Fading of India," *Washington Post* (May 5, 1974), p. 3.

92. J. D. Gould, *Economic Growth History* (London: Methuen, 1972), 78.

93. Johnathan Swift, *Gulliver's Travels* (New York: Grosset and Dunlap: n.d.), p. 133.

94. *Ibid.*, pp. 178–79.

95. Robert W. Herdt, "A Disaggregate Approach to Aggregate Supply," *American Journal of Agricultural Economics*, Vol. 52, No. 4 (November 1970), pp. 512–20.

96. McInerney and Donaldson, *op. cit.*

97. Dr. Saleem Ahmed and Mr. S. Abu Khalid, "Why Did Mexican Dwarf Wheat Decline in Pakistan?" *World Crops* (July/August 1971), pp. 211–15.

98. S. M. Hussein, "Price Incentives for Producing Mexican Wheat," *Pakistan Development Review*, Vol. 10, No. 4, Winter (1970), p. 465. For a critique of this work, see Sarfraz Khan Qureshi, "Price Incentives for the Production of High-Yielding Mexican Varieties of Wheat: A Comment," *Pakistan Development Review*, Vol. 11, No. 1 (Spring 1971), pp. 54–61.

99. Richard B. Reidinger and John P. Parker, "Irrigation May Be an Answer to India's Urgent Food Needs," *Foreign Agriculture* (March 25, 1974).

100. Ghulam Mohammad cited in Colin Clark, *The Economics of Irrigation* (Oxford: Pergamon Press (1970), pp. 24–25.

101. Montgomery and Sisler, *op. cit.*

102. Paglin Morton, " 'Surplus' Agricultural Labor and Development: Facts and Theories," *American Economic Review*, Vol. 55, No. 4 (September 1965), pp. 815–33, esp. p. 825.

103. A. M. Khurso, "Agricultural Revolution and the Price Mechanism," *Indian Journal of Agricultural Economics* (January/March 1969), pp. 1-13.

104. J. D. Gavan and J. A. Dixon, "India: A Perspective on the Food Situation," *Science*, Vol. 188, No. 4188 (May 9, 1975), pp. 541-49.

105. John W. Mellor, *The New Economics of Growth, a Strategy for India and the Developing World* (Ithaca: Cornell University Press, 1976); p. 33. Pakistani sources give almost identical figures for water losses. See S. M. Ayoob, "Measures for Better Utilization of Irrigation Potential in the Arid and Semi Arid Zones of West Pakistan," *CENTO Seminar on Agricultural Aspects of Arid and Semi Arid Zones, Tehran, 1971* (Tehran: CENTO, 1972), pp. 64-65.

106. Gunnar Myrdal, *Asian Drama: An Inquiry into the Poverty of Economics* (New York: Twentieth Century Fund, 1968), Vol. 3, Appendix 10, p. 2134. See also Erik P. Eckholm, *Losing Ground: Environmental Stress and World Food Prospects*, (New York: Norton, 1976), p. 120.

107. Eckholm, *op. cit.*, p. 12.

108. S. V. Ciriacy-Wantrup, "Natural Resources in Economic Growth: The Role of Institutions and Policies," *American Journal of Agricultural Economics*, Vol. 15, No. 5 (1969), pp. 1320-23.

109. Marvin Harris, "The Withering of the Green Revolution," *Natural History* (March 1973), pp. 20-22.

110. *Ibid.* See also Stephen Merrett, "Indian Fertilizer Manufacture: Some Lessons for Industrial Planning," *Journal of Development Studies*, Vol. 8, No. 4 (July 1972), p. 402.

111. Anon., "A Fist Waved at Goliath," *The Economist* (August 28-September 3, 1976).

112. Reidinger and Parker, *op. cit.*

113. Kenneth R. Farrell, "Food and Agriculture in the Next Quarter Century," paper delivered at a Conference on Planning for the Fourth Quarter Century, sponsored by the International Affiliation of Planning Societies and the Planning Executives Institute in San Francisco (May 23, 1975).

114. John W. Mellor and R. V. Moorti, "Dilemma of State Tube Wells," *Economic and Political Weekly*, Vol. 2, No. 13 (March 27, 1971), pp. 1-20.

115. Donald Ugent, "The Potato," *Science*, Vol. 170, No. 3963 (December 11, 1970), pp. 1161-66.

116. IRRI, *op. cit.*, pp. 55, 63, 83.

117. Robert F. Chandler, Jr., "New Developments in Rice Research in Agribusiness Council," *Agricultural Initiative in the Third World: A Report on the Conference: Science and Agribusiness in the Seventies* (Lexington, Mass.: Lexington Books, 1975), pp. 27-40; see also Peter R. Kann, "The Food Crisis: 'Green Revolution' Is Easing Hunger Slower Than Hoped," *Wall Street Journal* (November 18, 1974), p. 1.

118. *New Scientist* (August 7, 1975). The U.S. Department of Agriculture estimates that only 300,000 acres were attacked. See Verle E. Lanier, "Indonesia Gained Last Year in Push to Up Farm Output," *Foreign Agriculture*, Vol. 14, No. 32 (August 9, 1976).

119. Sinaga and Collier, *op. cit.*, p. 33.

120. H. Garrison Wilkes and Susan Wilkes, "The G.R," *Environment*, Vol. 14, No. 8 (October 1972), p. 32-39; and Edgar Anderson, *Plants, Man and Life* (Boston: Little, Brown, 1952).

121. Nicholas Wade, "Green Revolution (II): Problems of Adopting a Western Technology," *Science*, Vol. 180, No. 4170 (December 27, 1974), p. 1191.

122. Anon., "Breeding Resistance in Rice," *Agricultural Research*, Vol. 11, No. 21 (May 1973), p. 13.

123. Arthur Galston, "Molding New Plants," *Natural History* (November 1974), pp. 94-96; and Björn Sigbjörnsson, "Induced Mutations in Plants," *Scientific American*, Vol. 229, No. 1 (January 1971).

124. Wade, *op. cit.*

125. W. David Hopper, "The Mainsprings of Agricultural Growth" *Rajendra Prasad Memorial Lecture*, developed at the 18th Conference of the Indian Society of Agricultural

Statistics (January 1965), cited by K. M. Raj, "Some Questions Concerning Growth, Transformation and Planning of Agriculture in the Developing Countries," *Journal of Development Planning* (1969), pp. 15-38.

126. Kazuo Saito, "On the Green Revolution," *The Developing Economies*, Vol. 9, No. 1 (March 1971), pp. 16-30.

127. David Spurgeon, "Updating the Green Revolution," *Nature*, Vol. 254 (April 1975), pp. 642-43.

128. Kasturi Rangan, "Subsiding Floods Leave Dacca Desperate for Aid," *New York Times* (August 18, 1974).

129. Robert Allen, "New Strategy for the Green Revolution," *New Scientist*, Vol. 63, No. 909 (August 8, 1974), pp. 320-21.

130. Gail Bronson, "Workers' Right to Know," *Wall Street Journal* (July 1, 1977), p. 6, editorial.

131. Randolph Barker, "The Evolutionary Nature of the New Rice Technology," *Food Research Institute Studies in Agricultural Economics, Trade and Development*, Vol. 10, No. 2 (1971), pp. 117-30.

132. Richard W. Franke, "Miracle Seeds and Shattered Dreams in Java," *Natural History*, Vol. 83, No. 11 (January 1974); and Cheryl Payer, "Food Is Rice," *Pacific Research and World Empire Telegram*, Vol. 7, No. 3 (March-April 1976).

133. IRRI, *op. cit.*, pp. 282-83.

134. Folke Dovring, "Macro Constraints on Agricultural Development in India," *Indian Journal of Agricultural Economics*, Vol. 27, No. 1 (January/March 1972), pp. 46-66.

135. Gajendra Singh, *Energy Inputs and Agricultural Production Under Various Regimes of Mechanization in Northern India*, unpublished dissertation, University of California (Davis, 1972).

136. United States Department of Agriculture, *Agricultural Statistics*, 1976, pp. 463 and 465.

137. Falcon, *op. cit.*, p. 717.

138. René Dumont, *Socialism and Development*, Rupert Cunningham, tr. (New York: Praeger, 1973), p. 227.

139. Hari P. Sharma, "The Green Revolution in India: Prelude to a Red One in Imperialism," in Kathleen Gough and Hari P. Sharma, eds., *Revolution in South Asia*, (New York: Monthly Review Press, 1973), pp. 77-102.

140. *Ibid.*, p. 85.

141. William Hinton, *Fanshen: A Documentary of Revolution in a Chinese Village*, (New York: Vintage, 1966), p. 35, fn.

142. *Ibid.*, p. 34.

143. *Ibid.*, p. 39.

144. Dovring, *op. cit.*

145. *Ibid.*

146. Anon., "The Green Revolution—Past and Prologue," *The Farm Index*, Vol. 15, No. 16 (June 1966), pp. 3-6.

147. *Ibid.*

148. "How a Man Can Shape His Destiny," *RF Illustrated*, Vol. 3, No. 1 (July 4, 1976), p. 10.

149. Dana G. Dalyrmple, "High Yielding Varieties of Grain," from *Technological Change in Agriculture: Effects and Implications for Developing Countries*, United States Department of Agriculture (Washington, D.C.: April, 1969), reprinted in part in *The Symposium on Science and Foreign Policy: The Green Revolution, op. cit.*, p. 166-174.

150. *Ibid.* See also V. S. Vyas, D. S. Tyagi, and V. N. Misra, *Significance of the New Strategy for Agricultural Development for Small Farmers: A Cross Section Study of Two Areas* (Vollabh Vidyanagar: Agro Economic Research Center, Sardar Patel University, 1968).

151. John W. Mellor, *The New Economics of Growth: A Strategy for India and the Developing World* (Ithaca: Cornell University Press, 1976), p. 59.

152. Kann, *op. cit.*, p. 1.

153. Franke, "Miracle Seeds. . . ," *op. cit.*; and Payer, "Food. . . ," *op. cit.*

154. Harris, "The Withering. . . ," *op. cit.*

155. Franke, "Miracle Seeds. . . ," *op. cit.*; and Payer, "Food. . . ," *op. cit.*

156. *Ibid.*

157. Franke, "Miracle Seeds. . . ," *op. cit.*

158. Karl Marx, *Capital*, Vol. 1 (Chicago: Kerr, 1906), p. 533.

159. Yujiro Hayami and Vernon Ruttan, *Agricultural Development: An International Perspective*, (Baltimore: John Hopkins Press, 1971), pp. 39-43.

160. Sol Tax, *Penny Capitalism: A Guatemalan Indian Economy*, Smithsonian Institution, Institute of Anthropology, Publication No. 16 (1953) and David Hopper's unpublished Ph.D. thesis, Cornell University (Ithaca, June 1957). See also David Hopper, "Allocative Efficiency in Traditional Indian Agriculture," *Journal of Farm Economics*, Vol. 46, No. 3 (August 1965).

161. Richard Franke, "Solution to the Asian Food Crisis: 'Green Revolution' or Social Revolution?" *Bulletin of Concerned Asian Scholars*, Vol. 6, No. 4 (November/December 1974), pp. 2-13.

162. Theodore W. Schultz, *Transforming Traditional Agriculture* (New Haven: Yale University Press, 1964), p. 50.

163. Theodore W. Schultz, "Diminishing Returns in View of Progress in Agricultural Production," *Journal of Farm Economics*, Vol. 14 (October 1932), pp. 640-49.

164. Schultz, *Transforming. . .*, *op. cit.*, p. 17.

165. J. G. Harrar, President Emeritus of the Rockefeller Foundation, quoted in George, *op. cit.*, p. 103.

166. Don Paarlberg, "Food for More People and Better Nutrition," in Clifford M. Hardin (ed.) *Overcoming World Hunger* (Englewood Cliffs: Prentice Hall, 1969), pp. 73-74.

167. Lewis M. Simons, "Fading of India's Green Revolution," *Washington Post* (May 5, 1974), p. C3.

168. "Food and World Interdependence," reprinted in *Agriculture World*, Vol. 2, No. 5 (June 1976), pp. 5-6.

169. *FAO News*, cited in *Planet N. Abstracts*, Vol. 6, No. 9, Collier Carbon and Chemical Corporations, n. d.

170. Wade, *op. cit.*, p. 1191.

171. Sterling Wortman, *The World Food Situation: A New Initiative*, prepared for the Subcommittee on Science, Research and Technology and the Subcommittee on Domestic and International Scientific Planning and Analysis of the United States House of Representatives (Washington, D.C.: September 23, 1975).

172. Carol Ulinski and Ann Becker, "IRRI Designs Small Scale Farm Equipment for Developing Country Production," *Development Digest*, Vol. 14, No. 1 (January 1976), pp. 62-78.

173. "Simple, Sound Machinery," *The Farm Index*, Vol. 15, No. 4 (April 1976), pp. 10-12.

174. Robert Rodale, "The Greening of the Green Revolution," *Organic Gardening and Farming*, Vol. 23, No. 7 (July 1976), pp. 34-40.

15

THE FERTILIZER STORY

FERTILIZER FOR PROFIT

I do not know what is precisely meant by ammoniac manure. If it means guano, superphosphate or any other artificial product of that kind, we might as well ask the people of India to manure their soil with champagne.
—Lord Mayo, Viceroy of India, 1870[1]

Fertilizer is an essential ingredient of the Green Revolution. In fact, the characterization of the Indian program for the Green Revolution by John W. Mellor, Chief Economist for the State Department's Agency for International Development, holds true for the Green Revolution as a whole: it is "primarily a fertilizer scheme."[2]

Fertilizer is also big business now that farmers can no longer purchase a new acre of land for less money than it costs to fertilize it, as was the case in the days of Thomas Jefferson. As we mentioned in Part I, the fertilizer industry today is the fourth largest basic manufacturing industry (after petroleum, steel and cement). From one-third to over one-half of the crop production in the U.S. is attributed to fertilizer use.[3]

The fertilizer industry has always been highly concentrated.[4] The industry took on a new color, however, during the early 1960's when petroleum corporations took over the bulk of its assets. In 1963, for example, Cities Service took over the Tennessee Corporation; Socony Mobil, the Virginia-Carolina Chemical Company; and Gulf, Spencer Chemical.[5]

Since natural gas, which was a by-product of oil production, is the major raw material used in producing nitrogen fertilizer, the acquisitions seemed predictable enough.* In addition, the production of nitrogen fertilizer requires so much energy that one source estimates that by the year 2000, the equivalent of 25 per cent of the 1973 world energy budget will be required to satisfy the global demands for nitrogen.[6]

---

*The industry did not confine its activities to nitrogen because potash and potassium fertilizers could be distributed through virtually the same networks.

The fertilizer industry had another special attraction. According to a report prepared by Esso Chemicals published by the court during an antitrust action:

A gradual increasing need for fertilizers is undeniable: the inexorable growth of world population will create in 35 years a need for twice today's food production. . . Inevitably, lands now lying fallow because of their submarginal fertility will come back into cultivation—but only with heavy applications of fertilizers. . . the fertilizer raw materials seem almost uniquely free of the threat of substitution and of dependence upon industrial growth.[7]

During the middle 1960's, the fertilizer industry was thrown into disarray by a new technical developoment. M. K. Kellogg Co. invented a new process for manufacturing ammonia which cut production costs in half. Prior to this process, the typical plant would produce 300 tons of ammonia per day at a cost of $40 per ton. Using the Kellogg system, a plant would manufacture 1,000 tons per day at a cost of $20 per ton.[8] "When the companies saw the production costs," said Kellogg President Warren L. Smith, "they knew that they could not afford *not* to buy the new plants."[9] As the industry adopted the new plants, the supply of fertilizer skyrocketed; the price of fertilizer suffered tremendously. Domestic production seemed certain to outrun consumption unless the bottom were to drop out of the price structure of the fertilizer market. The industry was desperate for an outlet.

The new strategy for coping with the surplus was outlined by Lester Brown, the same Department of Agriculture representative who welcomed the new social relations of the Green Revolution so warmly. Writing in the *Columbia Journal of World Business* in 1967, Brown estimated that if the Third World could be induced to use only one-fourth as much fertilizer per acre as Japan, the U.S. could export $7 billion worth of fertilizer instead of the existing level of $1 billion.[10] Although the resulting profits to U.S. manufacturers might be attractive, the cost for the Third World was nothing short of phenomenal. In the same year in which Brown was writing, India was already paying 20 per cent of its export earnings for fertilizer imports, according to Brown's own figures.[11]

The foreign exchange shortage could be circumvented by constructing factories within the Third World. Initially, this strategy might seem paradoxical. Why construct new factories in the face of a glut? The fertilizer companies had several reasons.

Firstly, because the demand for gasoline relative to other petrochemicals was light in the Third World, refineries in that part of the world produced a surplus of naphtha. The product either had to be used or to be flared. Since naphtha could be used in place of natural gas, any future increase in refining capacity would be more profitable with a complementary increase in fertilizer production.*[12]

---

*During this period, nitrogen fertilizer manufacturers were predominantly oil companies. Since that time, some of these firms have sold off their operations.

Secondly, future fertilizer exports were threatened by the attempt at self-sufficiency by some Third World countries. Whatever the corporations could do to forestall this move would protect their future control of those markets. Locating a factory in a Third World nation was an ideal tactic for maintaining future access to a foreign market.

The politics of fertilizer exports were complicated by questions about the future role of the U.S. government. Traditionally, the government of the U.S. helped stimulate demand for fertilizers by subsidizing exports. The World Bank estimates that about half of all purchases in the Third World were financed through government aid programs or cheap credit.[13] However, fertilizer corporations had no guarantee that this support would continue.

Third World attempts at self-sufficiency did not turn out to be very successful. In countries such as India and Pakistan, contracts for constructing fertilizer plants were awarded to high-priced Western firms. Lack of foreign exchange caused long delays in construction.[14] These problems, combined with poor planning, resulted in far more expense than the governments had anticipated.[15]*

Political pressure was even more crucial in determining the course of the fertilizer industry in India. As early as 1964, the left wing of the ruling Congress Party in India was declining in influence. High-ranking government officials began wooing U.S. investors, but they could not reach an accord on prices.[19] The Indian policy was to set prices at a high enough level that public enterprises would earn 12½ percent profit. The Indian representatives assumed that the greater efficiency of U.S. firms would make a higher rate of profit feasible. The U.S. representatives held out for a higher rate of return. More importantly, they demanded the right to set prices and to control marketing, distribution and the oil feedstock supply.

When India applied to the World Bank for a loan to build the factory on her own, the bank stalled. India waited for almost two years for the loan, but by the end of 1965, India recognized that her agricultural situation was taking a drastic turn for the worse. India informed the U.S. of her need of between 10 and 14 million tons of grain to carry the people through 1966.[20] Since the U.S. was the only nation with a large enough

---

*Although some writers argue that attempts at fertilizer self-sufficiency for nations such as India are irrational,[16] data provided by John Mellor suggests that this judgment is mistaken. According to Mellor, the cost of importing fertilizer would amount to about 30 per cent of the cost of constructing a fertilizer production capacity, assuming that the plant operates at 65 per cent of full capacity.[17] At higher operating levels, the cost of developing the fertilizer manufacturing capacity would be still lower.

When he was deputy chairman of the Indian Planning Commission, Asoka Mehta took an even stronger position than Mellor. Mehta estimated that with 12 crores (120 million) of rupees of foreign exchange, "it would be possible to import 100,000 tonnes of nitrogen equivalent of fertilizers. But with this 12 crores of foreign exchange, we will be able to put up one plant of fertilizer which will be capable of producing 200,000 tonnes of nitrogenous fertilizer for all years to come."[18]

grain surplus to make a substantial contribution to the Indian shortfall, the U.S. power over India was unmistakable.*

In spite of the human needs in India, President Johnson continued current policy of abstaining from signing a year-long food agreement with India. As the screws tightened, India began to give way. The New York Times editorialized:

Call them "strings", call them "conditions", or whatever one likes, India has little choice now but to agree to many of the terms that the U.S., through the World Bank, is putting on its aid. For India simply has nowhere else to turn.[22]

In a classic example of understatement, one fertilizer company executive told a Congressional committee, "We certainly would not be in India . . . were it not for our effort at economic assistance."[23] The assessment of the Indian Congress Party seemed more to the point:

It appears that the American government and the World Bank would like to arrogate for themselves the right to lay down the framework in which our economy must function.[24]

Other nations offered less resistance to the activities of the U.S. fertilizer industry. In the Philippines, for example, ESSO built a fertilizer plant with a capacity of 1,000 tons per day next to its Bataan Peninsula refinery.[25] To market the fertilizer, ESSO developed a network of 400 "agro-service centers" where farmers could purchase seed, pesticides and farm implements as well as fertilizer from the ESSO dealer.[26]

In spite of every outward appearance of success, the worldwide plans of the fertilizer industry came to naught. Due to the worldwide glut of fertilizer, ESSO could not sell nearly as much as it could produce at the existing price level. Rather than lower prices, it chose to operate the plant at much less than full capacity. After years of deficits, ESSO sold its plant at a substantial loss.[27]†

The overconfidence of the fertilizer companies is easily understandable. Looking at aggregate figures, they could see that the average farmer could grow about $3 worth of rice for each $1 invested in fertilizer.[29] In these terms, the market for fertilizer in the Third World appeared quite lush, but the use of fertilizers is restricted by socio-economic conditions. In India, for example, nearly 80 percent of the total consumption of nitrogenous fertilizer remains confined to about 100 of the 330 districts in the country."[30] Use of fertilizer is restricted by soil conditions, cropping patterns and the availability of credit. In addition, each successive dose of fertilizer adds less to total production. Finally, the actual profit from the application of fertilizer depends upon weather and market conditions.

The more money a farmer has invested in fertilizer, the greater the

---

*President Johnson also wanted to use the food as a lever to pressure Mrs. Gandhi to abandon her criticism of the U.S. policy in Viet Nam.[21]

†Although the demand for fertilizer fell far short of the industry's expectations, fertilizer use increased dramatically. Between 1960 and 1970, world consumption of nitrogen fertilizer trebled; in Asia, the amount increased by 435 percent during the same period.[28]

potential risk from a failure to anticipate variations in the weather or markets. Even farmers who adopt Green Revolution practices tend to hedge against risk by purchasing less than the recommended level of fertilizer.[31] Besides the reluctance of farmers to consume as much fertilizer as expected, the fertilizer companies absorbed the added sales expense of serving many small farmers, each usually purchasing a minimal amount of fertilizer.[32]

By 1969, a worldwide glut of fertilizer had driven prices from $90 per ton of ammonia down to $20 per ton.[33] According to the division vice president for marketing for IMC, one of the world's largest fertilizer producers, the industry attempted to correct for the over-supply of fertilizer by shutting down plants, ceasing new research and keeping maintenance on operating plants to a minimum.[34]

As of 1974, none of the existing nitrogen fertilizer plants in the U.S. had been completed between 1970 and early 1974. In Europe, only seven plants were built during the same period.[35]

Few additional operations were expected to be completed in the near future. Only four new factories were under construction in western Europe. In the U.S., the situation was even more bleak with two factories under construction, one of which belonged to a farm cooperative.[36]

At the same time the fertilizer industry was restricting growth in capacity, demand for fertilizer was expanding, although the pace was not as rapid as the industry had expected. Demand was especially buoyant in the Third World, where fertilizer consumption was encouraged by government support of agricultural prices and outright subsidies for fertilizer consumption.* Subsidies of the cost of fertilizer of 50 percent and even more are not uncommon.[39]

By 1973, the pendulum had swung the other way. Fertilizer had become short in supply. As a result of new agricultural policies, farmers in the U.S. were rapidly expanding their planting. Between 1972 and 1974, the harvested acreage increased by 36 million acres, or about 13 percent.[40] The domestic demand for fertilizer grew accordingly. Naturally, prices rose and supplies on the world market tightened.

The results in the Third World were disastrous. In Bangladesh, fertilizer consumption declined by 11 percent.[41] Indian farmers managed to maintain their level of fertilizer consumption, only because the government had reserves on hand.[42] Even in the U.S., according to the industry, shortages of fertilizer were estimated to be reducing production by about 20 million tons of grain.[43] In the year when the shipping of 16 million tons to Russia stirred up so much controversy, the loss of 20 million tons of grain was very significant.

---

*At the same time that the U.S. pressured India into relinquishing control of her domestic fertilizer industry, the U.S. demanded that India adopt these policies which would increase fertilizer consumption.[37] Fertilizer subsidies for basic food crops are less expensive than price supports, but the administration of subsidies is complicated because of the profits which can be made by diverting the fertilizer to high-priced luxury crops which offsets the potential efficiency of the subsidy program.[38]

In the less developed nations, the effect was far more severe. By 1974, the United States Food and Agricultural Organization estimated that fertilizer shortages resulted in the loss of 15 million tons of grain in the Third World, enough to sustain about 90 million Asians or Africans for an entire year.[44]

Who was responsible for this enormous human tragedy? *Business Week* speculated at the time that if the demand for U.S. agricultural exports had not been so brisk, the status of the agrochemical industry would certainly be the focus of several sweeping government investigations.[45] Two representatives of the office of the U.S. agricultural attaché in Holland reported, in an aside, that Dutch fertilizer producers explicitly agreed to limit production.[46] By 1976, a federal grand jury had indicted eight fertilizer companies for conspiring to restrict the supply of potash and to stabilize its price.[47]

The full story of the nitrogen producers has yet to be fully revealed. We do know that the major feedstock for producing nitrogen in the U.S. is natural gas. Although several of the oil companies are still in the fertilizer business, more than 10 times as much natural gas is flared at the oil wells as is used for the manufacture of fertilizer.[48]* We saw that the fertilizer industry was hesitant to invest more for fertilizer factories; instead, they continued their program of shutting down plants, even during the height of the fertilizer shortage. Phillips Petroleum closed an 800-ton-per-day plant at Etter, Texas.[50] Grace's Baltimore plant also ceased to operate in 1973.[51] After acquiring 17 plants in Georgia, Agrico proceeded to shut down 10 of them.[52]† As supplies tightened, the international price of fertilizer skyrocketed.

Within the U.S., prices were officially contained by the existing system of wage and price controls. Rather than accept controlled prices in the U.S., the industry exported as much fertilizer as possible. In addition, ammonia, which had sold at $20 a ton a few years ago, was selling on the black market in the U.S. for as much as $330 per ton.[55]

Official government reaction showed a callous disregard for the people of the Third World. After the U.S. had pressured the Third World to adopt a system of farming which depended on manufactured fertilizers, about 125 members of the House of Representatives called for an embargo on fertilizer exports.[56] The Agency for International Development of the State Department responded to the fertilizer shortage by cutting back on exports of fertilizer as a form of aid.[57] The cutback would have been much more severe except that more than half of these exports were being used as

---

*In 1975, the U.S. met with officials of the Saudi Arabian government to "consider plans for . . . the use of flared gas for expanding the production of fertilizer."[49]

†The situation would have been far worse without the existence of the farm co-ops which made up 35 percent of the total sales of agri-chemicals in 1974.[53] These operations had no interest in raising prices or in curtailing production. Besides constructing plants when the industry was shutting down factories, in at least one case a co-op was able to purchase an inoperative factory. Either the farmers or we may question the motives for not continuing to utilize the operation.[54]

a form of military aid to the governments of South Vietnam and Cambodia.[58]

Eventually, the government recognized that unless it were prepared to meet the fertilizer industry head-on, it would have no choice except to capitulate. On October 25, 1974, the price of fertilizer was decontrolled. The only condition extracted by the government was a promise to divert 1 to 5 million tons of fertilizer from foreign to domestic markets.[59]

The effects were immediate. Ammonia delivered at a stated cost of $62.50 per ton east of the Rockies was selling at $95 to $125 a ton by mid-December.[60] By the spring of 1975, fertilizer prices were about 215 percent higher than they had been two years before.[61]

The industry blamed the higher prices on higher costs, especially for energy. Between 1970 and 1974, rising energy costs amounted to an extra $4.60 for each ton of nitrogen; the prices paid for the same quantity of fertilizer rose by $107.20.[62]

Profits naturally bounded upwards. The industry was making between 30 and 65 percent in nitrogen operations and 33 to 50 percent on phosphorous.[63] In 1974, Williams Companies, the parent company of the firm which shut down the 10 plants in Georgia, enjoyed a higher rate of return than any other of the 500 largest companies in the U.S. for the decade 1964-74.[64]

The industry did not accept responsibility for the fertilizer shortage; instead, it shifted the blame to others. Phosphate producers complained about the environmentalists who interfered with their plans to exploit the rich Florida deposits. Others explained that efforts to distribute materials more equitably were hampered by a shortage of boxcars.[65]

The lion's share of the blame was reserved for the federal government which regulated the price of natural gas. For years, the industry had saved on its energy bill by purchasing natural gas under interruptable contracts which gave the suppliers the right to stop delivery during emergencies. By 1974, this rarely-used option was being used with a vengeance. In Louisiana, the average nitrogen plant was out of operation almost two months per year; in California, shutdowns were reaching three and four months per year.[66]

The natural gas industry was holding the world food supply for ransom. Unless profits on natural gas were increased, the basic raw materials for producing nitrogen would be withheld. Within about a month after fertilizer prices were freed from controls, natural gas price ceilings were raised by the government.*[67]

---

*The shortages of natural gas compounded the overall shortage of energy, resulting in about 1.5-2 million extra barrels of oil consumed per day.[68] The natural gas industry continues to threaten the nation with economic disaster, predicting that unless it is free to raise its prices at will, California alone will lose 800,000 jobs by 1981.[69] The author of the report on which this claim is supposed to be based says that the study is being totally misrepresented.[70] Those elements of the fertilizer industry which are optimistic about the future demand situation are protecting themselves against future curtailment by building their new nitrogen capacity abroad.[71] Our increasing dependence on foreign fertilizer supplies makes the U.S. vulnerable to disruptions in fertilizer imports.

The bountiful financial statements of the fertilizer industry at the time indicate that the industry was not suffering very much from inadequate supplies of natural gas; on the contrary, the natural gas suppliers appear to have done the industry a great service by restricting the supply of fertilizer. In this regard, we might note that Williams Companies, the most successful of the major fertilizer producers at the time, was getting heavily involved in the natural gas industry.[72]

No matter who was to blame, much of the burden was borne by the same Third World farmers whom the industry had been courting only months before. In 1972, fertilizer factories in the Third World had about 40 percent of their fertilizer producing capacity lying idle.[73] When energy supplies became restricted in 1973, the situation deteriorated still further.

In India, rising prices plus disruption of the domestic fertilizer industry led to a trebling of the cost of imported fertilizer between 1974 and 1975.[74] Throughout the world, farmers responded to the inflated prices of fertilizer by cutting back on consumption. In India, for example, fertilizer use declined by 9 percent between 1973-74 and 1974-75.[75]

This trend in fertilizer use had serious consequences for world food production. A pound of fertilizer, on the average, produces about 90 percent more food in the Third World than in the developed nations.[76] Since fertilizer is sold according to how much the buyer will pay rather than according to need, many Third World farmers had to drop out of the market while much of the fertilizer in the U.S. was used in ornamental cultivation. According to one Department of Agriculture report, only 85 percent of the fertilizer in the U.S. was consumed on the farm in 1973-74.[77] If the other 15 percent had been sent to the developing countries in Asia instead of being spread on cemeteries, lawns and golf courses, fertilizer consumption in those nations could have risen by 62 percent.[78]*

Some people may take heart that the cycle is now entering a new phase. The boom years have induced a new wave of investment.[80] European fertilizer producers have begun to complain that the U.S. industry is dumping phosphorous and potassium fertilizer at prices low enough to constitute unfair competition.[81] Nitrogen prices are falling, making earlier industry fears of oversupply more credible.[82]

Reviewing the cycle of boom and bust in the fertilizer industry, *Business Week* editorializes that the eventual decline in prices proves that government intervention is not always a superior means to price stability.[83] True, prices came down, just as certainly as they will go up later; but the fact that the wild gyrations of the market eventually return to the same level does not validate the market; even a broken watch tells the right time twice a day.† Instead, we must judge the market by the suffering caused by the needless instability in the system.

---

*This statistic is not accepted by at least one industry source.[79]

†Compare *Business Week's* analysis of the cyclical behavior of prices with that of the chief economic advisor to the President of the U.S.: "One of the major damages which the very sharp increases in oil prices did to our economy was that it occurred so rapidly that it distorted the whole capital structure of industry, both in the U.S. and in Western Europe

At this point, it would be appropriate to consider traditional agricultural social relations. We have seen that they were an institutional arrangement which minimized the danger of potential disruptions in the economy. Schultz recognized that within this system, peasants were extremely efficient in using the resources available to them. This efficiency is made possible by decades and even centuries of experience in a relatively static environment. Accommodation can be made for the periodic occurrence of floods or droughts because everything else is well known.

When the economy becomes more commercialized, traditional relations among producers are replaced by market relations. Planning for the sort of instability which results from market relations is much more difficult. Under these conditions, traditional peasant agriculture is not able to make maximum use of its resources.[85]

Schultz recognized the reluctance of peasants to adopt new technology because of the potential risk. To overcome their fears, government policies fell in line with Schultz's recommendation to take the appearance of risk out of the Green Revolution. Grain prices were kept artificially high, while farm input prices were kept artificially low. The apparent stability these market relationships showed was an effective device for luring peasants into a dependence on the market. Once they came to rely on the market, the cruel hoax of stability became exposed. Governments could no longer afford to subsidize the cost of fertilizer. In India, for example, if the government had continued to attempt to maintain the subsidy of fertilizer consumption at previous levels, this program would have cost the government $500 million.[86]*

The subsidies of fertilizers encouraged the Third World in the false hope that Schultz's vision of agricultural progress was valid; that cheap manufactured fertilizer would substitute for land. In following this vision, they lost sight of some of their own resources.

The significance of the recent history of the fertilizer industry cannot be understood simply in terms of the problems associated with chemical fertilizers or of an accounting of who benefits from them. We can see in the gargantuan fertilizer industry, besides its technological achievements, a display of the human ingenuity typical of capitalistic production methods. While one group of employees in this industry struggles to make the operation cheaper, another group connives to shut down factories and to manipulate supplies.

Neither group learns to tap the experience of the people who will work with or produce its product. Instead, both groups function with total

---

and Japan. I would hate to see prices come down . . . and then have the price go back up again. We would be in a state which would be worse than if in fact the prices didn't change at all."[84]

*Much of the potential social benefits from keeping fertilizer prices low is dissipated. Much of the fertilizer is used on luxury crops.[87] Also, some of the fertilizer is resold at black market prices.[88] The overall effect of resulting redistribution is unclear. In Pakistan, for example, an estimated 25 percent of the total fertilizer supplies are traded on the black market.[88]

disregard for the people affected by their work. Most damning of all, the people who control the industry stand in the way of making the production process an experience which will develop the expertise and human potential of all involved.

In modern China, we find a different set of social relations, with correspondingly different results. In the first place, substantial amounts of fertilizer are produced by recycling all unconsumed organic matter through the pig—which Mao once called a "walking fertilizer factory."[89] In addition, Chinese peasants have learned to build small (by Western standards) home-made fertilizer plants.[90] This sort of effort not only insulates China from the wild gyrations of the world fertilizer market, but it educates the people about modern technology without losing sight of the rational kernel of traditional peasant methods.[91]*

With the discovery of rich oilfields, the Chinese seem to be relying more on larger operations,[92] combined with intensive efforts at composting, as the most efficient method of providing agriculture with enough nutrients.† Since this choice is made on the basis of social needs rather than profit, it will probably prove to be the correct one for the present situation in China. The Chinese experience is of great importance, because it demonstrates the hidden potential of the people of the Third World.

FERTILIZERS FOR FERTILITY

Capitalist production, by collecting the population in great centres, and causing an ever increasing preponderance of town population . . . disturbs the circulation of matter between man and the soil; i.e., prevents the return to the soil of its elements consumed by man in the form of food and clothing; it therefore violates the conditions necessary to the lasting fertility of the soil. By this action it destroys at the same time the health of the town labourer.

—Karl Marx, *Capital.*[95]

It is no exaggeration that the problem of the conversion of the excremental wastes of towns and people and the refuse of factories into useful materials is now engaging as much of the attention of intelligent minds throughout the world as any social question.
—*Scientific American,* "Sanitary Notes—Sewerage and Sewage."[96]

The concentration of "population in great centres" is responsible, in part, for the necessity of manufactured fertilizer in the U.S. The great distances between farms and markets make the return of organic matter to the soil seem uneconomical. A U.S. government report from 1934 estimated that the shipments of produce from farms resulted in an annual loss of

---

*The withdrawal of Soviet technicians in 1960 taught China about the risks of being dependent on foreign technology. The peasant-built fertilizer plants will help to disseminate the types of expertise which are essential to a modern industry. In this sense, any lack of efficiency in this indigenous technology might be considered a form of insurance against the possible danger of being overly reliant on a technology which they cannot fully control.

In this light, we should mention that industry sources question whether even the U.S. has

more than 30 million tons of potassium, almost 40 million tons of calcium, about 12 million tons of magnesium and more than 220 million tons of organic matter from U.S. soils.[97] Had locally available animal manures not been added to the soil during that period, losses would have been significantly greater.

By contrast, in the Orient almost every pound of nutrient was returned to the soil. For example, in 1911 F. W. King estimated an almost exact balance between nutrients removed from and returned to the soil in Japan.[98]

In the U.S., the continued depletion of the soil has forced farmers to turn to the market for nutrients to make their crops grow. In effect, the process of mining the topsoil was limited by mining other resources instead. The modern commercially manufactured fertilizers help to boost crop yields and even contribute somewhat to the buildup of soil humus,[99] but they are far less effective in this respect than manures or other organic fertilizers. With the deterioration of the soil structure, soils become more susceptible to erosion.. The loss of nutrients is intensified.[100]* Manures break down slowly, gradually making nutrients available to plants. Manufactured fertilizers, on the other hand, tend to dissolve very rapidly. Because so much is made available for a brief period of time, plants can absorb only a portion of the fertility. On the average, crops in the U.S. are able to use only about one-half of all the nitrogen applied to U.S. fields.[102]

Some of the unused nitrogen percolates into the groundwater, sometimes even making it poisonous for children.[103] One study shows that the infant mortality rate for females in Illinois is 5.5 per 1000 when nitrate levels in drinking water are high, and only 2.5 in months with low nitrate levels.[104]

Runoff of fertilizers' salts increases the salinity of surface waters. In the San Francisco Bay and Delta areas, about $11 million worth of damage is borne by municipalities and industries such as commercial fishing and recreation because of excess salinity in agricultural drainage water.[105] Homeowners also are affected by salinity from fertilizers which shorten the lifetime of their plumbing fixtures. More importantly, the accumulation of salts in arid lands destroys the fertility of the soil.† Salination has already ruined many farms in California's Imperial Valley,[106] and destroyed the fertility of others in the San Joaquin Valley.[107]

---

a satisfactory understanding of the complex technology of a synthetic ammonia plant. H. S. Robinson, chief engineer of the Oil Insurance Association, suggests that U.S. technology may be overly sophisticated. He wrote, "These are 'go or no go' plants in that if any link in the rather simple chain of operations is impaired, the entire plant is shut down. Our recent experience tells us that many of these plants are almost as much 'no go' as 'go'."[93] Robinson explained that as the size and complexity of equipment increases, so does the period of idleness: "Lead time for ordering equipment, if anything, is getting longer. Not only is this true for the large, expensive items, but often minor parts can hold up the entire plant for weeks. Replacing an ammonia converter may take 12 to 18 months for delivery."[94]

†This choice does not contradict the rationale of the small-scale plants. The experience accumulated in building and operating them has been invaluable.

*Nitrogen fertilizers have other environmental effects.[101]

†This problem was briefly discussed in "The Green Revolution."

To some extent, the problem of salinity can be offset by applying more irrigation water to wash away the salts, but this method is very expensive, especially in the Western states where the shortage of water is becoming more severe.[108]* As a result, expensive desalinization plants costing as much as $100 million[109] will be required to get the salts out of the water. The bulk of the cost of desalinization facilities will not be borne by the farmers or even by the giant fertilizer manufacturers, but by the government. Once again the close relationship between the seemingly technical question of soil fertilization and the organization of society becomes apparent.

This relationship is also influential in determining the direction of research. The fertilizer industry is big business. Almost 10 billion pounds of commercial fertilizer was sold in 1973.[110] The government has not displayed much enthusiasm about pursuing any line of research which might reduce agriculture's dependence on that industry.

Biological nitrogen fixation is a case in point. Bacteria have the ability to manufacture nitrogenous fertilizers from the air without any reliance on expensive inputs. As recently as 1974, the Department of Agriculture admitted to employing the equivalent of only four full-time researchers in this area.[111] The Department argued that it had to direct its research efforts towards "more pressing needs."[112]

As a result, a major potential source of fertilizer has until recently been overlooked. Although the ability of bacterial nodules attached to the root systems has long been known, scientists have begun to learn that biological fixation is far more widespread than ever imagined. One report even found a nitrogen-fixing bacterium in the gut of a marine shipworm.[113]† According to one estimate, more than four times as much nitrogen is fixed biologically‡ as industrially.[114]

Biological nitrogen fixation is already playing a role in Asian rice paddies where blue-green algae convert about 60 kilograms of nitrogen per hectare into valuable nutrients.[115]** Undoubtedly further research in this field could considerably improve the performance of the blue-green algae. Many other crops could benefit from free nitrogen by inoculating them with cultures of nitrogen-fixing bacteria.[118]

Other nutrients cannot be produced from the air. To halt the depletion of soil fertility, nutrients either have to be mined or organic matter must be returned to the soil. The importance of the latter approach is illustra-

---

*To provide enough water for expanding municipal demands as well as agriculture is proving all but impossible for California, where water is measured in million acre feet (enough water to cover an acre of land with a million feet of water).

†This discovery helps to explain how some insects are able to survive on a wood-based diet.

‡This figure includes nitrogen fixed by lightning.

**Albert Howard, the English mycologist who devoted much of his life to scientifically investigating the interactions between the soil and organic matter, suggested research along this line in 1943.[116] Recent work suggests that nitrifying bacteria even live in the mud of streams.[117]

ted by phosphorous.* In 1974, more than 40 million tons of phosphorous was sold for agricultural purposes.[120] Presently, we have only about 60 years of known reserves of phosphorous.[121]† Many of these deposits can be mined only with considerable environmental damage.[123] Because the Florida phosphorous deposits contain 3 to 5 percent fluorine, the process of converting the rock into the fertilizer triple super-phosphate creates significant additional air pollution problems.[124]

A substantial amount of phosphorous and other nutrients could come from animal manures. A United Nations report estimated that in 1970–71 unused manures in the Third World contained 7 to 8 times the quantity of nutrients as the inorganic fertilizer used.[125]

The benefits from the utilization of the manure can be multiplied by fermenting it in the absence of oxygen. This process gives off methane gas which can be substituted for natural gas. Pacific Gas and Electric Company estimates that it could produce 30 million cubic feet of gas per day from the feedlots in three Southern California counties.[126]‡

In addition to animal manures, human excreta could be returned to the soil.** Although this practice was in use for centuries in many parts of Asia, it was rejected in the U.S. during the 19th Century for health reasons.[129] The dangers of using sewage or night soil on the land are real enough. One survey of prerevolutionary Chinese found that as much as one-third of their body weight consisted of intestinal worms.[130] Today modern techniques are available which can eliminate the dangers to human health.††

The current problem with returning sewage to the fields is not biological, but social. Industries are allowed to release high concentrations of heavy metals and chemicals into sewage systems. As a result, returning sewage to the land could injure plants or render them inedible. Since it

---

*Arnold Schultz suggests that a deficiency of phosphorous along with calcium may explain the strange behavior of the lemmings, the small rodents which periodically reduce their population through mass migrations into the sea. According to this theory, the grazing together with burrowing and tunneling reduces the organic insulation of the soil. As a result, the soil thaws deeper. Minerals then are free to leach down below the root zone. This spreading of the nutrients over a larger area results in deficiencies in the vegetation. Stress builds up leading to the population crash.[119] Phosphorous deficiencies limit the effectiveness of biological nitrogen fixation.

†This statement is not a prediction that all the world's reserves of phosphorous will be depleted in 60 years. According to the U.S. Bureau of Mines no comprehensive studies of phosphorous reserves have ever been made. The statistic above only refers to known reserves.[122]

‡This process also produces ethylene gas, which stimulates the ripening of tomatoes and also serves as a building block for many plastics.[127]

**Returning sewage to the land also increases the available amount of ground water under proper conditions. The soil acts as a living filter which purifies the water before it reaches the aquafers.[128]

††Some U.S. fields are still fertilized with untreated human excreta, because toilets are too expensive to provide. The Occupational Health and Safety Administration is trying to correct this problem,[131] but the Council on Wage and Price Stability argues that these measures are too expensive.[132]

cannot be used as fertilizer, it is discharged into waterways or piled up as sludge. The environmental damages caused by these discharges must be included in any assessment of the rationality of alternative fertilizer systems.*

Besides animal manures, organic waste products could be composted into valuable fertilizer. Compost has long been recognized as an effective source of plant nutrients, but its commercial use has been limited. The major economic disadvantage of compost is its bulkiness; rather than get involved in the time and expense of moving tons of bulky compost, most U.S. farmers prefer to order a few sacks of fertilizer.

While the reluctance to recycle organic matter might make some sense in the U.S., it is totally irrational in the Third World, where labor is cheap and abundant. The Indian government, for example, even after the experience of the fertilizer shortage, is putting an only modestly higher priority on composting. By 1978–79, it expects composting facilities to be only 50 percent larger than the small 1976 capacity of about 5 million tons.[135] Most other Third World countries do not seem to be matching even this scant effort.

The neglect of the potential of composting has been encouraged by the biases in the study of agronomy. Much of the bulk of compost consists of organic materials which are beneficial to the soil. Many agronomists forget that organic material improves the structure of the soil. In India, for example, rain is concentrated in monsoons. Manufactured fertilizers tend to wash away. Organic materials which release nutrients more slowly act as a sponge holding the valuable moisture in place. Organic materials also improve the health of the plants. Again, agronomists tend to obscure this point by analyzing fertilizer in the same terms in which it is marketed. For them, it is nothing more than a mix of so much nitrogen, potassium or phosphorous, whether it comes from the factory or the barnyard. Even today, most textbooks reflect the same state of ignorance.

This theory is now coming to grief as a consequence of new discoveries about plant feeding. Not only can plants absorb proteins and vitamins through their roots, but they even take up complex molecules through their leaves.[136]† The more complex compounds found in manures will affect plants differently than the simple salts sold by the fertilizer companies. Organic material also has the advantage of giving off carbon dioxide,‡ which stimulates plant growth. It nourishes the mycorrhizal fungi (myco = fungus; rhizal = root) which are important for the health of many plants.[138]

---

*Municipal sewer systems play an important economic role in the U.S. At the time of this writing, official unemployment rates in the U.S. exceed 8 percent. Actual rates are much higher. In 1972, Congress authorized $18 billion to be spent for the federal grants for municipal treatment plants over a 3-year period.[133] An estimated 400,000 to 650,000 jobs are generated from these sewage grants.[134] Converting these plants to nutrient delivery systems would create more jobs, but it would also involve a changeover period during which the number of jobs created would be very, very small.

†The United States Department of Agriculture has reported that plants can absorb vitamin B$_{12}$.[137]

‡Unless it has been fully decomposed before being applied to the soil.

These fungi represent an extraordinary symbiotic relationship between soil fungi and plant roots. In many ways, the fungi appear, at first glance, to be similar to other fungal parasites on plant roots, but these fungi are quite different. Sometimes they are able to produce antibiotic chemicals to limit, or even prevent, plant diseases.[139] Mycorrhizal associations allow plants which would otherwise suffer from some nutrient deficiency to get a balanced intake of plant nutrients.[140] They protect other plants by forming a dense mass of hyphae (fungus roots) which act as a mechanical barrier to harmful organisms in the soil.[141] Mycorrhizal fungi also help plants to absorb water more efficiently.[142] This property is especially important in the desert where many plants might not otherwise survive. In fact, plants growing with the aid of mycorrhizal fungi are often twice the size of plants not infected by these beneficial fungi.[143]

Some other fungi form living lassos to capture and then devour destructive nematodes.[144]* Finally, fungal roots bind soil together, thereby helping to prevent erosion.[146] In addition to the fungi, organic matter stimulates the growth of soil animals and bacteria which promote plant life.

Organic matter also contains trace elements which are important to plant and human life. Experiments with lunar soil retrieved during the Apollo program demonstrate the importance of trace minerals to plants. Low in the elements most commonly comprising fertilizers (nitrogen, phosphorous, potassium and sulfur) but rich in iron, magnesium and manganese, lunar soil was found to stimulate plant growth. Concentrations of chlorophyll and carotenoid pigments also increased.[147] The concentration of the few nutrients in commercial fertilizer seems to result in a deficiency in some other important minerals in our food, whether or not these minerals are present in the soil. A study of English vegetables, for example, revealed that they contain three times as much potassium, but only about one-half as much magnesium, one-sixth as much sodium and one-third as much copper as they did in 1940, when commercial fertilizers were less generally used.[148]

The worsening imbalances in the soil, the loss of fertility, and the loss of soil itself by erosion reflect imbalances in society. Only by recognizing that fertility and agriculture in general are social phenomena, and by treating the soil as a resource to be preserved for all people, will any progress be made.

---

*Nematodes destroy about $1.6 billion worth of crops annually. Organic decomposition also creates volatile fatty acids and phenols which can be toxic to nematodes.[145]

REFERENCES

1. Cited by Stephen Merrett, "The Growth of Indian Fertilizer Manufacture: Some Lessons for Industrial Planning," *Journal of Development Studies*, Vol. 8, No. 4 (July 1972), pp. 395–410.

2. John W. Mellor, *The New Economics of Growth: A Strategy for India and the Developing World* (Ithaca: Cornell University Press, 1976), p. 43.

3. J. D. Beaton, "Fertilizers and Their Use in the Decade Ahead," in *Proceedings, 20th Annual Meeting of the Agricultural Research Institute* (Washington, D.C.: National Academy of Sciences, October 1971).

4. See Jesse W. Markham, *The Fertilizer Industry: a Study of an Imperfect Market* (Nashville: Vanderbilt University Press, 1958), p. 211.

5. John M. Blair, *Economic Concentration: Structure, Behavior and Public Policy* (New York: Harcourt Brace Jovanovich, 1972), p. 279.

6. Amory Block Lovins, "Energy in the Real World," *Stockholm Conference* ECO (San Francisco: Friends of the Earth, December 13, 1975), p. 9.

7. Blair, *op. cit.*, p. 47.

8. Thomas O'Hanlon, "All That Fertilizer and No Place to Grow," *Fortune* (July 1968).

9. *Ibid.*

10. Lester R. Brown, "The Stork Outruns the Plow," *Colombia Journal of World Business* (January/February 1967), p. 17.

11. Lester R. Brown, "New Directions in World Agriculture," Second International Conference on War on Hunger (Washington, D.C., February 20, 1968).

12. Michael Tanzer, *The Political Economy of International Oil and the Underdeveloped Countries* (Boston: Beacon Press, 1969), chapter 19.

13. Anon., "Fertilizer Investment Seen on Rise in Developing Lands," *Report: News of the World Bank Group* (September/October 1974).

14. Merrett, *op. cit.*, pp. 405-07.

15. Bruce F. Johnston and Peter Kilby, *Agriculture and Structural Transformation: Economic Strategies for Late-Developing Countries* (New York: Oxford University Press, 1975), pp. 328-52.

16. *Ibid.*, pp. 348-52.

17. Mellor, *op. cit.*, p. 64.

18. Cited in Mellor, *op. cit.*, p. 64n.

19. Michael Tanzer, *op. cit.*, chapter 19.

20. Cited in *ibid.*, p. 255.

21. See Mellor, *op. cit.*, p. 46n.

22. Tanzer, *op. cit.*, p. 255.

23. Susan George, *How the Other Half Dies: The Real Reasons for World Hunger* (Montclair, N.J.: Allanheld, Osmun, 1977), p. 132.

24. Cited in Henry John Frundt, *American Agribusiness and U.S. Agricultural Policy*, unpublished Ph.D. dissertation, Sociology Department, Rutgers University (New Brunswick, N.J., May 1975), p. 228.

25. Anon., "U.S. Agribusiness Shows the Way," *Business Week* (January 18, 1969).

26. Lester R. Brown, *Seeds of Change* (New York: Praeger, 1970), p. 61.

27. "U.S. Agribusiness Shows the Way," *op. cit.*; and Cleaver, *op. cit.*, p. 90.

28. University of California Food Task Force, *A Hungry World: The Challenge to Agriculture*, Division of Sciences, University of California (Berkeley, July 1974), p. 99.

29. Tanzer, *op. cit.*, p. 243.

30. Mellor, *op. cit.*, p. 63.

31. Joseph W. Willett, "The Ability of the Developing Countries to Meet Their Own Agricultural Needs in the 1980's," Speech at the Canadian Agricultural Economics Society, Agricultural Institute of Canada, Quebec City, Canada (August 6, 1974).

32. "U. S. Agribusiness Shows the Way," *op. cit.*

33. Anon., "Boom in Agrichemicals," *Business Week* (June 8, 1974), pp. 52-62.

34. Mr. Neal Schenet, "The World Fertilizer Crisis," *Feeding the World's Hungry: The Challenge to Business, An International Conference Sponsored by Continental Bank, Chicago* (Chicago, May 20, 1974), p. 95.

35. David Brand, "Fertilizer Industry Warns of Shortage, Prices May Go Up Higher Than Predicted," *Wall Street Journal* (February 19, 1974).

36. Anon., "Boom in Agrichemicals," *op. cit.* (June 8, 1974), pp. 52-62.

37. "U.S. Agribusiness Shows the Way," *op. cit.*

38. Randolf Barker and Yujiro Hayami, "Price Support versus Input Subsidy for Food Self-Sufficiency in Developing Countries," *American Journal of Agricultural Economics*, Vol. 58, No. 4 (November 1976), Part I, pp. 617–28.

39. Dana Dalrymple, "Fertilizer Subsidies," *Development Digest*, Vol. 14, No. 1 (January 1976), pp. 113–24.

40. *Agricultural Statistics* (1975), p. 434.

41. Richard B. Reidinger, "Fertilizer to Remain Tight, Prices High in 1975 and 1976," *Foreign Agriculture*, Vol. 51, No. 48 (December 23, 1974).

42. Richard B. Reidinger and John P. Parker, "New Plants Up India's Fertilizer Output," *Foreign Agriculture*, Vol. 12, No. 48 (December 2, 1974).

43. Edwin M. Wheeler, President of the Fertilizer Institute in *Fertilizer Shortage Situation*, Hearings before the Subcommittee on Department Operation of the Committee on Agriculture, House of Representatives, 93rd Congress, 1st Session (September 26 and October 3, 4, and 9, 1973), p. 49.

44. Erik P. Eckholm, *Fertilizer Scarcity and the Food Outlook*, Communiqué on Development Issues, No. 26, Overseas Development Council (October 1974).

45. "Boom in Agrichemicals," *op. cit.*, p. 53.

46. Cline J. Warren and Herman Keyman, "Thriving Dutch Fertilizer Industry Plans to Expand Exports in 1975," *Foreign Agriculture*, Vol. 12, No. 47 (November 25, 1974).

47. Anon., "United States Charges Eight Potash Makers with Conspiracy," *Wall Street Journal* (June 30, 1976), p. 11.

48. Senator Mark Hatfield, *Congressional Record*, 93rd Congress, 2d Session, Vol. 120, No. 157 (October 16, 1974).

49. Bernard Gwertzman, "Milestone Pact Signed by United States and Saudi Arabia," *New York Times* (June 9, 1975), p. 1.

50. *Fertilizer Shortage Situation, op. cit.*, p. 116; also see "Why Fertilizer Is in Such Short Supply," *Business Week* (October 6, 1973), pp. 84–87.

51. *Fertilizer: Supply, Demand and Prices*, Hearing before the Subcommittee on Agricultural Credit and Rural Electrification of the Committee on Agriculture and Forestry, United States Senate, 93d Congress, 2d Session (February 19, 1974), p. 80.

52. *Ibid.*, p. 87.

53. Anon., "Why Farm Co-Ops Have Become Powerhouses," *Business Week* (June 8, 1974), p. 54.

54. See *Future Supply, Demand and Price Situation for Fertilizer, Fuel and Pesticides*, Hearings before the Subcommittee on Agricultural Credit and Rural Electrification of the Committee on Agriculture and Forestry, United States Senate, 93d Congress, 2d Session (July 24, 25, 1974), pp. 270–71.

55. Statement of Governor James Exon of Nebraska in *Fertilizer: Supply, Demand and Prices*, Hearings before the Subcommittee on Agricultural Credit and Rural Electrification of the Committee of Agriculture and Forestry of the United States Senate, Omaha, Nebraska, 93d Congress, 2d Session (March 8, 1974) (Washington, 1974), p. 239.

56. Roy Reed, "United States Fertilizer Shortage Expected to Be Damaging Many Poorer Nations," *New York Times* (April 4, 1974), p. 47.

57. Statement of John M. Hill of A.I.D. in *Fertilizer Shortage Situation, op. cit.*, p. 3.

58. *Ibid.*, p. 12.

59. United States General Accounting Office, "The Fertilizer Situation: Past, Present, and Future" (September 5, 1974).

60. Morgan Guaranty Survey, "Why Fertilizer Is Scarce" (May 1974), pp. 4–8.

61. United States Department of Agriculture, Economic Research Service, *Index Numbers of Prices Received and Paid by Farmers* (January 1965–April 1976; revised, May 28, 1976), p. 41.

62. Barry Commoner, "Energy and Rural People," Address before the National Conference on Rural America, Washington, D.C. (April 17, 1975).

63. "Boom in Agrichemicals," *op. cit.*, p. 53.

64. Williams Companies, *Annual Report* (1975).

65. *Fertilizer Shortage Situation, op. cit.,* pp. 141–65.

66. *Ibid.,* pp. 68 and 119.

67. James W. McKie, "The United States," pp. 73–90 in Raymond Vernon, ed., *The Oil Crisis* (New York: W. W. Norton, 1976), p. 75.

68. *Ibid.*

69. Anon., "The Natural Gas Shortage Gets Worse . . . Worse . . . Worse," *Business Week* (September 27, 1976).

70. Robert E. Fullen, "A Misinterpreted Report: Letter to Editor," *Business Week* (November 1, 1976).

71. "John H. Williams Gets Riches Out of the Ground," *Business Week* (October 13, 1975), pp. 73–76.

72. *Ibid.*

73. United States Department of Agriculture, Economic Research Service, *United States and World Fertilizer Outlook, 1974 and 1980,* Agricultural Economics Report No. 257 (Washington, D.C.: May 1974), p. 20.

74. John B. Parker, Jr., "Export Earnings Ease Indian Trade Problems," *Foreign Agriculture* (March 10, 1975).

75. India, 1976, New Delhi: Government of India, Ministry of Broadcasting and Information.

76. Statement of Raymond Ewell in Hearings before the Select Committee on Nutrition and Human Needs, United States Senate, 93d Congress, 2d Session, *Nutrition and the International Situation of National Nutrition Policy Study* (June 19, 1974), Part 2, p. 361.

77. United States Department of Agriculture, Economic Research Service, *Fertilizer Situation,* FS-4 (Washington, D.C.: January 1974).

78. United States Department of Agriculture, Economic Research Service, *United States and World Fertilizer Outlook, 1974 and 1980,* Agricultural Economics Report No. 257 (Washington, D.C.: May 1974), pp. 16, 22, and 24.

79. Joseph P. Sullivan, President, Estech, Inc., "Outlook for Fertilizer," *1975 Agricultural Outlook, Papers Presented at the National Agricultural Outlook Conference Sponsored by the United States Department of Agriculture* (Washington, D.C.: December 9-12, 1974), pp. 105–10.

80. Anon., "Why the Fertilizer Forecast Was Wrong," *Business Week* (April 19, 1976).

81. Anon., "Unfair Competition in Fertilizer Sales?" *Business Week* (July 5, 1976).

82. Anon., "John H. Williams Gets Riches Out of the Ground," *Business Week* (October 13, 1975), pp. 76–77.

83. Anon., "Economics Lesson," *Business Week* (October 10, 1975), p. 146.

84. Alan Greenspan, Chairman, Council of Economic Advisors (June 10, 1976), in "Notes from the Joint Economic Committee, United States Congress," Vol. 11, No. 14 (August 1976), p. 27.

85. Scott R. Dittrich and Ramon H. Myers, "Resource Allocation in Traditional Agriculture: Republican China, 1937-1940," *Journal of Political Economy,* Vol. 79, No. 4 (July/August 1971).

86. Dalrymple, "Fertilizer Subsidies," *op. cit.,* p. 118.

87. Dana G. Dalrymple, *Evaluating Fertilizer Subsidies in Developing Countries,* A.I.D. Discussion Paper No. 30, United States State Department (Washington, D.C.: July 1975), pp. 33–35 and 60.

88. *Ibid.,* p. 20. Muhammad Afzal *et al., The Pricing of Agricultural Capital Inputs in Pakistan* (Islamabad: Pakistan Institute of Development Economics), pp. 15–17.

89. Cited in John Neville Maxwell, "Learning frpm Tachai," *World Development,* Vol.

90. Eric Simon, "A Peasant-Built Ammonia Plant," *Chemical Technology,* Vol. 5, No. 10 (October 1975), pp. 582–84.

91. See Julian M. Sobin, "China: the fertile market," China Trade Report of the *Far Eastern Economic Review* (June 1976) reprinted by International Minerals and Chemical Corporation, Boston, Mass.

92. See Kang Chao, "The Production and Application of Chemical Fertilizers in China," *The China Quarterly*, No. 64 (December 1975), pp. 721–29.

93. Cited in John M. Blair, *Economic Concentration: Structure, Behavior and Public Policy* (New York: Harcourt Brace Jovanovich, 1972), pp. 92–93.

94. *Ibid.*

95. Karl Marx, *Capital*, Vol. 1 (Chicago: Kern, 1906), p. 554.

96. Scientific American, "Sanitary Notes—Sewerage and Sewage," *Scientific American*, n.s., Vol. 28 (June 28, 1873), p. 405.

97. National Resource Board Report, December 1934, cited in Richard T. Ely and George S. Wehrwein, *Land Economics* (Madison: University of Wisconsin Press, 1964), p. 209.

98. F. W. King, *Farmers of Forty Centuries: or Permanent Agriculture in China, Korea and Japan* (Emmaus, Pa.: Rodale Press, n.d.), p. 215.

99. See S. R. Aldrich, "Some Effects of Crop-Production on Environmental Quality," *BioScience*, Vol. 22, No. 2 (February 1972), pp. 90–95.

100. National Academy of Sciences, Committee on Agriculture and the Environment, *Productive Agriculture and a Quality Environment* (Washington, D.C.: N.A.S., 1974), p. 53.

101. John Phillips, "Problems in the Use of Chemical Fertilizers," in M. Taghi Farvar and John P. Milton, eds., *The Careless Technology: Ecology and International Development* (Garden City, N.Y.: Natural History Press, 1972), pp. 549–66.

102. Edward Groth, III, "Increasing the Harvest," *Environment*, Vol 17, No. 1 (January/February 1975).

103. Barry Commoner, *The Closing Circle* (New York: Bantam, 1971), chapter 5.

104. *Ibid.*, p. 90.

105. See Gerald L. Horner, "Internalizing Agricultural Nitrogen Pollution Externalities: A Case Study," *American Journal of Agricultural Economics*, Vol. 57, No. 1 (February 1975), pp. 33–39.

106. See Thomas W. Bush, "Salt Turning the Imperial Valley Bitter—Salinity Driving High Value Crops Out of Area, Farmers Complain," *Los Angeles Times* (October 20, 1968).

107. California Department of Water Resources, "Status of San Joaquin Valley Drainage Problems," Bulletin No. 227-74, Sacramento (December 1974).

108. See Jay Noel, Charles V. Moore, Frank Robinson and J. H. Snyder, "Effect of Water Quality and Irrigation Frequency on Farm Income in the Imperial Valley," *California Agriculture* (November 1975).

109. Stanton D. Anderson, Acting Assistant Secretary, Department of Interior, and John C. Whitaker, Under Secretary, Department of Interior, "Letter to Carl Albert, Speaker of the House of Representatives, 7 February 1974," in Subcommittee on Water Resources of the Committee on Insular Affairs, House of Representatives, *Colorado River Basin Salinity Control Act, Hearings*, 93d Congress, 2d Session (March 4, 5, and 8, 1974), pp. 59–63.

110. *Agricultural Statistics, 1975.*

111. T. W. Edminister, Director, Department of Agriculture, Agricultural Research Service, "Letter to George McGovern, 9 April 1974," in Subcommittee on Agricultural Credit and Rural Electrification of the Committee on Agriculture and Forestry, United States Senate, *Future Supply-Demand Situation for Fertilizer, Fuel and Pesticides*, 93d Congress, 2d Session (July 25 and 27, 1974).

112. *Ibid.*

113. Edward J. Carpenter and John L. Culliney, "Nitrogen Fixation in Marine Shipworms," *Science*, Vol. 187, No. 4176 (February 14, 1975), pp. 551–52.

114. R. W. F. Hardy and U. D. Havelka, "Nitrogen Fixation Research: A Key to World Food?" *Science*, Vol. 188, No. 4188 (May 1975), pp. 633–43.

115. Robert F. Chandler, Jr., "New Developments in Rice Research," *The Agribusiness Council, Agricultural Initiative in the Third World: A Report on a Conference* (Lexington, Mass.: Lexington Books, 1975), p. 33.

116. Albert Howard, *An Agricultural Testament* (Emmaus, Pa.: Special Rodale Press Re-edition, 1972), pp. 15-16.

117. Collier Carbon and Chemical Corporation, Los Angeles, *Planet N. Abstracts*, Vol. 6, No. 11 (n.d.).

118. Rex L. Smith, J. H. Boulton, S. C. Schank and K. H. Queensberry, "Nitrogen Fixation in Grasses Inoculated with *Spirillum lipoferum*," *Science*, Vol. 193 (September 10, 1976).

119. See Arnold M. Schultz, "The Nutrient-Recovery Hypothesis for Arctic Microtine Cycles, II: Ecosystem Variables in Relation to Arctic Microtine Cycles," in D. J. Crisp, ed., *Grazing in Terrestrial and Marine Ecosystems* (Oxford: Blackwell, 1964), pp. 57-68.

120. *Agricultural Statistics, 1975*, p. 469.

121. Institute of Ecology, *Man in the Living Environment, Report on the Workshop on Global Ecological Problems* (Madison, Wisc.: Institute of Ecology, 1971), pp. 48-59. A recent cartel of major phosphate producers has been formed. See Anon., "Cartel Formed," *The Elements* (January 1977), p. 12.

122. James Ridgeway, "Stripmine," *Elements*, No. 30 (May 1977).

123. Neil Maxwell, "Conservation vs. Fertilizer: Fierce Opposition to New Mining Stymies Phosphate Industry Expansion in Florida," *Wall Street Journal* (July 14, 1976), p. 34.

124. Thomas D. Crocker and A. J. Rogers III, *Environmental Economics* (Hinsdale, Ill.: Dryden Press, 1971), p. 96.

125. Jeff Cox, "A New Understanding of Soil Health," *Environmental Action Bulletin* (May 17, 1975).

126. Timothy C. Gardner, "Converting Manure to Fuel," *San Francisco Chronicle* (November 1, 1976), p. 57.

127. Anon., "Energy Roundup," *Business Week* (September 8, 1975).

128. Lewis T. Kardos, "A New Prospect," *Environment*, Vol. 12, No. 2 (March 1970).

129. Joel A. Tarr, "From City to Farm: Urban Wastes and the American Farmer," *Agricultural History*, Vol. 49, No. 4 (October 1975), pp. 598-612.

130. John Cameron Scott, *Health and Agriculture in China* (London: Faber, 1952).

131. *Federal Register*, Vol. 41, No. 82 (April 27, 1976), pp. 17576-80.

132. Council on Wage and Price Stability, "Comments before the Occupational Safety and Health Administration and Press Release" (August 6, 1976).

133. Council on Environmental Quality, *Environmental Quality, 1975: The Sixth Annual Report on the Council on Environmental Quality* (1975), p. 68.

134. Council on Environmental Quality, *Environmental Quality, 1976: The Seventh Annual Report of the Council on Environmental Quality* (1976), p. 153. See also Robert Ball and Joseph T. Finn, "Labor and Materials Requirements for Sewer Works Construction," *Monthly Labor Review*, Vol. 99, No. 11 (November 1976), pp. 38-41. This report stresses the labor-saving innovations in this field.

135. Government of India, Ministry of Information and Broadcasting, *India, 1976*, p. 186. See also Glen Ames, "Can Organic Manures Improve Crop Production in Southern India?" *Compost Science*, Vol. 17, No. 2 (March-April 1976), pp. 7011.

136. M. M. Kononova, *Soil Organic Matter: Its Nature, Its Role in Soil Formation and Fertility*, 2d ed., trans. Nowakowski and Newman (Oxford: Pergamon Press, 1966), p. 215.

137. See United States Department of Agriculture, Agricultural Research Service, *The Effects of Soils and Fertilizers on the Nutritional Quality of Plants*, Agricultural Information Bulletin No. 299 (October 1965).

138. Albert Howard, *op. cit.*, pp. 62, 100 and 166.

139. N.C. Schneck, "Mycorrhizal Fungi," *Sunshine State Agricultural Report* (November 1970), pp. 12-15.

140. *Ibid.*

141. Edward Hackskayle, "Mycorrhiza: The Ultimate in Reciprocal Parasitism?" *Bio-Science*, Vol. 22, No. 10 (October 1972), pp. 577-83.

142. R. R. Safir *et al.*, "Mycorrhizal Enhancement of Water Transport in Soybean," *Science*, Vol. 172, p. 581.

143. Schneck, *op. cit.*

144. C. L. Duddington, *The Friendly Fungi* (London: Faber, 1957), chapter 2.

145. See Anon., "Organic Soil Conditioners Reduce Root-Knot Damage on Plants, Say USDA Researchers," *Organic Farming and Gardening* (December 1974), p. 8; and anon., "Soil Amendments Reduce Root-Knots," *Agricultural Research* (October 1974), p. 17.

146. Kononova, *op. cit.*, p. 200.

147. Michael Blake, *Concentrated Incomplete Fertilizers* (London: Crosby Lockwood, 1967), p. 14.

148. C. H. Walkinshaw *et al.*, "Results of Apollo 11 and 12 Quarantine Studies on Plants," *BioScience*, Vol. 20, No. 24 (December 15, 1970), pp. 1297–1302; and John D. Weete and Charles H. Walkinshaw, "Apollo 12 Lunar Material: Effects on Plant Pigment," *Canadian Journal of Botany*, Vol. 50, No. 1 (1972), pp. 101–04.

16

THE HIDDEN POWER
OF THIRD WORLD AGRICULTURE

Frankly, I think the agricultural system we've been following is self defeating. We've been concentrating on an elite—but "trickle down" doesn't work.

As regards China: they have put *every* resource into farm level development—to the extent of putting every research scientist into the field. And they are carrying the people with them. My question is: Can we come up with a system *fast enough* to keep this system from overwhelming us?

—Sterling Wortman, Vice President of
the Rockefeller Foundation[1]

An Asian educated in the West recently had dinner with Mao after having spent a week studying the agricultural system of China. Mao asked the visitor what was the primary lesson he had drawn from his examination. The visitor suggested that Mao make some of his agricultural experts available to the Third World. Mao said that the primary impression should have been that the complex system the Chinese use had evolved over many years and had entailed many mistakes. Mao said that it would be wrong to attempt to apply the Chinese approach elsewhere, and the only thing that was replicable from the Chinese experience was the slow, painful, dialectical process of experimentation that the Chinese had pursued over a number of years.

—Elliot R. Morss[2]

The agricultural potential of the Third World is truly phenomenal. To show how scientific methods could revolutionize agricultural production in the Third World, Richard Bradfield, an agronomist working in the Philippines, demonstrated that a single acre of land was capable of growing two to four tons of rice, 10 tons of sweet potatoes, one ton of soybeans, plus 18,000 ears of sweet corn and 6,000 pounds of soybean pods,[3] enough calories for 29 people and enough protein for 53.[4] The same acre produced about 13 tons of stalks, vines and leaves which could nourish livestock. Production could be intensified still further by draining the manure into ponds which would yield at least a ton of fish per acre.[5]

We must be careful not to turn this experiment into the doctrine that modern inputs and science are sufficient for development. Technology is, of course, not neutral. It affects each class differently. The specific technology used by Bradfield may not be appropriate for agriculture in the Third World. This particular experiment relied heavily on expensive chemicals, and the amount of labor is not given. Nevertheless, it does demonstrate the type of results which can be expected from the application of scientific methods in the Third World.

The lack of scientific work on plants specifically tailored to the needs of the Third World is a significant handicap, because the crops which form the basis of temperate agriculture have been selected to take full advantage of the concentration of photosynthetic activity during the four- to eight-month growing season typical of the temperate lands.[6] Since many tropical lands have the potential of a year-long growing season, much of the work which has gone into developing crops suited for temperate agriculture is not of much value for the environment of the tropics.*

Instead of attempting, for example, to produce vegetable oils from soybeans, which do well in temperate zones, the Third World can turn to crops such as the oil palm. An acre of palm oil trees in Malaysia produces about 12 times as much oil as a soybean field of comparable size.[8]† We might expect that this exceptional performance would be a cause for rejoicing. Here is a poor Third World nation which is able to produce a major product at a substantially cheaper cost than the most advanced nation in the world—yet the official reaction in the U.S. was chilling.

Rather than applauding the prospect in increasing agricultural exports, the Department of Agriculture questioned the wisdom of the World Bank in financing the expansion of the palm oil plantings. The Department demanded that:[10]

. . . extreme caution should be taken when providing assistance for production aimed at export. In such circumstances, care should be taken to avoid disrupting markets of other exporters.

Both the palm oil plantings and Bradfield's experiment demonstrate the ability to multiply the productive capacity of Third World agriculture. Other technologies of the simplest type could substantially improve the availability of food in the Third World. In India, where harvests are notoriously erratic, a simple program of grain storage could do much to

---

*Tree crops and other perennials would appear to have more of an advantage in the tropics. Besides the ability of nondeciduous trees to take advantage of the twelve-month growing season, such crops do not require annual plowing which takes so much energy and lays the soil bare to erosion.[7]

†Because the quality of soybean meal is superior to that of the palm oil fruit, the value of an acre of oil palms is only about four times as much as an acre of soybeans.[9]

eliminate the disasters resulting from periodic shortfalls in grain production. Facilities for storing the 1976 Indian grain crop were so inadequate that grain was kept in ballrooms and dining halls.[11] A total of 5 million tons of grains was estimated to be rotting under tarps, according to the U.S. Department of Agriculture.[12] So much of this grain was lost that 1975–76 imports of rice were expected to rise by 14 percent.[13] Even Bangladesh could not store all the grain it had on hand in mid-1976. As a result, the U.S. Department of Agriculture had to halt all shipments to that nation.[14]

According to the President's Science Advisory Committee appointed by President Johnson, reducing worldwide storage losses would save 55 million tons of grain. Distributing this grain among the needy could bring the diets of 500 million people up to an adequate caloric level.[15] Of course, the construction of adequate storage capacity is just a temporary stopgap. To develop the full potential of Third World agriculture requires deeper social and political changes which are not always desired by the ruling classes. Bhaduri has shown why money lenders who control the villages in West Bengal strongly resist economic progress which would let the poor farmers escape from their deep indebtedness.[16]* Richard Franke confirmed the same phenomenon in Java, where wealthy landlords were able to keep poor families from taking advantage of government programs to supply the needy with cheap credit and access to modern technology.[18]

In 1963, 12 students at the Indonesian Institute of Agriculture at Bogor demonstrated the agricultural potential of social and political action. To help the peasants, they chose to live and work in the villages near the school. Besides offering technical advice on farming, they attempted to eliminate the institutional disadvantages of the peasants by forcefully interceding with local government and private organizations on the peasants' behalf.[19] As a result, yields rose by an astounding 50 percent. Within a year, the Indonesian Department of Agriculture took over the program, and by September 1965, about 1,200 students were participating.†

The economic potential of political action can be seen most clearly in land reform policies. In spite of the commitment of an ever-expanding portion of the land in the Third World for the production of luxury crops for Europe and the U.S., the Third World still has a reservoir of idle land. A 1962 report of the United Nations Food and Agricultural Organization

---

*Marx had already dealt with the usurer's disinterest in accelerating economic development,[17] but a complete analysis of the conflicts of interest with the ruling class of the Third World and between the ruling classes of the Third World and capitalist nations has yet to be worked out. Merchants, employers in the cities and others generally benefit from the Green Revolution. Others engaged in supplying traditional inputs might be threatened. Much more work on this subject remains to be done.

†Its success was tragically cut short by the overthrow of the government and the subsequent slaughter of between 200,000 and 1,000,000 known or suspected communists on Java alone.

estimated that only about 45 percent of the potential cropland in the Third World was then being cultivated. Although some expenses would be incurred in bringing parts of this land into production, the FAO calculates that about 12 to 16 million acres could be brought into production at a reasonable cost.[20]

Besides land which lies idle, many people are idle in the Third World. No technical genius is required to know that if these unemployed people are given a chance to farm previously uncultivated land, they can increase food production.* Of course, some of this land would take time before it would be ready for cultivation.

The Third World has the capacity to increase production significantly even without increasing the area used for agriculture. To begin with, it could take advantage of the frequently confirmed fact that yields per acre are highest on small farms.[21] Small farms have the added advantage of consuming fewer industrial inputs, in effect relying on labor instead of manufactured materials and producing more food with fewer resources.† Consequently, a greater reliance on the small farm can increase employment at the same time as the requirements for manufactured agricultural inputs are reduced. The industrial capacity freed by such a policy could be used to increase the rate of investment and/or raise the levels of consumption.

The actual performance of small farms in the Third World is better than official statistics indicate. Crops grown for home consumption or the production of clothing or furniture are often overlooked when the criterion of output per acre is used. The amount of labor required for small farm production is easily overstated, because the farm family labor force often includes children or aged workers. A further overestimate of the labor involved in small-scale agriculture in the Third World arises where farmers devote part of their labor to other employments. In Asia, for example, many small farmers hire themselves out to larger farmers for part of the year. A 1938 survey of Ghanian cocoa farmers confirmed the importance of outside employment in that nation. About one-third of the farmers earned a significant portion of their income from other occupations, working as palm wine tappers, armadillo hunters, masons, and so on.[23] A later survey of Nigerian cocoa farmers found a higher proportion engaged in employments off the farm.‡

Land reform entails an upheaval in social relations. Large landholders are made obsolete; unemployed and underemployed workers become productive; and, as was just mentioned, society produces more food with fewer resources. Nevertheless, land reform does not require a thoroughgoing revolution in social relations, and it is for this reason that many

---

*Keeping in mind that poor peasant farmers consume very few agricultural inputs.

†Hassain's study of Bangladesh and Berry's work on Colombia both indicate that the small farm (over 2.5-5.0 acres) consumes fewer resources even if labor, valued at the wage rate, is included as a resource.[22]

‡J. D. Gould points out that early estimates of economic activity in India, as well as Meiji, Japan, suffer from this same bias.[24]

reformers have embraced land reform as a means of increasing economic productivity. It remains a limited solution, however. To harness the hidden power of Third World agriculture requires a total transformation of social relations.

Nowhere has the transformation of agriculture been more complete than in China. The demands of landlords, moneylenders, merchants and government officials consumed about one quarter of the national income.[25] Tapping this pool of wealth by restructuring social relations allowed the Chinese to substantially increase the standard of living of the masses at the same time as the level of investment was doubled.[26] The previously wasted potential of unemployed workers, averaging almost two months per year for every able-bodied man[27] was mobilized for productive activities. Barry Richman, a professor of management at UCLA, has pointed out that the most important of all the changes in the Chinese economy has been the success of the government in inspiring the vast majority of the people to work for the common goal of economic and social development.[28]

A striking example of this new mentality is the case of Tachai, a village of 88 households located on a barren hillside strewn with rocks. Traditionally the area had been one of the poorest in China, with only about 140 to 150 frost-free days a year.[29] The peasants of Tachai literally remade their environment, carving terraces out of the mountains by hand. In 1955, the peasants set to work terracing the hills and gullies which made up the bulk of the village farmland. Even in subzero temperatures the peasants carved their fields out of barren lands of Tachai with only hand tools and wheelbarrows for equipment. The following spring flash floods washed away the terraces and stone walls. Undaunted, they rebuilt the terraces. Again in 1963, a week-long deluge washed away 90 percent of their work.[30] Again the people rebuilt their terraces, with no help from the central government except for some assistance in building an irrigation canal. Each acre of land required at least 1,200 worker days to complete.[31]

The transformation of Tachai from a mountainous wasteland to a food exporter demonstrates the potential of Third World agriculture.* Progress in Tachai cannot be credited to new technology. The Chinese have discovered that raising the consciousness of the people is far more effective than adopting modern equipment.[33]† In Mao's words, "We pay chief attention to the revolution of man's thinking and, through this

---

*Reclamation projects are not limited to Tachai. China reports that in the period between October 1975 and the end of January 1976, China added and improved 2 million hectares of irrigated land, freed 1.3 million hectares from waterlogging, transformed another 1.3 million hectares of low-yielding fields, terraced 1 million hectares and levelled 4.6 million acres. In Kiangsu Province and the suburban areas of Shanghai, where the land is already improved, the government is planning to produce more land capable of yielding 15 tons of grain per hectare.[32]

†Although the commune uses some modern inputs, they were not a major factor in its success. On the other hand, most observers agree that the nature of the work in China has been altered to make it as pleasant as possible.[34]

command, guide and promote the work of mechanization and modernization."[35] As a result, the Chinese have been able to dissipate much of the
mutual suspicion and distrust which plagued the traditional village.[36]*

In practice, the Chinese model for development engages the masses of
people in the actual decision-making process. For example, China
estimates that more than 10 million workers are engaged in scientific
experiments.[39]† Only a small portion of these people are trained scientists; some, no doubt, are illiterate; yet their contributins are vital to the
Chinese success. Besides increasing the awareness of workers who are
engaged in research projects, this degree of mass participation serves to
educate the experts.[41] For instance, a practical observation by workers
with experience in growing melons taught the experts the importance of
digging the soil very deeply to minimize the dangers of flooding and to
conserve valuable moisture.[42]‡

The results of the Chinese system have been extraordinary. Flies and
mosquitos** have been virtually eliminated in China.[45] A combination
of human efforts plus astute application of biological forces minimizes
the requirements for pesticides. To control insect pests, ducks are herded
through rice paddies, turning insects into a traditional Chinese delica-
cy.[46] As a result, insecticide use on early rice has been cut by 87 percent.[47]

Sterling Wortman, vice president of the Rockefeller Foundation, was
surprised that he "didn't see a bad field of rice in all of China."[48] Unlike
many other parts of the Third World, agricultural progress has occurred
in China. In Tachai, with its unfavorable climate, grain fields reached
8.25 tons/hectare,[49] slightly higher than corn yields in the most productive state in the U.S. during the same year.[50] As a result of progress in
agriculture, nutrition has improved in China.[51] Infants and children are
now substantially taller and heavier than before the revolution.[52]

The Chinese system is also paying unexpected environmental dividends. Although Marx had analyzed ecological mismanagement as a
symptom of capitalistic social relations,[53] most socialists forgot this
aspect of Marxism until after the Chinese revolution. In China, the
people are told that pollutants are nothing more than useful products for
which no purpose has been discovered. They are asked to use their
ingenuity to turn waste products into useful by-products.[54]

---

*In Tachai, villagers joined the collective once they discovered that yields were lower on
private plots. Another benefit of collectivization was the elimination of the inefficiencies
resulting from extreme fragmentation of the land. In 1974, the village was divided into
about 50 plots per household.[37] This situation is not exceptional. One small farmer in India
is known to have worked 200 tiny plots of land scattered around his village.[38]

†Although the active participation of the working class in scientific affairs is uncommon today, the working class made significant contributions to English science during the
sixteenth century.[40]

‡Development economists give wide credence to a story about an Indian soil scientist who
continued to have his soil samples sent from New York to extend his doctoral research.[43]
The contrast between this scientist, whether he is apocryphal or not, and the workers of
Tachai reveals much about the divergent paths of India and China.

**The elimination of the mosquito may have some harmful consequences, however,
especially for fish.[44]

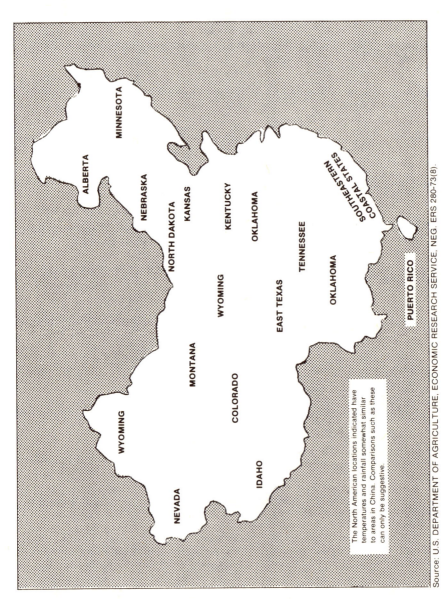

The North American locations indicated have temperatures and rainfall somewhat similar to areas in China. Comparisons such as these can only be suggestive.

FIGURE 4   United States and China: Climatic Analogues

Source: U.S. DEPARTMENT OF AGRICULTURE, ECONOMIC RESEARCH SERVICE, NEG. ERS 280-73(8).

The Chinese are making great strides in recycling human wastes. The government estimates that human feces and urine together are capable of replacing an annual production of 10 million tons of ammonium sulfate fertilizer.[55] The cost of producing a factory with a comparable capacity would come to almost $1 billion.[56] This estimate seriously understates the value of the resulting fertilizer. In the first place, this fertilizer would be superior to a corresponding amount of inorganic materials because of the other elements it contains. In addition, the Chinese have learned to extract silver, mercury and other metals from sewage, thereby converting potentially harmful contaminants into economically useful materials.[57] Harmful pollutants from industrial smokestacks have been turned into fertilizers.[58]* For example, workers in the Tientsin Chemical Works succeeded in producing precipitated calcium sulfate and ammonium humate from waste hydrochloric acid. Subsequently they assisted two production brigades of a rural people's commune set up two fertilizer factories using the wastes as raw materials.[59]

The phenomenal success of China is built on an environmental consciousness which contrasts sharply with that which is typical of profit-oriented societies. To be sure, the Chinese mine fossil fuels to some extent, and even look forward to a rapid development of their energy industries; but great efforts are made to eliminate the needless use of resources. The emphasis on reusing waste products has transformed the country into a national recycling center. As a result, the Chinese have succeeded in building up the stocks of some resources, especially topsoil.

Rather than calculate the appropriate rate of resource depletion, as was suggested by Professor Scoville (cited in the section on mining), the leader of the Tachai commune echoed the environmental vision of Marx. In evaluating the 1,200 days required to terrace an acre of land, he suggested that the immediate benefits might not justify the effort: "We must look farther ahead; we must ask how much food this land could produce over the next 50 years."[63]† In fact, Tachai is now tearing down some of its terraces in order to transform the landscape more radically. As a means of erosion control, the soil from the tops of hills is being used to fill gullies.[65]

The Chinese are also building up their environmental resources through a massive program of reforestation. In Hunan Province, with a population about two-thirds that of Britain, the amount of *new* forest planted since 1964 exceeds the total forested area of Britain.[66]

While other nations appoint commissions and hold conferences about the environment, the Chinese are actually building their natural resource

---

*The Chinese consider chemical fertilizers harmful when overused. Western observers dismiss the Chinese concerns as "peasant superstition,"[60] or as "rationalization,"[67] but the leaders of the Tachai commune describe how the soil becomes "like steel slabs" when too much chemical fertilizer is applied.[62]

†This perspective is not inconsistent with modern economic theory. One critic of the Scoville article argued that the future benefits of building up the soil might well invalidate Scoville's justification of mining.[64] In practice, Scoville's analysis still reflects the underlying reality of economic behavior in this economy. The high discount rate common to capitalist economies makes future benefits fall into insignificance except when the payoff is extraordinarily large.

base at the same time in which they are recognizing the dignity of the workers who toil on the land. Here is the potential of Third World agriculture!

REFERENCES

1. Sterling Wortman, Vice President of the Rockefeller Foundation, *Second Bellagio Conference: Strategies for Agricultural Education in the Developing Countries* (New York: Rockefeller Foundation, January 1976), p. 40.

2. Elliot R. Morss, reported in *Land Tenure Center, Newsletter*, University of Wisconsin, No. 19 (July-September 1975), pp. 10-11.

3. Caroll P. Streeter, *Reaching the World's Small Farmers: A Special Report from the Rockefeller Foundation* (New York: Rockefeller Foundation, March 1975), chapter 7.

4. Richard Bradfield, "Increasing Food Production in the Tropics by Multiple Cropping," in Daniel G. Aldrich Jr., ed., *Research for the World Food Crisis, American Association for the Advancement of Science Symposium*, Vol. 92 (Washington, D.C.: AAS, 1970), pp. 229-42, and Streeter, *op. cit.*

5. Bradfield, *op. cit.*, and Streeter, *op. cit.* For a description of the potential of recycling by way of ponds and even producing energy from the system, see Jose A. Eusebop, B. Rabino, and E. C. Eusebio, "Recycling system in integrated plant and animal farming," Technical Report, Vol. 1, No. 1 (Laguna: University of the Philippines at Los Banos College, n.d.).

6. See David Gates, "The Flow of Energy," *Scientific American*, Vol. 225, No. 3 (September 1971).

7. For an analysis of the potential of trees, see J. Russell Smith, *Tree Crops: A Key to a Permanent Agriculture* (New York: Devin Adair, 1953).

8. United States Department of Agriculture, Economic Research Service, *Analysis of Fats and Oils Industry to 1980 with Implications for Palm Oil Imports*, ERS-627 (May 1976), p. 14.

9. *Ibid.*

10. Richard E. Bell, Assistant Secretary of Agriculture for International Affairs and Commodity Programs, "Statement before U.S. House of Representatives, Committee on Agriculture, Subcommittee on Oil Seeds and Rice" (March 1976), reprinted in *Foreign Agriculture*, Vol. 14, No. 15 (April 12, 1976).

11. Anon., "India Achieves the Impossible Dream, It Has Food to Spare," *New York Times* (June 21, 1974), p. 4.

12. United States Department of Agriculture, "Weekly Roundup of Production and Trade" (June 16, 1976).

13. John B. Parker Jr., "India Increases Imports of Grain," *Foreign Agriculture*, Vol. 34, No. 23 (August 23, 1976). Parker gives other reasons for expanded demand for imports. See also Robert C. Tetro, "Bumper Grain Crops Strain India's Storage Capacity," *Foreign Agriculture*, Vol. 14, No. 12 (October 18, 1976).

14. Anon., "U.S. Delays Sending Grain to Bangladesh," *San Francisco Chronicle* (June 23, 1976), p. 19; Subcommittee on Foreign Assistance of the Committee on Foreign Relations, U.S. Senate, *Commodity Storage Conditions in Bangladesh, A Staff Report*, 94th Congress, 2d Session (September 1976); Denis M. Neill, Assistant Administrator, Agency for International Development, "Letter to Senator Henry Bellmon" (January 13, 1977). See also Barry Kramer, "Still Surviving, Despite Many Political Woes, Bangladesh is Stirring Unexpected Optimism," *Wall Street Journal* (December 29, 1976).

15. President's Science Advisory Committee, *The World Food Problem*, Vol. II, *Report of the Panel on the World Food Supply* (Washington, D.C.: The White House, May 1967), p. 554.

16. A. Bhaduri, "Agricultural Backwardness Under Semi-Feudalism," *Economic Journal*, Vol. 33, No. 329 (March 1973), pp. 120–37.

17. Karl Marx, *Capital*, Vol. 1 (Chicago: Kerr, 1906), p. 183.

18. Richard W. Franke, "Miracle Seeds and Shattered Dreams in Java," *Natural History*, Vol. 83, No. 11 (January, 1974).

19. *Ibid.*

20. Anon., "An Elusive Balance," *The Farm Index*, Vol. 14, No. 2 (February 1975).

21. See R. Albert Berry, "Cross Country Evidence on Farm Size/Factor Productivity Relationships in Developing Nations," in George F. Patrick *et al.*, eds., *Small Farm Agriculture: Studies in Developing Nations*, Purdue University, Department of Agricultural Economy, Station Bulletin No. 101, West La Fayette, Indiana (September 1975), pp. 3–27; Erven J. Long, "The Economic Basis of Land Reform in Underdeveloped Economies," *Land Economics* (May 1961), pp. 113–23; James P. Grant, "Growth From Below: A People-Oriented Development Strategy," Overseas Development Council Occasional Paper No. 16 (December 1963); Peter Dorner, *Land Reform and Economic Development* (Baltimore: Penguin, 1972), chapter 5.

22. Mahabub Hassain, "Farm Size and Productivity in Bangladesh: A Case of Phulpur Farms," *The Bangladesh Economic Review*, Vol. 11, No. 1 (January 1974), pp. 469–500; and Albert Berry, "Farm Size, Income Distribution and the Efficiency of Agricultural Production: Colombia," *American Economic Review*, Vol. 72, No. 2 (May 1972), pp. 403–8.

23. Johnston and Kilby, *op. cit.*, p. 26.

24. J. D. Gould, *Economic Growth in History* (London: Methuen, 1972), p. 78.

25. See Leon Stover, *The Cultural Ecology of Chinese Civilization, Peasants and Elites in the Last of the Agrarian States* (New York: New American Library, 1974), p. 183. The potential of cutting off the demands of unproductive elements in society is not limited to China. Keith Griffin estimates that about 15 percent of the value of agriculture in West Pakistan was siphoned out of the countryside. Of that flow, about 80 percent was used for luxury consumption in urban areas. See Keith Griffin, *The Political Economy of Agrarian Change: An Essay on the Green Revolution* (Cambridge: Harvard University Press, 1974), p. 119.

26. Victor Lippit, *Land Reform and Economic Development in China* (White Plains, N.Y.: International Arts and Sciences Press, 1975), p. 157.

27. R. P. Sinha, "Chinese Agriculture: Past Performance and Future Outlook," *Journal of Agricultural Economics*, Vol. 25, No. 1 (January 1974), pp. 37–52.

28. Barry Richman, "Chinese and Indian Development: An Interdisciplinary Environmental Analysis," presented at the American Association for the Advancement of Science Meeting, San Francisco (March 24-April 1, 1974).

29. Ch'en Yung-kei, "On Scientific Farming," *Chinese Economic Studies*, Vol. 6 (Summer 1973), pp. 56–74; and Chia Wen-Ling, "The Story of Tachai," from his *The Seeds and Other Stories* (Peking: Foreign Language Press, 1972), pp. 168–93, reprinted in David Milton, Nancy Milton and Franz Schurman, *People's China* (New York: Vintage, 1974), pp. 39–43.

30. Neville Maxwell, "Learning from Tachai," *World Development*, Vol. 3, Nos. 7, 8 (July–August 1975), pp. 473–95.

31. Ch'en, *op. cit.*

32. Anon., "Large-Scale Winter Farmland Capital Construction," *Peking Review*, Vol. 19, No. 14 (April 2, 1976), p. 3.

33. Benedict Stavis, *Making Green Revolution: The Politics of Agricultural Development in China*, Cornell University, Rural Development Committee Monograph Series, Rural Development Monograph No. 1 (Ithaca, N.Y.: 1974), p. 97.

34. John Gurley, "Capitalist and Maoist Economic Development," *Monthly Review*, Vol. 22, No. 9 (February 1971), pp. 15–35; and Arthur Galston, "Down on the Commune," *Natural History* (October 1972), pp. 50–59.

35. Cited in Gurley, *op. cit.*

36. On this, see Stover, *op. cit.*, p. 136.

37. Maxwell, *op. cit.*, p. 474.

38. Albert and Gabrielle L. C. Howard, *The Development of Indian Agriculture* (Oxford: Oxford University Press, 1927), p. 75.

39. Anon., "China Develops Science and Technology Independently and Self-Reliantly," *Peking Review*, No. 46 (November 15, 1974), pp. 13-15.

40. Christopher Hill, "London Science and Medicine," *The Intellectual Origins of the English Revolution* (Oxford: Oxford University Press, 1965), pp. 15-84.

41. See Chao Hung-Chang, "Thirty Years in Search of Better Wheat Strains," *Peking Review*, No. 27 (July 7, 1972), pp. 15-18; and Jack Westoby, "Whose Trees? Whose Science?" *New Scientist*, Vol. 71, No. 103 (August 12, 1976), pp. 341-43.

42. Ch'en, *op. cit.*, p. 65.

43. See Bruce F. Johnston, "Review of Robert E. Evanson and Yoav Kiselev, Agricultural Research and Productivity," *Journal of Economic Literature*, Vol. 14, No. 4 (December 1976), pp. 1342-43.

44. See George Perkins Marsh, *Man and Nature, or Physical Geography as Modified by Human Action*, in David Lowenthal, ed. (Cambridge, Mass.: Belknap Press, 1965), p. 96.

45. Leo A. Orleans and Richard P. Suttmeier, "The Mao Ethic and Environmental Quality," *Science*, Vol. 170 (December 11, 1970), pp. 1173-76.

46. Anon., "Chinese Insect Control Integrates Old and New," *Chemical and Engineering News*, Vol. 54, No. 11 (March 15, 1976), pp. 30-31.

47. See Robert L. Metcalf, "China Unleashes its Ducks," *Environment*, Vol. 18, No. 9 (November 1976), pp. 14-17.

48. Anon., "U.S. Team's Long Look at China's Agriculture," *RF Illustrated*, Vol. 2, No. 2 (March 1975).

49. Maxwell, *op. cit.*, p. 475.

50. *Agricultural Statistics, 1975*, p. 31.

51. Maxwell, *op. cit.*, p. 475.

52. Anon., "Healthy Children," *Peking Review*, No. 24 (June 14, 1974), p. 22.

53. Michael Perelman, "Natural Resources and Agriculture: Karl Marx's Economic Model," *American Journal of Agricultural Economics*, Vol. 57, No. 4 (November 1975).

54. Chi Wei, "Turning the Harmful into the Beneficial," *Peking Review*, No. 4 (January 28, 1972), pp. 5-7.

55. See Leo Orleans, "China's Environomics: Backing into Environmental Leadership," in Joint Economic Committee of the United States Congress, *China: A Reassessment of the Economy, A Compendium of Papers*, 94th Congress, First Session (Washington, D.C.: July 10, 1975), pp. 116-44.

56. Based on estimates of about 2.2 million tons of nitrogen in 10 tons of ammoniam sulfate and $400 capital cost per ton of capacity. See Raymond Ewell, "Estimates of Fertilizer Production/Consumption in 1980 and 1985," presented at the Ninth National Fertilizer Seminar, New Delhi (December 14-15, 1973), reprinted in United States Senate, Select Committee on Nutrition and Human Needs, *National Nutrition Policy Study—1974 Hearings, Part 2, Nutrition and the International Situation* (June 19, 1974), pp. 391-408.

57. Roger Blobaum, "China Recycles Her Wastes by Using Them on the Land," *Compost Science*, Vol. 16, No. 5 (Autumn 1975), pp. 16-17.

58. See Orleans and Suttmeier, *op. cit.*

59. Anon., "Pesticide Production Develops in Tientsin," *Peking Review*, Vol. 19, No. 30 (July 23, 1976), pp. 22-23.

60. See John Kenneth Galbraith, *A China Passage* (Boston: Houghton Mifflin, 1973), p. 129.

61. Harold C. Champeau, "Five Communes in the People's Republic of China; Part 2, Massive Farm Production Inputs Spark Gains in China's Harvests," *Foreign Agriculture*, Vol. 13, No. 30 (July 28, 1975), pp. 7-9.

62. Ch'en, *op. cit.*, p. 69.

63. *Ibid.*, p. 61.

64. Roger W. Weiss, "Mr. Scoville on Colonial Land Wastage," *Southern Economic Journal*, Vol. 21, No. 1 (July 1954), pp. 87–90.

65. See Maxwell, *op. cit.*, p. 474.

66. Westoby, *op. cit.*

PART FIVE

Myth and Economics

17

MYTHS OF AGRICULTURE AND PRIMITIVE EFFICIENCY

Ancient poetry and mythology suggest, at least, that husbandry was once a sacred art; but it is pursued with irreverent haste and heedlessness by us, our object being to have large farms and large crops merely. We have no festival, nor procession, nor ceremony, not excepting our cattle-shows and so-called Thanksgivings, by which the farmer expresses a sense of the sacredness of his calling, or is reminded of its sacred origin. It is the premium and the feast which tempt him. He sacrifices not to Ceres and the Terrestrial Jove, but to the infernal Plutus rather. By avarice and selfishness, and a grovelling habit, from which none of us is free, of regarding the soil as property, or the means of acquiring property chiefly, the landscape is deformed, husbandry is degraded with us, and the farmer leads the meanest of lives. He knows Nature but as a robber.

—Henry David Thoreau, *Walden*[1]

Food production is a struggle in which mankind seizes its sustenance from the environment. The rules of the struggle reflect the pattern of social relations. In primitive societies where social relations are fossilized by firmly held tradition, society's relationship with the environment is expressed in myth and magical beliefs.[2]

Marx suggested that all "mythology masters and dominates and shapes the forces of nature in and through the imagination; hence it disappears as soon as man gains mastery over the forces of nature."[3] Where this mastery is lacking, mythology tends to persist. For example, an Indian psychologist, Sudhir Kakar, considers that the extreme unreliability of the Asian monsoon explains the conception of reality permeated with magic and animism which has not lost its hold in his land.[4] Even though myths are a very imperfect description of reality, they frequently embody an unconscious strategy for coping with the material world.

Because many primitive societies are almost completely dependent on their local habitat, environmental stability is a prerequisite for survival.*

---

*Many primitive societies live in environments with a considerable margin of survival. Pleistocene hunters, for example, were apparently able to hunt their prey intensively before causing them to become extinct.[5]

Myths serve the purpose of direction behavior in ways that keep the environment intact.

The ability of myths to restrain behavior which might damage the environment is especially important in the tropics where the topsoil is generally very fragile.[6] One common belief in these regions is that gods live in the mountains and the hillsides cannot be farmed because they are sacred. As a result, soil erosion is minimized. Guatemalan Indians believe that seeds become "homesick" and "pine away" if they are planted away from their "birthplace."[7] Consequently each village preserves the genes in its own particular strains of seeds and the genetic diversity of the plants is maintained.

The benefits of the stability resulting from myth-based behavior are to some extent offset by a tendency towards stagnation. Hills which could be used to good effect with the proper precautions are left untouched. Potential improvements in seeds cannot be shared among small villages. A more rational management of resources could improve the wealth and welfare of society, but only if social relations were consciously improved.*

Anthropologists have collected a wide array of examples of cultural systems with built-in mechanisms for environmental protection.[8] One of the most famous of these is the ritual system of the Tsembaga Maring of Highland New Guinea, which has been described in detail by Roy Rappaport.[9] According to Rappaport, the behavior of this people is guided by an involved system of rituals that is regulated by the number of pigs. As long as there are few pigs, they assist society by weeding the gardens and clearing the area of human excrement. When the pig population gets too large, the animals become a nuisance; in effect, the pigs cease to work for people and people have to work hard in order to care for the pigs. Their diet has to be supplemented with food grown for human consumption.

As the density of the pig population increases, the domestic tranquility of the village is upset. Neighbors squabble over gardens that are rooted up by errant pigs. As the disputes become more intense, preparations for war begin with the wholesale slaughter of pigs. Once the short period of martial activity ceases, a taboo on the consumption of pigs is reimposed. Pork cannot be eaten except during certain rituals performed during times of stress such as sickness, death or other occasions when the physical demands for protein are maximal. In time, the pig population recovers and the cycle of war is re-initiated.

The Tsembaga Maring say that they perform rituals to rearrange their relations with the spiritual world.[10] In fact, they are rearranging their relations with the material world. Periodic prohibitions of the slaughter

---

*If we include the adoption of new technology as an example of improved use of resources, it is possible that social welfare could be improved within the framework of existing social relations; but as the example of the Green Revolution shows, this possibility is not necessarily realized.

of pigs, as well as marsupials and eels, protect the food supply from overexploitation.

Rappaport compares the working of the ritual cycle with a computer which signals appropriate behavior in response to changes in social and environmental conditions.[11]* We may appreciate the intricacy of this homeostatic ritual system, but we should keep in mind that Tsembaga Maring have enough experience with their environment to manage it directly without having recourse to any ritualistic system. No matter how much we might admire the nobility of primitive life, we should not forget that this remarkable system of rituals and myths required considerable destruction of property and human life during the wars.†

In any case, ritual tended to hold primitive societies within the limits imposed by their environments. Cultures that were able to keep from destroying their natural resource base tended to follow rituals celebrating humanity's existence as part of nature rather than its mastery over nature. One of the most common of this type of ritual appears to be sacrifice, either of plants or animals or even of other humans. Frazer gives a particularly detailed description of an Indian king dismembering himself in the process of carrying out one such ritual of human sacrifice.[13] The purpose of this type of sacrifice is not so much to appease gods as to proclaim the unity of human life within the cycle of nature.

The violence of these sacrificial rituals should not blind us to their basic vision: Each individual could identify with both the king *and* the plant. The lives of both were seen to be not finite, but part of a continual process whereby the life of each successive generation continues from the cuttings of the last. The basic myth, the myth of the dying fertility god, echoes in almost every religion in the world. The resurrection of Christ is not celebrated in the spring by accident. The nonrational nature of myth allows for a celebration of life to take the form of the destruction of life.

According to the best guesses of anthropologists, the ritual of the dying fertility god probably began in the tropics where agriculture required only the planting of cuttings from tuberous roots.[14]‡ People may have noticed more vigorous growth near burial sites, suggesting a connection between the life cycle of humans and plants. This connection was then incorporated into the myth that plants were the gift of a semidivine figure who was sacrificed in order that mankind could receive nourishment from it.[16]

*Gregory Bateson sees Balinese culture from a similar vantage point. He sees their culture as one geared to the maintenance of "the steady state of the system—that is, in preventing the maximization of any single variable, the excessive increase of which would produce irreversible change. . . . The ordinary Balinese term for the world before the coming of the white man is 'when the world was steady.'"[12]

†We have our own rituals and myths to govern our economic behavior. Our money, banks, and account books are also costly to maintain. More importantly, the wars which periodically break out to serve the needs of our high priests of finance and industry are far more devastating than the spears and rocks hurled by the Tsembaga Maring.

‡Gras notes that the nomadic Australian Aborigines had long developed the practice of returning part of "wild" yam heads back to the soil.[15]

This pre-scientific insight would have been very useful in teaching people about the technique of planting tubers. Repeating the ritual, time and again, allowed society to garner some indirect understanding of cause and effect. For example, the earth (mother) becomes fertile through implanting a cutting or a seed. The event is celebrated over the years until people begin to notice that turning the soil produces beneficial results. From this experience, people learn how to make digging sticks and then plows.* Wheels, carts, and even the castration of cattle seem to have developed out of ritual practices.[19] The connection between ritual and agricultural technology is reflected in the Latin root of the word, "cultivate," which has the two-fold meaning of "tilling" and "worship."

Myth and ritual contributed to an involvement with the environment. Consequently, primitive societies accumulated an immense store of biological information. According to Edgar Anderson, modern society has not domesticated a single plant during the last 5,000 years which was not used by primitive cultures.[20]† As an example of the biological knowledge of primitives, Anderson points out that they managed to discover all five natural sources of caffeine: tea, coffee, the cola plant, cacao, yerba mate and its relatives.[24] As a result of their accumulation of biological information, primitive cultures developed the capacity to manipulate the environment. This progressive aspect of ritual probably lay dormant for long periods until the effectiveness of ritualistic restraints declined.

After traditional myths lost their power to protect the environment, many societies developed without any regard to their resource base. According to Plato, the Greek orator Critias compared once lush hills near Athens to the skeleton of a sick man, "all the fat and soft earth wasted away, only bare hills left."[25] Their fertility, once wasted away, has never

---

*Even after they developed improved technology, myth and supersitious beliefs tended to affect their use. The act of plowing filled the Celts, the Germans, and the Slavs with an intense fear because the earth was considered to be a living being. To divert the anger of the earth, they pretended that the plow was not a machine, but an animal with its own will. Therefore the Anglo-Saxons called the plow "pig's nose," the Letts called it "bear," and the Rhinelanders called it "wolf"—as if to put the blame on the animal for having dug up the earth. . . . [The fear of plowing was so great that] dreaming of a plow meant death, for the earth thrown up by the plow was akin to the graveyard earth turned up by the spade.[17] Quite likely, this attitude contributed to the success of the European peasant, even well into the twentieth century, in protecting the fertility of the land.[18]

†Triticale, added since Anderson's book, is the sole exception, although crosses, mutations and polyploidal varieties have all increased the list of domestic crops. On the other hand, with the passage of time society actually experiences a reduction in the number of food sources produced in any given location. Primitive hunters and gatherers found on the order of 100 different sources of food within a very limited area.[21] Over time, the most advanced agricultural environments became simplified with miles and miles of farmland planted to the same crops.[22] Meanwhile, in 1970 the typical supermarket carried 7,800 different food items. In 1975, the food industry introduced a total of 7,200 new food products, down from 9,400 in 1972.[23] This variety depends, in part, on the ability to draw on a worldwide network of food suppliers. More importantly, the use of food gimickry multiplies the number of products. The amount of biological wisdom involved in the process is open to question.

been restored. The experience of the Greeks was not unique. Vladimir Simkhovich, a noted historian, has traced the fall of Rome to the root cause of faulty agriculture.[26] The strength of the Middle East, North Africa, and many parts of Southern Europe as well as China was sapped by devastating soil erosion.[27]*

Parallel to the changes in the relationship between society and the environment, new social relations develop so that society can turn its expanding intellectual powers to controlling and profiting from the environment. People learned to control other human beings more effectively. Mumford estimates that the mass of people that made up the human labor machine was equivalent to between 25,000 and 100,000 horsepower.[28] Gradually, the rule of the priests and lords common to antiquity gave way to the rule of bankers, industrialists and merchants. The masses were freed from direct slavery or serfdom, but the relationship between worker and employer was still characterized by exploitation.

Under these new social relations, technical knowledge and productivity multiplied even more rapidly. As Marx and Engels wrote in the *Communist Manifesto* of 1848, "the bourgeoise has been the first to show what man's activity can bring about."[29] They go on to say that "It has accomplished wonders far surpassing Egyptian pyramids, Roman aqueducts, and Gothic cathedrals."[30]

Although a contemporary list of technical marvels would fill an entire encyclopedia, the majority of people in the world still suffer from a degrading poverty which cannot be explained by myths or technical backwardness.

---

*Other civilizations, however, were able to survive their careless agricultural practices. In Mesopotamia, for instance, empires were able to outlast the fertility of their soils by militarizing their society to harvest, not food, but plunder and loot. For centuries Egypt, too, was able to waste much of its fertility since its soil received annual infusions of nutrients washed down from the African hills.

REFERENCES

1. Henry David Thoreau, *Walden, or Life in the Woods* (New York: Holt, Rinehart & Winston, 1964), p. 137.

2. Karl Marx, "The British Rule in India," *New York Daily Tribune*, June 6, 1853, reprinted in Karl Marx, *Surveys From Exile*, David Fernbach, ed. (New York: Vintage, 1974) pp. 393 and 406, and Karl Marx, *Economic and Philosophical Manuscripts of 1844* (New York: International Publishers, 1964), p. 115.

3. Karl Marx, *The Grundrisse* (New York: Harper & Row, 1972), p. 45. The Nicolaus translation (New York: Vintage, 1973), p. 110, is slightly less free, but is also less clear.

4. Dr. Sudhir Kakar, letter to V. S. Naipul in the latter's "India: A Defect of Vision," *The New York Review of Books*, Vol. 23, No. 13 (August 5, 1976), pp. 9–14; see also Albert and Gabrielle L. C. Howard, *The Development of Indian Agriculture* (Oxford: Oxford University Press, 1927), p. 12.

Engels states that ".... these various false conceptions of nature, of man's own being, of spirits, magic forces, etc., have for their most part only a negative economic factor as their basis; the low economic development of the prehistoric period is supplemented and also partially conditiond by and even caused by the false conceptions of history." See Frederick Engels, "Letter to Conrad Schmidt, October 27, 1890," in Karl Marx and Frederick Engels, *Selected Correspondence*, 3d ed., (Moscow: Progress Publishers, 1975), p. 400.

5. Paul Martin, "Prehistoric Overkill," in Thomas R. Detwyler, ed., *Man's Impact on Environment* (New York: McGraw-Hill, 1971), pp. 612-25.

6. For a review of this and other problems of managing tropical ecosystems, see David H. Janzen, "Tropical Agroecosystems; These Habitats are Misunderstood by the Temperate Zone and Mismanaged by the Tropics," *Science*, Vol. 182 (December 21, 1974), pp. 1212-19. See also E. M. Bridges, *World Soils* (Cambridge: Cambridge University Press, 1970), pp. 72-73, and Mary McNeil, "Lateritic Soils," *Scientific American*, Vol. 221, No. 5 (1964), pp. 96-102, and her "Lateritic Soils in Distinct Tropical Environments, Southern Sudan and Brazil," in M. Taghi Farvar and John P. Milton, *The Careless Technology: Ecology and International Development* (Garden City, N.Y.: Natural History Press, 1972), pp. 591-608. An articles that minimizes the problems of tropical soils is P. A. Sanchez and S. W. Buol, "Soils of the Tropics and the World Food Crisis," *Science*, Vol. 188, No. 4188 (May 9, 1975), pp. 598-603.

7. Barbara Pickersgill, "The Domestication of Chili Peppers," in Peter J. Ucko and G. W. Dimbleby, eds., *The Domestication of Plants and Animals* (Chicago: Aldine, 1969), p. 446.

8. Andrew P. Vayda, *Environment and Cultural Behavior: Ecological Studies in Cultural Anthropology* (Garden City, N.Y.: Natural History Press, 1969).

9. Roy A. Rappaport, *Pigs for the Ancestors: Ritual in the Ecology of a New Guinea People* (New Haven: Yale University Press, 1967), p. 233. Rappaport's work is summarized in his article, "Ritual Regulation of Environmental Relations of a New Guinea People," *Ethnology*, Vol. 6 (1967), pp. 17-20 and reprinted in Yehudi Cohen, ed., *Man in Adaptation* (Chicago: Aldine, 1971), pp. 226-36, and in Vayda, *op. cit.*, pp. 181-201. Later citations refer to the latter version.

10. *Ibid.*

11. Roy Rappaport, "Ritual, Sanctity and Cybernetics," *American Anthropologist* Vol. 73, No. 1 (February 1971), p. 69. See also Francis Bacon, *Novum Organum*, Book II, Section 29.

12. Gregory Bateson, "Bali: The Value System of a Steady State," in his *Steps to an Ecology of Mind* (San Francisco: Chandler Publishing Co., 1972), pp. 121 and 125.

13. James Frazer, *The Golden Bough* (London: Macmillan & Co., 1922), pp. 274-75. See also Charles Heiser, *From Seed to Civilization: The Story of Man's Food* (San Francisco: W. H. Freeman, 1973), pp. 23-24.

14. Lewis Mumford, *The Myth of the Machine* (New York: Harcourt, Brace, & World, 1966), p. 50.

15. N. S. B. Gras, *An Introduction to Economic History* (New York: Harper & Bros., 1922), p. 39. For a further elaboration of the planting of tubers, see Marston Bates, *Where Winter Never Comes* (New York: Charles Scribner & Sons, 1952), p. 55 citing E. J. Payne, *History of the World*, Vol. 1 (Oxford: Oxford University Press, 1892).

16. Charles B. Heiser, Jr., *Seed to Civilization: The Story of Man's Food* (San Francisco: W. H. Freedman, 1973), pp. 22-23.

17. H. E. Jacob, *Six Thousand Years of Bread* (Garden City, N.Y.: Doubleday, 1944), p. 117.

18. Siegfried Ciriacy-von Wantrup, "Soil Conservation of European Peasant Farm Management," *Journal of Farm Economics*, Vol. 20, No. 1 (February 1938), pp. 86-101.

19. Eric Isaac, "Myths, Cults and Livestock Breeding," *Diogenes* (Spring 1963), p. 75. That myths should pay such dividends is not surprising, in one sense. Paul Radin points out that the basic purpose of myths is to coerce the world. See Paul Radin, *Primitive Man as Philosopher* (New York: Dover, 1957), pp. 19-40.

20. Edgar Anderson, *Plants, Man and Life* (Boston: Little Brown & Co., 1952), pp. 132-33.

than a person with a hoe, but the tractor is not used to make the job easier for the farm worker.* Instead, it allows a single driver to replace several hoers.

The rising level of unemployment is proof of a divorce between economic behavior and fundamental social and biological rationality. If machines were specifically used to help society meet the increasing workload resulting from the functioning of the law of diminishing returns, we could hardly expect to see millions of people unable to find employment. In reality, technology responds to what are called the laws of supply and demand. Nevertheless, the law of diminishing returns continues to be invoked to explain hunger and unemployment, especially as they exist in the Third World. As the economy multiplies the number of unemployed people, visions of overpopulation are conjured up to account for the malfunctioning of the economic system. We return to the dismal vision of Garrett Hardin and the lifeboats.

---

up of the tempo of production. Although a precise measure of the speedup is hard to determine, David Gordon suggests that the rate of industrial accidents might serve as a proxy.[33] In addition, the time devoted to breaks seems to have decreased.[34]

*The word "easier" is not readily defined. The amount of muscular activity required from the tractor driver is not great compared to the demands from hoeing, but the driver will be subjected to other stresses. Dust, noise, and vibrations all undermine the physical well-being of the tractor operator, in addition to the continual danger to life and limb discussed in the Prologue.[35]

Occasionally, technical change involves little more than a change in design. In such cases we are more justified in speaking in terms of an increase in efficiency. For example, the traction power of animals used in Pakistan agriculture could be increased by an estimated 60 percent with an improved yoke.[36] According to Lynn White, the perfection of the yoke used in Europe was one of the most important technical improvements in medieval technology.[37] The effect of improvements in the design of the yoke were no less profound in China during the same period.[38]

REFERENCES

1. John Stuart Mill, *Principles of Political Economy*, in "Collected Works of John Stuart Mill," J. M. Robson, ed. (Toronto: Toronto University Press, 1965), Vol. 2, p. 174.

2. J. R. Harlan and D. Zohary, "Distribution of Wild Wheats and Barley," *Science*, Vol. 153 (1966), p. 1078; and J. R. Harlan, "A Wild Wheat Harvest in Turkey," *Archaeology*, Vol. 20, No. 3 (1967), p. 198.

3. Philip Morison, "Review of Jack Harlan, *Crops and Man*, Madison, Wisconsin: American Society of Agronomy," *Scientific American* (September 1976).

4. Kent V. Flannery, "Origins and Ecological Effects of Early Domestication in Iran and the Near East," in Peter J. Ucko and G. W. Dimbley, eds., *The Domestication of Plants and Animals* (Chicago: Aldine Press, 1969), p. 81. See also Philip E. L. Smith, "Land Use, Settlement Patterns and Subsistence Agriculture," in Ucko *et. al.*, *Man, Settlement and Urbanism* (Cambridge, Mass: Schenkman Publishing Co., 1972), p. 416.

5. F. Hole and K. Flannery, "The Prehistory of Southwestern Iran: A Preliminary Report," *Proceedings of the Prehistory Society*, Vol. 33 (1963), p. 201; Ester Boserup, *The Conditions of Agricultural Growth* (Chicago: Aldine Press, 1965), pp. 45–46; Edward Hyams, *Soil and Civilization* (New York: Thames & Hudson, 1952), p. 48; and Karl Marx, *Capital*, Vol. 1 (Chicago: Kerr, 1906), pp. 562–63.

6. James Mill, *The History of British India*, Vol. 1 (London, 1817), p. 343, cited by William J. Barber, *British Economic Thought and India,1600–1858, A Study in the History of Development Economics* (Oxford: Oxford University Press, 1975), p. 130.

7. Richard Wilkenson, *Poverty and Progress, An Ecological Perspective on Economic Development* (New York: Praeger, 1973), p. 169, citing *John Smith, Works, 1608–1631*, ed. Edward Arden (Birmingham, 1884), p. 149.

8. Wilkenson, *op. cit.*, p. 147, citing Frederick J. Turner, *The Frontier in American History* (New York, 1922), p. 4. For an excellent review of the literature on labor requirements in pre-modern agriculture, see Mark Nathan Cohen, *The Food Crisis in Prehistory: Overpopulation and the Origins of Agriculture* (New Haven: Yale University Press, 1977), pp. 28–35. Also see Ester Boserup, *Conditions of Agricultural Growth* (Chicago: Aldine Press, 1965), p. 63; and D. B. Grigg, *The Agricultural Systems of the World: An Evolutionary Approach* (Cambridge: Cambridge University Press, 1974), pp. 63 and 70. The Work of John Rae, referred to in Part II. "The Meaning of Mining," is also relevant here.

9. Vivian Wiser, "Women in American Agriculture," in *1976 Agricultural Outlook: Papers Presented at the National Agricultural Outlook Conference Sponsored by the U.S. Department of Agriculture, 17–20 November 1975*, Prepared for the Committee on Agriculture and Forestry of the U.S. Senate, 94th Cong., 1st Session (December 18, 1975), pp. 89–94.

10. K. F. Mathur, *Enough to Spare* (New York: 1944), cited by J. J. Spengler, "The Economist and the Population Problem," *American Economic Review*, Vol. 56, No. 1 (March 1966), p. 21.

11. Keith Sward, *The Legend of Henry Ford* (New York: Atheneum, 1972), p. 280.

12. Eugene Ayres and Charles A. Scarlott, *Energy Sources—The Wealth of the World*, (New York: McGraw Hill, 1952), p. 221.

13. Barry Commoner, *The Closing Circle* (New York: Alfred A. Knopf, 1969), p. 160.

14. Emma Rothschild, "What is the Energy Crisis?" *New York Review of Books* (August 9, 1973), p. 33.

15. Pei-Sung Tang, *Green Thraldom: Essays of a Chinese Biologist* (London: George Allen & Unwin, 1949), p. 53.

16. *Agricultural Statistics*, 1975, p. 57.

17. F. H. King, *Farmers of Forty Centuries: or Permanent Agriculture in China, Korea, and Japan* (Emmaus, Pa.: Rodale Press, n.d.), pp. 314 and 319.

18. Cited in "The Roots of Agriculture in the United States," above.

19. Joseph A. Schumpeter, *History of Economic Analysis* (Oxford: Oxford University Press, 1954), pp. 258–61.

20. Commoner, *op. cit.*, pp. 84–85.

21. See Jeffrey Finke, "Nitrogen Fertilizer: Price Level and Sales in Illinois," *Illinois Agricultural Economics*, Vol. 13, No. 1 (January 1973), pp. 34–40.

22. Stephen Enke, "The Economic Aspects of Slowing Population Growth," *Economic Journal*, Vol. 76, No. 1 (March 1966), pp. 44–56.

23. Paul R. and Anne H. Ehrlick, *Population, Resources, Environment: Issues in Human Ecology*, 2d ed. (San Francisco: W. H. Freeman, 1972), p. 263.

24. See Finke, *op. cit.*

25. Data from David Pimentel, L. E. Hurd, A. C. Bellotti, M. J. Forster, I. N. Oka, O. D. Sholes, and R. J. Whitman, "Food Production and the Energy Crisis," *Science*, Vol. 182 (November 2, 1973), pp. 443–49, Table 1.

26. See Zvi Griliches, "Hybrid corn and the economics of innovation," *Science* (July 29, 1960), pp. 275–80. A confusion between Illinois and national statistics flaws the work of Sterling B. Hendricks, "Food from the Land," in National Academy of Sciences, Committee on Resources and Man, *Resources and Man* (San Francisco: W. H. Freeman, 1969), pp. 65–86.

27. Pimentel *et. al., op. cit.*

28. *Ibid.*

29. Anon., "Why Recovering Economies Don't Create Enough Jobs," *Business Week* (March 22, 1976).

sources (including labor) are required to meet the demands of a growing population. It reinforces the teaching commended in the *Examiner* of 1830 that "want and labour spring from the niggardlyness of nature and not from the inequality which is consequent of the institution of property."[18]

THE LAW OF DIMINISHING RETURNS

Naturally, the privileged classes prefer to divert attention from exploitation and the irrationalities of the market system. They intellectualize their attitude by recognizing an eternal known as the law of diminishing returns. This law, commonly associated with Malthus, states that successive increases of labor or any other input will result in smaller and smaller increments of additional production, without some improvement in technology.[19]

Within the context of the law of diminishing returns, the situation of the primitive food gatherer is perceived to be identical with that of the modern farm worker. Both must submit to the increasing demands of a growing population. More people simply mean more work.

Of course, this attitude is utter nonsense. The market system has long ago severed any direct links between needs and work. Today everything is mediated through the market.

The influence of social organization on resource use is illustrated by the recent history of nitrogen fertilizer. The application of this nutrient is commonly cited as an example of the workings of the law of diminishing returns. Between 1945 and 1948, when relatively little artificial fertilizer was used, corn production in Illinois was about 50 bushels per acre; in 1958, about 70 bushels per acre was an average yield. Illinois farmers were then using about 100,000 tons of nitrogen fertilizer per year. By 1965, they were using 500,000 tons to obtain an average yield of 90 bushels per acre.[20]*

The first increase of 20 bushels per acre required only 100,000 tons of fertilizer: to produce a further increase of 20 bushels, an additional

---

consumed, one-third is in the form of proteins, one-half in the form of carbohydrates, and one-twentieth in the form of fats, totaling some eleven calories in the form of chemical energy. Of this amount of chemical energy consumed, only one calorie is returned in the form of the machine that is the body of the mature larva. Thus, for the production of one kilogram of silk, about forty-seven kilowat hours, which is the equivalent of 40,000 calories, are required.[15]

The 40,000 calories required for the manufacture of the kilogram of silk do not represent much energy. If the kilogram of silk were converted to an equivalent weight of water, this much energy would raise its temperature by about 75°, substantially less than the temperature is raised for the purpose of synthetic fiber production. It should also be borne in mind that the mulberry tree is a renewable energy source and that some by-products of the process serve useful functions.

A comparison between cotton and silk is very difficult. In 1974, cotton yields were 442 pounds per acre.[16] At the turn of the century, silk yields were about one-third as large.[17] Of course, the two fibers differ a great deal in quality.

*These figures overstate Illinois nitrogen fertilizer use in 1965.[21]

their traditional farming methods designed for the populous lands of the Old World, they frequently adopted the less time-consuming aboriginal techniques.[7] Even the settlers who accompanied Captain John Smith, long revered for their strenuous efforts, had plenty of free time. In the words of Captain Smith himself, work required only four hours a day, leaving the settlers free to enjoy "the rest in pastimes and merry exercise."[8]*

Eventually, population increases forced nations to turn first to more labor-intensive methods of extracting the fruits of nature and later to the substitution of mineral and synthetics for organic materials. More than three decades ago, one observer commented:

A hundred years ago, nearly 80 percent of the things men used was derived from the plant and animal kingdoms, with only about 20 percent from the mineral kingdom. Today only about 30 percent of the things used in industrialized countries comes from things that grow; about 70 percent have their origins in mines and quarries.[10]

These words were written in 1944, in the days when Henry Ford looked forward to an automobile made entirely from wheat.[11] Since then, we have increased our reliance on inorganic materials by leaps and bounds.

Shifting sources of fibers offer a good example of the way society comes to rely more heavily on inorganic materials. In nations with sparse populations, animal hair is an excellent source of fiber. Wool, for instance, requires very little effort to produce as long as plenty of land is available; but in the U.S., one acre of cotton produces about 150 times as much fiber as an acre devoted to grazing sheep.[12]† As populations increase, people turn to growing vegetable fibers where the land is appropriate for growing them, even though the cultivation and harvesting of the fiber demands much more effort.

The adoption of synthetic textiles frees land which would otherwise be used for cotton or wool. In effect, synthetic fibers substitute fossil fuel for land. Besides consuming the petroleum or natural gas which forms the basic raw material for synthetic fiber production, the manufacturing process requires extremely high temperatures. Nylon, for example, involves a series of six to ten chemical reactions which require temperatures ranging from 200° to 700° F.[13] However, because cotton growers in the U.S. use particularly energy-intensive farming methods, synthetic fibers require only about five times as much energy as cotton.[14]**

The sequence from animal hair to vegetable fibers and finally to synthetics appears to follow a pattern in which increasingly more re-

---

*Women may not have shared in the leisure equally in the colonies. In the Dutch colony of New Netherlands (New York), women tilled the soil while the men went off to hunt.[9]

†This ratio does not measure the relative productivity of wool and cotton, because sheep are used for meat and cottonseed for oil.

**The enormous scale of energy use in synthetic fiber production is better revealed in a comparison with oriental silk manufacture. The basic resource demand of silk production is a supply of mulberry leaves. During the larval life of the silkworm:

. . . from the time of hatching to the time of cocoon formation, it consumes mulberry leaves to a total of about three grammes dry weight. . . . Of the three grammes of food materials

18

RESOURCES AND THE LAW
OF DIMINISHING RETURNS

This general law of agricultural industry is the most important proposition
in political economy.
—John Stuart Mill, *Principles of Political Economy*[1]

POPULATION AND AGRICULTURAL DEVELOPMENT

On fertile, sparsely populated land, early hunters and gatherers could
supply their own needs with very little effort. One modern plant scientist
demonstrated this observation. Jack Harlan, choosing a naturally rich
area, armed himself with a flint-bladed sickle and harvested enough wild
wheat in an hour to produce one kilo of clean grain. Harlan's wild wheat
harvest suggests that a family of experienced plant collectors, working
over the three-week period when wild grain comes ripe, could easily
harvest more than it could hope to consume in a year.[2] Harlan matched
the energy efficiency of the Chinese wet-rice farmers by producing 50
calories of food for each calorie of his own energy he expended.[3] The wild
grain, after chemical analysis, proved to be almost twice as rich in protein
as domestic wheat.

The naturally rich land, such as Harlan studied, was limited. Cultivation was an effort to reproduce optimum conditions on the margin of the
optimal zone.[4] Even so, these primitive methods of farming did not
require much labor compared to more modern techniques. For example,
European settlers in the sparsely populated lands of North and South
America quickly realized that the popular image of society consumed by
drudgery did not apply in the new world.[5]* Rather than continue to use

---

*Of course, drudgery is common in the harsh economies of the Third World societies of
today. This condition does not reflect backwardness or primitiveness or even overpopulation, but rather the role assigned to these economies in the modern world economy. James
Mill, whose monumental book on India won him a high position in the East India
Company in the early nineteenth century, compassionately wrote of "the pain of idleness"
which the people of India had to endure prior to the introduction of European civilization.[6]

21. John Robson, "Changing Food Habits in Developing Countries," *Ecology of Food and Nutrition*, Vol. 4 (1976), pp. 251-56.

22. United States Department of Agriculture, Task Force on Spatial Heterogeneity in Agricultural Landscapes and Enterprises, *Monoculture in Agriculture: Extent, Causes and Problems* (Washington, D.C.: October 1973).

23. Anon., "The Hard Road of the Food Processors," *Business Week* (March 8, 1976), pp. 50-54, and Larry Traub, "Food Technology Sparks Concern," *The Farm Index*, Vol. 15, No. 8 (August 1976), p. 12.

24. Anderson, *op. cit.*, p. 119. For a study of the botanical knowledge of ancient India, see Ferdinand S. Hammett, "Agriculture and Botanical Knowledge of Ancient India," *Osiris*, Vol. 9 (1950), pp. 211-26. See also the review of literature on the extent of biological knowledge among primitives in Mark Nathan Cohen, *The Food Crisis in Prehistory: Overpopulation and the Origins of Agriculture* (New Haven: Yale University Press, 1977).

25. Cited by Tom Dale and Vernon Gill Carter, *Topsoil and Civilization* (Norman: University of Oklahoma Press, 1955), p. 105. For a more standard translation, see B. Jowett, *The Dialogues of Plato*, 4th ed. (Oxford: Clarendon Press, 1953), Vol. III, pp. 793-94.

26. Vladimir Simkhovitch, *Toward the Understanding of Jesus and Two Additional Historical Studies* (New York: The MacMillan Co., 1937).

27. W. C. Lowdermilk, "Conquest of Land Through Seven Thousand Years," United States Department of Agriculture, Soil Conservation Service, Agricultural Information Bulletin No. 99, reissued, and Nos. 12 and 14 (Washington, D.C.: 1975).

28. Mumford, *op. cit.*, p. 196.

29. Karl Marx and Frederick Engels, "Communist Manifesto," pp. 98-137, in Karl Marx and Frederick Engels, *Selected Works, Three Volumes* (Moscow: Progress Publishers, 1969), Vol. 1, p. 111.

30. *Ibid.*

ing returns from labor. As we have repeatedly seen, the amount of labor required to grow corn or just about any other product has fallen off dramatically throughout the last two centuries. To speak of diminishing returns when some inputs are increasing slower than output is illogical; to do so when the products themselves are as different as hybrid and open-pollinated corn is downright foolish.

The law of diminishing returns is irrelevant to market economics. It predicts that the demand for labor should be increasing, but, in fact, unemployment has become an apparently "normal" feature of the U.S. economy. The editors of *Business Week* estimate that reducing the current level of unemployment only 2 percentage points by 1980 will require 12 million new jobs, more than have ever been created within such a short time except during war years.[29]

The increasing profitability to agriculture of this displacement of labor by materials is reflected in the U.S. Department of Agriculture's index of output per unit of input. In 1930, this index stood at 53, exactly where it had been 20 years earlier.[30] By 1941, it had increased to only 64. During the next two decades when the use of energy-intensive agriculture was becoming more widely adopted, the index jumped to 110.

Recently, the flow of benefits from this form of technology seems to have been tapering off.* Between 1971 and 1974, the index fell to 107 and then skipped back up to 113 in 1975. An influential report from the National Academy of Sciences reveals a widespread fear in the agricultural research community that some sort of technical plateau is at hand.

A closer examination of the figures on which the index is based, as well as an analysis of the National Academy of Sciences report, shows that the indications of technological stagnation in agriculture are due to an overreliance on high energy-based inputs. This situation has two causes. Firstly, the price of energy has been very low; and secondly, capitalistic economies place an undue emphasis on technologies which reduce employment regardless of whether or not alternative jobs exist.

We cannot explain the adoption of hybrid corn technology or any other technology by a physical law such as the law of diminishing returns.† Technologies are selected or rejected according to how well they serve the interests of the privileged class. In capitalist society, machinery is not introduced to save work, but to save *labor*.** As John Stuart Mill suggested, "Hitherto it is questionable if all the mechanical inventions yet made have lightened the day's toil of any human being."[32] In other words, machinery is not used to reduce the work of individual workers, but to increase their production.‡ A farm worker on a tractor can turn more soil

---

*Industrial productivity has also been sluggish during the past decade.[31]

†The law of diminishing returns does become relevant when the shortage of a particular resource begins to constrict economic development.

**Labor is a commodity sold by workers. Work is a measure of the effort expended in production.

‡Of course, the average length of the work week in the U.S. and other industrialized nations has been falling. Some of the reduction in the working hours is offset by the speeding

400,000 tons were necessary. In other words, the quantity of fertilizer needed to increase yields by an additional 20 bushels per acre rose by 400 percent. Extrapolating from these statistics, we could expect fertilizer requirements to grow far more rapidly than increases in yields. If this conclusion is correct, then maintaining the same standard of living in the face of rising population would be very difficult.

The law of diminishing returns gives rise to the mistaken populationist interpretation of poverty. It implies that, as population expands, either the average standard of living must fall or people will have to work harder, again assuming constant technology. Following this logic, the route to economic betterment begins with population control, not changes in social relations.[22] A typical example of its application reads:

The law of diminishing returns is . . . operative in increasing food production to meet the needs of growing population. Typically, attempts are made both to overproduce on land already farmed and to extend agriculture to marginal land. The former requires disproportionate energy use in obtaining water, fertilizer, and pesticides. Farming marginal land also increases per capita energy use, since the amount of energy invested per unit yield increases as less desirable land is cultivated.[23]

Such simplistic applications of the law of diminishing returns demonstrate why this kind of reasoning does so little to explain poverty. The critical point is that fertilizer applications and other energy-intensive inputs have not been required to keep ahead of population growth; they are and have been geared to making a profit. Between 1945 and 1965 nitrogen prices fell by more than 30 percent.[24] No wonder artificial fertilizer was used more intensively!

National figures for the U.S. indicate an apparent reversal of diminishing returns between 1949 and 1959.[25] This national trend is explained by the expanded usage, during that period, of hybrid corn, which was specifically bred to respond to commercial fertilizers.*The overall benefits from hybrid corn are open to dispute, but the new corn technology accomplished its immediate purpose: it did succeed in overcoming diminishing returns from fertilizer. Pimentel and his associates have shown that partially as a result of increasing fertilizer use, energy use in corn production has risen far faster than production itself,[27] but again, this trend reflects a market in which energy could be purchased very cheaply.†

Diminishing returns from energy, fertilizer, or any other resource in corn production was willingly accepted by farmers in return for *increas-*

---

*The divergent trends for Illinois and the U.S. result from the earlier adoption of hybrid corn in Illinois.[26]

†Since fertilizer production required more energy than any other aspect of growing corn, considerable savings in energy are possible by using manures or by rotating corn with legumes.[28] With biological fixation of nitrogen, the diminishing returns from energy could be easily reversed.

Engels states that ".... these various false conceptions of nature, of man's own being, of spirits, magic forces, etc., have for their most part only a negative economic factor as their basis; the low economic development of the prehistoric period is supplemented and also partially conditiond by and even caused by the false conceptions of history." See Frederick Engels, "Letter to Conrad Schmidt, October 27, 1890," in Karl Marx and Frederick Engels, *Selected Correspondence*, 3d ed., (Moscow: Progress Publishers, 1975), p. 400.

5. Paul Martin, "Prehistoric Overkill," in Thomas R. Detwyler, ed., *Man's Impact on Environment* (New York: McGraw-Hill, 1971), pp. 612-25.

6. For a review of this and other problems of managing tropical ecosystems, see David H. Janzen, "Tropical Agroecosystems; These Habitats are Misunderstood by the Temperate Zone and Mismanaged by the Tropics," *Science*, Vol. 182 (December 21, 1974), pp. 1212-19. See also E. M. Bridges, *World Soils* (Cambridge: Cambridge University Press, 1970), pp. 72-73, and Mary McNeil, "Lateritic Soils," *Scientific American*, Vol. 221, No. 5 (1964), pp. 96-102, and her "Lateritic Soils in Distinct Tropical Environments, Southern Sudan and Brazil," in M. Taghi Farvar and John P. Milton, *The Careless Technology: Ecology and International Development* (Garden City, N.Y.: Natural History Press, 1972), pp. 591-608. An articles that minimizes the problems of tropical soils is P. A. Sanchez and S. W. Buol, "Soils of the Tropics and the World Food Crisis," *Science*, Vol. 188, No. 4188 (May 9, 1975), pp. 598-603.

7. Barbara Pickersgill, "The Domestication of Chili Peppers," in Peter J. Ucko and G. W. Dimbleby, eds., *The Domestication of Plants and Animals* (Chicago: Aldine, 1969), p. 446.

8. Andrew P. Vayda, *Environment and Cultural Behavior: Ecological Studies in Cultural Anthropology* (Garden City, N.Y.: Natural History Press, 1969).

9. Roy A. Rappaport, *Pigs for the Ancestors: Ritual in the Ecology of a New Guinea People* (New Haven: Yale University Press, 1967), p. 233. Rappaport's work is summarized in his article, "Ritual Regulation of Environmental Relations of a New Guinea People," *Ethnology*, Vol. 6 (1967), pp. 17-20 and reprinted in Yehudi Cohen, ed., *Man in Adaptation* (Chicago: Aldine, 1971), pp. 226-36, and in Vayda, *op. cit.*, pp. 181-201. Later citations refer to the latter version.

10. *Ibid.*

11. Roy Rappaport, "Ritual, Sanctity and Cybernetics," *American Anthropologist* Vol. 73, No. 1 (February 1971), p. 69. See also Francis Bacon, *Novum Organum*, Book II, Section 29.

12. Gregory Bateson, "Bali: The Value System of a Steady State," in his *Steps to an Ecology of Mind* (San Francisco: Chandler Publishing Co., 1972), pp. 121 and 125.

13. James Frazer, *The Golden Bough* (London: Macmillan & Co., 1922), pp. 274-75. See also Charles Heiser, *From Seed to Civilization: The Story of Man's Food* (San Francisco: W. H. Freeman, 1973), pp. 23-24.

14. Lewis Mumford, *The Myth of the Machine* (New York: Harcourt, Brace, & World, 1966), p. 50.

15. N. S. B. Gras, *An Introduction to Economic History* (New York: Harper & Bros., 1922), p. 39. For a further elaboration of the planting of tubers, see Marston Bates, *Where Winter Never Comes* (New York: Charles Scribner & Sons, 1952), p. 55 citing E. J. Payne, *History of the World*, Vol. 1 (Oxford: Oxford University Press, 1892).

16. Charles B. Heiser, Jr., *Seed to Civilization: The Story of Man's Food* (San Francisco: W. H. Freedman, 1973), pp. 22-23.

17. H. E. Jacob, *Six Thousand Years of Bread* (Garden City, N.Y.: Doubleday, 1944), p. 117.

18. Siegfried Ciriacy-von Wantrup, "Soil Conservation of European Peasant Farm Management," *Journal of Farm Economics*, Vol. 20, No. 1 (February 1938), pp. 86-101.

19. Eric Isaac, "Myths, Cults and Livestock Breeding," *Diogenes* (Spring 1963), p. 75. That myths should pay such dividends is not surprising, in one sense. Paul Radin points out that the basic purpose of myths is to coerce the world. See Paul Radin, *Primitive Man as Philosopher* (New York: Dover, 1957), pp. 19-40.

20. Edgar Anderson, *Plants, Man and Life* (Boston: Little Brown & Co., 1952), pp. 132-33.

been restored. The experience of the Greeks was not unique. Vladimir Simkhovich, a noted historian, has traced the fall of Rome to the root cause of faulty agriculture.[26] The strength of the Middle East, North Africa, and many parts of Southern Europe as well as China was sapped by devastating soil erosion.[27]*

Parallel to the changes in the relationship between society and the environment, new social relations develop so that society can turn its expanding intellectual powers to controlling and profiting from the environment. People learned to control other human beings more effectively. Mumford estimates that the mass of people that made up the human labor machine was equivalent to between 25,000 and 100,000 horsepower.[28] Gradually, the rule of the priests and lords common to antiquity gave way to the rule of bankers, industrialists and merchants. The masses were freed from direct slavery or serfdom, but the relationship between worker and employer was still characterized by exploitation.

Under these new social relations, technical knowledge and productivity multiplied even more rapidly. As Marx and Engels wrote in the *Communist Manifesto* of 1848, "the bourgeoise has been the first to show what man's activity can bring about."[29] They go on to say that "It has accomplished wonders far surpassing Egyptian pyramids, Roman aqueducts, and Gothic cathedrals."[30]

Although a contemporary list of technical marvels would fill an entire encyclopedia, the majority of people in the world still suffer from a degrading poverty which cannot be explained by myths or technical backwardness.

---

*Other civilizations, however, were able to survive their careless agricultural practices. In Mesopotamia, for instance, empires were able to outlast the fertility of their soils by militarizing their society to harvest, not food, but plunder and loot. For centuries Egypt, too, was able to waste much of its fertility since its soil received annual infusions of nutrients washed down from the African hills.

REFERENCES

1. Henry David Thoreau, *Walden, or Life in the Woods* (New York: Holt, Rinehart & Winston, 1964), p. 137.

2. Karl Marx, "The British Rule in India," *New York Daily Tribune*, June 6, 1853, reprinted in Karl Marx, *Surveys From Exile*, David Fernbach, ed. (New York: Vintage, 1974) pp. 393 and 406, and Karl Marx, *Economic and Philosophical Manuscripts of 1844* (New York: International Publishers, 1964), p. 115.

3. Karl Marx, *The Grundrisse* (New York: Harper & Row, 1972), p. 45. The Nicolaus translation (New York: Vintage, 1973), p. 110, is slightly less free, but is also less clear.

4. Dr. Sudhir Kakar, letter to V. S. Naipul in the latter's "India: A Defect of Vision," *The New York Review of Books*, Vol. 23, No. 13 (August 5, 1976), pp. 9-14; see also Albert and Gabrielle L. C. Howard, *The Development of Indian Agriculture* (Oxford: Oxford University Press, 1927), p. 12.

30. United States Department of Agriculture, Economic Research Service, "Changes in Farm Production and Efficiency, A Special Issue Featuring Historical Series," Statistical Bulletin No. 561 (September 1976), p. 68.

31. See Joint Economic Committee of the United States Congress, *U.S. Economic Growth from 1976 to 1986: Prospects, Problems, and Patterns*, Vol. 1. *Productivity Studies Prepared for the Use of the Joint Economic Committee*, 94th Congress, 2d Session (October 1, 1976).

32. John Stuart Mill, *op. cit.*, Vol. 3, p. 756.

33. David Gordon, "Capital vs. Labor: The Current Crisis in the Sphere of Production," in David Mermelstein, ed., *The Economic Crisis Reader* (New York: Vintage, 1975), p. 395.

34. Edward Pesser, "Labor from the Revolution to the Civil War," *Monthly Labor Review*, Vol. 99, No. 6 (July 1976), pp. 17–25. Pesser describes long and frequent breaks for snacking as well as drinking alcohol during the day.

35. See Graham F. Donaldson, *Farm Machinery Safety*, Royal Commission on Farm Machinery Study No. 1 (Ottawa: Queen Printer, 1969).

36. The figure of 60 percent comes from Swadesh R. Bose and Edwin H. Clark II, "Some Basic Considerations on Agricultural Mechanization," *Pakistan Development Review*, Vol. 60, No. 3 (Autumn 1969), pp. 271–300.

38. Lynn White, *Mediaeval Technology and Social Change* (New York: Oxford University Press, 1963).

38. See Joseph Needham, *The Grand Titration: Science and Society East and West* (Toronto: University of Toronto Press, 1969), pp. 87–90.

19

BLAMING THE PEOPLE:
THE POPULATION MYTH

A continuation of the 2 percent rate of world population growth from the present population of about three billion would provide enough people, in lock step, to reach from the earth to the sun in 237 years. . . . It would generate a population which would weigh as much as the earth itself in 1,566 years.

—Philip M. Hauser[1]

Our city slums are packed with youngsters—thousands of them idle, victims of discontent and drug addiction. And millions more will pour into the streets in the next few years at the present rate of procreation. You go out after dark at your own peril. Last year one out of every four hundred Americans was murdered, raped or robbed. Birth control is an answer.

—Newspaper advertisement of the
Campaign to Check the Population Explosion[2]

Without the modern input of chemicals, of pesticides, of antibiotics, of herbicides, we simply couldn't do the job. Before we go back to an organic agriculture in this country, somebody must decide which 50 million Americans we are going to let starve or go hungry.

—Earl Butz, Secretary of Agriculture[3]

Although unemployment, poverty and the necessity for questionable technologies are said to be justified by the requirements of a growing population, the truth is that population growth is essential to a capitalist economy. Measures to control population growth are temporary expedients used only when the rate of population growth begins to exceed the rate desired by the ruling class.

Take the case of Japan. This country has more people per cultivated acre than any other nation in the world. The average price of land sold for agricultural use rose from $3,891 per acre in 1965 to $18,160 in 1972. During the same period, land used for housing increased from $13,833 per acre to $59,940, and land used for industry, which sold for only $15,182 in

1972, reached a spectacular $65,067 by late 1974.[4] The soaring value of land seemed clearly to fall in line with the predictions of the overpopulationists. Too many people were bidding up the price for scarce land. Rising rents would inflate the costs of food and shelter, bringing down the standard of living for all.

This view of the Japanese economy deserves a closer look. How much of the cost of land can be explained by speculation? A partial answer came in 1975 when the Japanese real estate market went sour. Of the 8,600 bankruptcies recorded in the first seven months of that year, at least 500 were directly blamed on real estate; many others fell as a result of repercussions from the real estate collapse.[5] The editors of *Business Week* reported almost one million acres of raw land, about 40 percent of the land purchased by industrial concerns between 1969 and 1974, "lying undeveloped and largely unsalable."[6]

Even if we remove the effects of speculation, land values in Japan are still high and can be expected to go still higher. Do these residual values confirm the law of diminishing returns? The answer to this question is affirmative. To reject the primacy of the law of diminishing returns in economic decision-making does not imply a denial of the technical relationships described by the law. It only means that they are of secondary importance. Here again, Japan is a case in point.

A reduction in population in Japan would help to relieve the crowding which is common in that land.* In fact, the Japanese seemed to be acting on the premise that population limitation was important for the welfare of the nation. A program of population control based on government-sponsored programs backed up by widespread propaganda was so successful that it was typically used as the prime example for Third World nations.[7] Then, in 1969, Minister Eisaku Sato announced to a group of Japanese newspaper editors that the government intended to reverse its policy and strive for an increase in the rate of population growth. According to a report in *Science*:[8]

. . . Sato's statement was no irrational, off-the-cuff remark by an uninformed politician. It was based on some cautiously worded recommendations by the Problems Inquiry Council, a cabinet-level group which included some of Japan's leading demographers.

Why would Japan, which acted in accordance with the principles of the overpopulationists, suddenly reverse its official policy? The answer lies in the relationship between population growth and the labor supply. During the period after World War II, migration from the farms provided a steady supply of labor for the Japanese factories.[9] Between 1950 and 1975 approximately 7 million laborers emigrated from the agricultural sector in Japan.[10]† Once the pool of cheap rural labor had been depleted,

---

*This statement does not mean that population control is necessarily the best method for mitigating crowding. Certainly, planning and a wiser use of resources would have a more immediate effect.

†In 1965, only 9 million wage earners were employed in manufacturing.[11]

workers were able to demand higher wages, which cut into profits. Monthly reports of the Bank of Japan and various other establishment periodicals voiced serious concern about the supply of labor. For example, the Bank of Japan's monthly report for May 1969 stated:[12]

I may point out that there exists in all advanced countries a cycle of wage rise and price rise caused by a labor shortage. . . . Japanese managements have a *serious anxiety* as to how long the wage rise of over 10 percent can be absorbed in the years ahead.

Others are much more precise about the type of labor shortage which concerns them. The economist who heads the Family Planning Federation of Japan, for instance, says:[13]

The industrialists say that the labor shortage is severe. But I say what is deficient is young labor which is very cheap. So all we can say is that we lack cheap labor, only that.

The Japanese example reveals only one aspect of the need for population growth in advanced capitalist economies. Even if capitalism were to find an inexhaustible source of cheap labor, population growth would still be necessary to stimulate investment. For example, one of the major causes of the Great Depression was the slowdown in construction activity which can be traced to the slacking off of population growth.[14] One Nobel Prize-winning economist has gone so far as to call the "whole industrial revolution of the past two hundred years . . . nothing else but a vast secular boom, largely induced by the unparalleled rise in population."[15]*

Business publications concur on the importance of population. Ansley Coale cited a few examples of the typical attitude toward population growth; *Business Week* wrote on "The Why Behind the Dynamic 50's— Overall Population Growth Is One of the Mainsprings of Prosperity." *U.S. News and World Report* was more explicit with its "A Bonanza for Industry—Babies; Sixty Million More U.S. Consumers in the Next 19 Years."[16]

If capitalism fosters population growth, why is it that much higher rates of population growth exist in the underdeveloped nations where remnants of precapitalistic social relations continue to survive? We do know that some of the most important of the homeostatic rituals and practices in primitive cultures served to hold population growth in check. For example, in certain cultures marriage had to be delayed until the suitor could afford a cow. Extended periods of breast feeding reduced ovulation. Many cultures had developed herbal methods of limiting fertility.[17]

With the destruction of traditional systems of social relations, cultural methods of population control have been destroyed. This connection is suggested by A. M. Carr-Saunders, author of one of the most comprehensive studies of primitive systems of population control, who observed:

*Agriculture did not share in that prosperity.

... that which is common to these races, where overpopulation is suspected, is the absence of hope and fear alike, of ambition and a standard of living; they are contented to live on what will just support life. . . . [We] always seem to find that political misfortunes have overtaken these people. . . . They have suffered from oppression in one form or another and gradually the old customs have been lost, hope and ambition alike have faded from their outlook. In consequence of oppression, the mass of people has by degrees sunk into a degraded condition.[18]

The destruction of traditional social relationships may be only partial, yet significant. The Tsembaga Maring certainly live more like their ancestors than those societies which came in more direct contact with the colonial powers. Yet even if the formal content of social relations remains intact in the shape of traditional village hierarchy, their effectiveness may be eliminated with the villagers' loss of control over the means of production.[19]

Engels singled out Java as the focus of a particularly vigorous effort to remake social relations.[20] Clifford Geertz's study of colonial relations in that land implied that the Dutch actually designed their policy to foster a more rapid increase in population.[21] Taxes were levied in the form of a family labor quota;[22] the larger the family, the less labor each individual would have to perform. This policy suited the Dutch because the more people they ruled, the more sugar they could extract.[23] Geertz's study suggests that the powerful western nations influence reproductive rates far beyond their borders.

With the worldwide exodus from farm to city stimulated by the Green Revolution, we hear much about overpopulation; as soon as the demand for labor catches up with the supply, however, we can expect as dramatic a turn-around in policy as was displayed in Japan.

Third World reproductive rates do differ from those of the industrialized lands in one crucial respect. In that part of the world, poverty creates an extra stimulus to population growth. One study in Gujarat found that families continued to have children until they had a reasonable certainty of having at least one male who would survive.[24] Even in the Punjab, where the people consume 50 percent more food than in states such as Bihar and West Bengal, half the women over 45 years of age had lost at least three children; only one woman in seven had lost no children.[25]

Children make good economic sense to the peasant family.* Children can care for the parents after they are too old to fend for themselves. In addition, children are a necessary component of the workforce for small farmers who are too poor to hire wage labor.[26]†

The exploitation of children within the family is not unique to the

---

*Children can be profitable to a family, at the same time as they are a burden to society. The poor farmer, for example, saves the cost of paying wages. But these wages are not a cost to society. They serve to maintain the laborer who would be unemployed. Here again the distortions of market-based decisions interfere with a rational functioning of society.

†Child labor perpetuates poverty by denying children education. In India, for example, children from small farms spend fewer days at school than children from more prosperous farms.[27]

contemporary Third World. Adam Smith, a shrewd observer of eighteenth-century economic life, thought that children would yield a sizable surplus to parents in the colonies, but not in England.[28] However, he seems to be referring only to the wages earned by children, rather than to their unpaid labor. By the nineteenth century, people of widely divergent opinions seem to agree that workers appeared to marry so that they could "squeeze money from children."[29]

The net result of a high birthrate coupled with high rates of infant mortality puts a heavy burden on society—much of the society's resources must be devoted to the rearing of children, many of whom never live to repay society. According to the United Nations Food and Agricultural Organization, prewar India spent 22.5 percent of its national income on raising children.* England, by comparison, spent only 6.5 percent of its national income on raising children.[31] If a decline in infant mortality allowed India to invest an extra 15 percent of its national income in productive facilities, the outlook for that nation would be brighter.†

Although rising population presents a technical hindrance to the economic development of the Third World, the fundamental causes of poverty are not technical at all.** Again, we have to consider population growth as a consequence of capitalist pressures.††

An increasing population does eventually take its toll. In attempting to meet the demands of a growing population, industry has to confront the law of diminishing returns. As wood becomes scarcer, plastics become common. Synthetic fibers replace cotton and wool. In agriculture, commercially produced fertilizers, pesticides, herbicides and preservatives are used in increasing intensity. In the process, the mining of resources accelerates and the environment becomes more polluted with dangerous

---

*An official of the U.S. Department of State who was chief of Food and Nutrition at the AID Mission in New Delhi wrote that prerevolutionary India spent 22.5 percent of its national income on raising children who would not live long enough to produce anything for society; he gave no source except to say that the estimate was made by Ghosh; so he may be misinterpreting the above statement, or he may have an even more damning story to tell.[30]

†The experience of England suggests that the high burden of a large percentage of children is not insurmountable. At the end of the seventeenth century, 38.4 percent of the population of England and Wales was under 15 years old.[32] By 1821, when the industrial revolution was in full gear, the percentage had risen to 39.1 percent.[33]

Conditions of the poor were so harsh that almost 60 percent of their children died before their fifth birthday, according to government documents cited by Engels in 1844.[34] In 1860, Marx wrote to Engels that more recent data showed that child mortaltiy had worsened since 1844.[35]

**The development of China would have certainly been a simpler task if the population had been less dense. The necessity of producing food on the terraces of Tachai was extremely costly in terms of the labor time required for their construction. On the other hand, such community efforts might be effective in building a spirit which made for more development in the long run. Also, we might ask, if China had been a less populous nation, would the foreign enemies of the revolution have been tempted to interfere in the affairs of China more actively?

††China has been extremely successful in limiting population.[36]

materials.* Between 1964 and 1974, the production of synthetic organic chemicals, for example, increased more than 250 percent.[37]

The costs of the resulting environmental insults go far beyond the loss of a few rare species or the destruction of pristine landscapes. The American Cancer Society estimates that 25 percent of all Americans will ultimately develop some form of cancer.[38] From 60 to 90 percent of these cases can be traced to environmental causes.[39] Even though the technical response to pollution problems has been painfully inadequate, the monetary costs of these measures have not been insignificant. Presently, about 1.5 percent of the National Product is absorbed by investments in pollution control equipment; by 1983, this figure is expected to reach 3 to 6 percent of the Gross National Product.[40]†

With proper social planning, effluents from one industry could be used as raw materials for another; as Engels suggested, under socialism

. . . . man's encroachments into nature will be rationalized, so that their remoter consequences will remain capable of control. . . . In this way, nature will be robbed step by step of the possibility of revenging itself on men for their victories over it.[42]

---

*Or, we might add, with materials which are not dangerous except when their concentrations become excessive.

†The pollution control industry, however, has created more than one million new jobs, according to Bureau of Labor Statistics estimates.[41]

REFERENCES

1. Philip M. Hauser, "The Population of the World," in Ronald Freeman, ed., *Population: The Vital Revolution* (Garden City, N.Y.: Anchor Books, 1964), p. 17.

2. Cited in Barry Commoner, *The Closing Circle* (New York: Bantam, 1972), pp. 233-34.

3. Earl Butz, "Meet the Press, Radio and Television Interview, NBC, 12 December 1971," in Alan F. Pater and Jason R. Pater, eds., *What They Said in 1971: The Yearbook of Spoken Opinion* (Monitor Book Co., 1972), p. 123.

4. Alan K. Hemphill and Bryant H. Wadsworth, "Japan's Farm Merger Program in Industrial-Urban Sqeeze," *Foreign Agriculture*, Vol. 12, No. 46 (November 18, 1974), p. 13.

5. Anon., "Japan: Heavy fallout from the real estate bust," *Business Week* (October 13, 1974), p. 50.

6. *Ibid.*, p. 50.

7. See Minoru Muramatsu, "Japan's Success Story," in H. Peter Gray and Shanti S. Tangri, eds., *Economic Development and Population Growth: A Conflict?* (Lexington, Mass.: D. C. Heath, 1970), pp. 124-36.

8. See Philip M. Boffy, "Japan: A Crowded Nation Wants to Boost Its Birthrate," *Science*, Vol. 167 (February 13, 1970), pp. 960-62.

9. See J. E. Heller, *Population Trends and Economic Development in the Far East* (Washington, D.C.: George Washington University, 1965), Population Project, pp. 7-8.

10. Ernest Mandel, *Late Capitalism*, London: NLB (1975), p. 171, citing Nasayoshi Namiki, *The Farm Population of Japan, 1872-1975*, Agricultural Development Series, No. 17, Tokyo (n.d.), pp. 42-43.

11. *Ibid.*, p. 171.

12. Reported in *Daily Summary of the Japanese Press*, Tokyo: American Embassy (2 July 1969), cited in Anon., "Population Control and Organized Capital," *Science for the People*, Vol. 2, No. 4 (December 1970), pp. 22–26.

13. Takuma Terao cited in Boffy, *op. cit.*

14. See Alvin Hansen, "Economic Progress and Declining Population Growth," *American Economic Review*, Vol. 29, No. 1 (March 1939), pp. 1–15. For a more complex analysis of the Great Depression which puts less emphasis on construction, see Peter Temin, *Did Monetary Forces Cause the Great Depression?* (New York: W. W. Norton, 1976), especially pp. 65–68.

15. John R. Hicks, *Value and Capital* (New York: Oxford University Press, 1939), chapter 24.

16. Cited in Ansley J. Coale, "Population Change and Demand, Prices, and the Level of Employment," in National Bureau of Economic Research, *Demographic and Economic Change in Developed Countries* (Princeton, N.J.: Princeton University Press, 1960).

17. See Yung Cheung-Kong *et al.*, "Potential Anti-Fertility Plants from Chinese Medicine," *American Journal of Chinese Medicine*, Vol. 4, No. 2 (Summer 1976), pp. 105–26; Richard Meier, *Science and Economic Development* (Cambridge, Mass.: MIT Press, 1966), p. 152; and *A Barefoot Doctor's Manual: Translation of a Chinese Instruction to Certain Chinese Health Personnel*, John E. Fogarty International Center for Advanced Study in the Health Sciences, United States Department of Health, Education and Welfare (1974), pp. 175–6.

18. A. M. Carr-Saunders, *The Population Problem, A Study in Human Evolution* (Oxford: Oxford University Press, 1922), pp. 213–14.

19. Kropotkin's *Mutual Aid* can be read as a chronicle of the gradual elimination of traditional social relations. See Petr Kropotkin, *Mutual Aid: A Factor in Evolution* (Boston: Extending Horizon Books, n.d.).

20. Frederick Engels, "Letter to Karl Kautsky, 16 February 1884," in Karl Marx and Frederick Engels, *Selected Correspondence*, 3d ed. (Moscow: Progress Publishers, 1975), p. 347.

21. Clifford Geertz, *Agricultural Involution* (Berkeley and Los Angeles: University of California Press, 1963).

22. *Ibid.*, pp. 52–53.

23. *Ibid.*, p. 75.

24. Alan Berg, "The Role of Nutrition in National Economic Development," *Technology Review* (February 1970), pp. 45–51.

25. *Ibid.*

26. Mahmood Mamdani, *The Myth of Population Control* (New York: Monthly Review Press, 1972), pp. 76–80. See also Colin Clark, *Population Growth and Land Use* (New York: St. Martin's Press, 1976); and Ester Boserup, *The Conditions of Agricultural Growth* (Chicago: Aldine, 1965). This view is disputed by Eva Mueller, "The Economic Value of Children in Peasant Agriculture," paper prepared for the Conference on Population Policy sponsored by Resources for the Future (February 28–March 1, 1975). Mueller makes the mistake of using money wage rates as a measure of the productivity of child labor, which underestimates its productivity.

27. See Richard L. Shortlidge Jr., "A Socioeconomic Model of School Attendance in Rural India," Cornell University, Department of Agricultural Economics, Technical Change in Agriculture Project, Occasional Paper No. 86 (January 1976).

28. Adam Smith, *An Inquiry into the Nature and Causes of the Wealth of Nations* (New York: Modern Library, 1937), pp. 71 and 532.

29. See Karl Marx, "Letter to J. Weydemeyer, 2 August 1851," in Karl Marx and Frederick Engels, *Letters to Americans: A Selection*, Alexander Trachtenberg, ed. (New York: International Publishers, 1953), p. 24. See also Karl Marx, *Capital*, Vol. 1 (Chicago: Charles H. Keen, 1906), p. 432; and Leonard Horner, "Letter to Nassau Senior, May 23, 1837," included in Nassau Senior, *Selected Writings on Economics, A Volume of Pamphlets*, 1827–1837 (New York: Augustus Kelly, 1966), p. 30.

30. See Berg, *op. cit.*, p. 46.

31. Ian Bowen, *Population* (Cambridge: Cambridge University Press, 1966), p. 116, citing United Nations Food and Agricultural Organization, *The State of Food and Agriculture* (Rome: FAO, 1948), p. 31.

32. D. C. Coleman, "Labour in the English Economy of the Seventeenth Century," *Economic History Review*, 2d Series, Vol. 8, No. 3 (April 1956), pp. 280–95.

33. *Ibid.*

34. Frederick Engels, *The Conditions of the Working Class in England in 1844*, in Karl Marx and Frederick Engels, "Collected Works," Vol. 4 (New York: International Publishers, 1974), p. 405.

Adam Smith gives a slightly more conservative figure, which is understandable, because it refers to an earlier period and includes both rich and poor. Adam Smith, *An Inquiry into the Nature and Causes of the Wealth of Nations* (New York: Modern Library, 1937), p. 68.

35. Karl Marx, "Letter to Frederick Engels, 11 January 1860," in Karl Marx and Frederick Engels, *Selected Correspondence*, 3d ed. (Moscow: Progress Publishers, 1975), p. 114.

36. Leo A. Orleans, *China's Experience in Population Control: The Elusive Model*, Prepared for the Committee on Foreign Affairs of the United States House of Representatives, 93d Congress, 2d Sess. (September 1974).

37. See Council on Environmental Quality, *Environmental Quality—1975* (Washington, D.C.: Council on Environmental Quality, 1975), p. 23.

38. *Ibid.*, p. 12.

39. *Ibid.*, p. 17.

40. Lewis J. Perl, "Ecology's Missing Price Tag," *The Wall Street Journal* (August 10, 1976), p. 16.

41. Russell W. Peterson, in Jeffrey A. Klein and Kenneth Ch'uvan-K'ai Leung, *The Environmental Control Industry: An Analysis of Conditions and Prospects for the Pollution Control Equipment Industry*, for the Council on Environmental Quality (Montclair, N.J.: Allanheld Osmun, & Co., Publishers, 1976), *Foreword*, p. viii.

42. Frederick Engels, *The Dialectics of Nature* (London: Lawrence, Wishart, 1940), p. 293.

IN PLACE OF A CONCLUSION

The ideas of the ruling class are in every epoch the ruling ideas.
—Karl Marx and Frederick Engels[1]

In primitive societies, the production of food could be said to be efficient, from the point of view of its members, because it taught the people about the harmony between human beings and nature at the same time as it reinforced the social relations which were necessary for survival. In later societies, agriculture was esteemed to be efficient because it produced good soldiers. In the early days of the United States, Thomas Jefferson considered agriculture efficient because it developed good citizens. In the contemporary United States, efficiency has become synonymous with profitability.

No matter how disruptive capitalist production methods may be, farmers in this society are still highly efficient in maximizing profits. They carefully apportion fertilizer, pesticides, labor and all other inputs according to their relative prices in the market. The market dictates the spraying of toxic chemicals, even though the full extent of their effects is not yet known. The market demands the adoption of technologies which squander resources and hurl workers into the depths of unemployment. When social benefits do occur, they are incidental to the mad rush for profits. The charge of inefficiency, then, cannot be traced to the behavior of individual farmers, but to the subordination of farming to market forces.

We have seen the enormous human and environmental costs resulting from capitalist agriculture. Because economic theory both reflects and influences reality, our critique of agriculture necessitated a parallel critique of the theory which is designed to justify capitalism.

The ideological nature of economic theory is understood even by as conservative an economist as George Stigler, who confesses that "the professional study of economics makes one politically conservative."[2] After a successful indoctrination in the theory of economics, the fledgling economist "cannot believe that a change in the *form* of society or social organization will eliminate basic problems.[3]*

In spite of the more explicit ideological element in economic training, we have seen that economists are by no means exceptional in the degree to which they consciously or unconsciously serve capital. A typical example of the effects of the capitalistic value system is the development of the tomato harvester. Whether the plant breeders and agricultural engineers who created this technology saw the problem as resulting from the unionization of farm workers in the U.S. or from competitive pressures from cheap labor in Mexico, they viewed the tomato fields entirely from the perspective of the growers. Society as a whole was not considered.

We are all conditioned to believe that what is good for capital is good for society as a whole. The effectiveness of this conditioning disintegrates as people come to realize that the present system of social organization can no longer meet their needs. Expensive food, deteriorating quality, financial disasters for small farmers, and hunger are a few of the symptoms of unmet needs. As the crisis in agriculture deepens, an expanding majority will be prepared to look to an improved system of social relations. This reconstruction of our lives will not come without a struggle, but the stakes are high enough to make it worthwhile. As Karl Marx was fond of writing, "De te fabula narratur" (It is of you the story is told).[6]

---

*Alain Enthoven, then chief economist at the Department of Defense, told the annual meeting of the American Economics Association, how advanced training in economics is necessary before the students submit to the ideology. In his words:

> The economic theory that we are using (in the department) is the theory most of us learned as sophomores. The reason Ph.D.'s are required is that many economists do not believe what they have learned until they have gone through graduate school and acquired a vested interest (in conventional economic theory.)[4]

Even when economists have no direct obligations to serve capital, their thinking remains colored by its requirements. Alex McCalla displayed an exceptional degree of intellectual honesty when he expressed what his fellow agricultural economists knew to be true, that "we have identified closely with our perceived clientele so often, after a couple of generations we begin to think like them, share their values, and come to perceive their sanctions of our activities as necessary and desirable."[5]

REFERENCES

1. Karl Marx and Frederick Engels, "Feuerbach: Opposition of the Materialistic and Idealistic Outlook," Chapter I of *The German Ideology*, in "Selected Works in Three Volumes" (Moscow: Progress Publishers, 1970), Vol. I, p. 47.

2. George Stigler, "The Politics of Political Economists," *Quarterly Journal of Economics*, Vol. 73, No. 4 (November 1959), pp. 522–33.

3. *Ibid.*, p. 528.

4. Alain C. Enthoven, "Economic Analysis in the Department of Defense," *American Economic Review*, Vol. 53, No. 2 (May 1963), pp. 413–23.

5. Alex McCalla, "Public Sector Research and Education and the Agribusiness Complex: Unholy Alliance or Socially Beneficial Partnership? Discussion," *American Journal of Agricultural Economics*, Vol. 55, No. 5 (December 1973), pp. 999–1002.

6. Marx, *Capital, op. cit.*, p. 13.

INDEX

Africa, 138, 209; colonial period, 110; exports of primary products from, 111; exports to, 107; luxury crops, 115; slaves, 108

Agency for International Development (AID), 115, 143, 169, 171n, 174 agribusiness, 6, 17–18; abuses, 87; antitrust laws and, 87; human costs, 5; marketing motive, 86, 87; as new feudalism, 79–93; view of land, 83; as source of credit, 90; Third World policies of, 111–23. *See also* farm size; large-scale farming

Agrico, 174

Agricultural Act of 1961, 84

Agricultural Development Council, 146, 159

agricultural research, 6–9, 75; in American South, 8; reordering priorities of, 8–9; and small farmer, 84, 98; on Third World food crops, 113

agriculture: capital requirements of, 17–18; colonialism and, 124–30; control of, 89–91; economic process, 43; investment appeal of, 82–83; labor-saving techniques, 34; potential efficiency of, 17; ramifications of, 3–4; myths of, 205–11; traditional, 131–33, 136–38, 145–46, 155, 159–61. *See also* farms and farming; U.S. agriculture

agronomy, 182

agro-nuclear complexes, 16

Alabama, 91

Albrecht, William Albert, 45

American Cancer Society, 225

American Chemical Society, 161

American Economic Association, 56

American Railroad Journal, 33

Anderson, Edgar, 208

Andrilenas, Paul A., 96

animal husbandry, 137

antibiotics, 134

antitrust laws, 87

anthropologists, 206

Argentina, 116, 134

Arkansas, 98

Army, T. J., 13

Asia, 142, 156, 160, 161, 176; exports to, 107; Green Revolution, 145–52, 153. *See also* names of countries

Australia, 24, 112, 133; aborigines, 207n

Austria, 6

automobiles, 15

Bairoch, Paul, 55n

Balinese culture, 207n

bananas, 112

Bangladesh, 155, 173, 193n

Bank of America, 90, 98

Bank of Japan, 222

Banking, 90

banks, 81, 88, 89, 117. *See also* credit

Bateson, Gregory, 207n

bell peppers, 90

Bellers, John, 23–24

Bengal, 156

Beresford, J. Tristamm, 95

biological nitrogen fixation, 180

Blake, Helen T., 96

bonanza farms, 79

Boon, G. K., 48n

Boone, Charles, 27

Borgstrom, Georg, 46n

Borlaug, Norman, 7–8, 143, 144, 145, 147

Borsoki, Ralph, 143n

Boulton, Mathew, 23

Boyle, Robert, 124, 127

Bradfield, Richard, 190–91

Brazil, 112, 116, 132n; food consumption patterns, 116; U.S. investors in, 119

Breeze, Sidney, 28

British East India Company, 108n

Brown, Lester, 146, 151, 170